THE REVOLUTION in the
NEW YORK PARTY SYSTEMS
1840-1860

KENNIKAT PRESS

NATIONAL UNIVERSITY PUBLICATIONS

SERIES IN AMERICAN STUDIES

General Editor

JAMES P. SHENTON

Professor of History, Columbia University

Mark L. Berger

THE REVOLUTION in the
NEW YORK PARTY SYSTEMS
1840-1860

National University Publications
KENNIKAT PRESS
Port Washington, N.Y. • London • 1973

Library of Congress Catalog Card No.: 72-89990
ISBN: 0-8046-9030-8

Manufactured in the United States of America

Published by
Kennikat Press, Inc.
Port Washington, N.Y./London

for Elinor

Acknowledgments

Every historian knows how much he has benefited from the assistance of other scholars. I am especially indebted to Professor Hans L. Trefousse who has afforded me the benefit of his advice at every stage of my work and has been a warm and concerned friend. I also appreciate the helpful criticisms and suggestions of Professors Ari Hoogenboom, Edward Pessen, and Harold C. Syrett. I want to thank Professor Charles M. Snyder of the State University of New York at Oswego for placing the recently discovered Millard Fillmore papers at my disposal and for his hospitality. Professor Eric Foner provided several useful suggestions about manuscript collections. I am grateful for the help of many librarians, but I want especially to thank the staff of the New-York Historical Society for their cordial cooperation.

My parents, Miriam and Samuel Berger, and my sister, Gail, have been patient with my academic endeavors and have always provided me with encouragement. Lastly, I want to thank my wife, Elinor Evenchick Berger, who has never failed to be a source of cheerfulness and encouragement.

M. L. B.

Columbus, Georgia
February, 1973

Contents

THE REVOLUTION in the
NEW YORK PARTY SYSTEMS
1840-1860

Introduction

Since the adoption of the Federal Constitution, only three national party systems, each consisting of two dominant political organizations, have been in existence. The first party system originated in the early years of the Republic during the struggles between Federalists and Jeffersonians; it lasted for approximately two decades. The second party system emerged in the early 1830's as a consequence of the conflict between the partisans of Andrew Jackson, the Democrats, and his opponents, the Whigs; it, too, survived for about twenty years.

During the period 1854-1856, the nation experienced one of the most profound political unheavals in its history. These years witnessed the disintegration of the second party system and gave rise to the third and most enduring political order. In this brief span of time the Whig party dissolved, so that ex-Whigs were left homeless; the Democratic party became committed to the course it kept until the Civil War; a new party, the Know-Nothing, enjoyed a brief triumph and then suffered a decline; and another upstart party, the Republican, arose to dominate the politics of the North.

These years of political revolution were filled with crises, with extraordinary tension, with unavoidable decisions. What generated this overpowering strain on the second party system? How did this stress operate to bring about a political transformation? What alternatives were open to politicians and voters and how were choices made? In short, how resilient was the American party system at a time of seemingly insoluble crisis? These are some of the questions which this study will seek to answer.

New York State provides the focus for this investigation. Because of her large and heterogeneous population, her geographical location and economic power, and the ambition and ability of her leaders, the

1

Empire State affected the entire nation and so did her politics. In many respects the revolution in the New York party system was unique; however, similar developments occurred in most Northern states. The importance of New York's political history is matched by its complexity. A wide spectrum of partisan activity must be examined.

By 1854, the New York Democratic party had been weakened by more than ten years of factional strife. During the early 1840's a rift developed between two sections of the New York Democracy, the "Barnburners" or "Radicals" and the "Hunkers"[1] or "Conservatives." State-wide issues and competition for power among ambitious politicians were the original sources of contention, but the dispute soon spilled over into the more dangerous problem of slavery. Accumulated grievances against Southern Democrats and their Hunker allies emboldened the Barnburners to support the Wilmot Proviso in 1846, and to bolt from the party in 1848 and join the Free Soilers in the presidential campaign of that year.

During the 1849 election a group of moderate Hunkers, known as the Soft Shells, established a shaky truce with the Radicals.[2] The Compromise of 1850 and the subsequent reduction in sectional tension strengthened this alliance. However, another group of Hunkers, known as the Hard Shells or Adamantines, refused to cooperate with former Free Soilers. In 1852, Barnburners, Softs, and Hards managed to submerge their differences, and they carried New York for Franklin K. Pierce and elected Horatio Seymour, a Soft, governor.

Factionalism reappeared after the Democratic triumph. The Hards were outraged when they failed to receive the choicest spoils from President Pierce. The selection of the Softs' chieftain, William L. Marcy, for Secretary of State—the post coveted by the Hard Shell leader, Daniel S. Dickinson—was especially galling. When the Democratic state convention met in 1853, the Hards bolted and established a separate organization and nominated their own ticket. The Whigs, of course, were the only beneficiaries of this conflict, and they easily carried the election of 1853.

Other difficulties exerted a great strain on the New York Democratic party. The old Jacksonian rallying cries of opposition to national banking, tariffs, and internal improvements—which had proved so potent in the past—were obsolete; large numbers of Protestant, native-born Democrats were attracted to causes such as temperance, anti-Catholicism, and nativism. These preoccupations threatened to alienate thousands of foreign-born Democrats, mainly of Irish stock. Some antislavery Barnburners had accepted the Compromise of 1850 with reluctance. Rebellious over Southern dominance of the national party, they eagerly looked for some way to revive the defiant spirit of 1848. All of these problems generated stress within the New York Democratic party and made it vulnerable to a strong shock, which could at last break weakened threads of loyalty.

The Whig party in New York also faced a crisis. Factionalism between radical Whigs piloted by William H. Seward and Thurlow Weed, and conservative Whigs led by Millard Fillmore and Francis Granger, racked the party. The slavery issue exacerbated this rift. Seward and Weed's antislavery pronouncements alarmed conservatives, who feared that agitation on this subject would destroy the North-South Whig alliance and endanger the Union itself. Economic motives also played significant roles: New York City's Whig merchants benefited from a lucrative trade with the South and blanched at the thought of secession. Other problems created pressure within the party. Temperance and nativist sentiment spread rapidly in central and western New York, the area of greatest Whig strength. Whigs divided sharply over how to deal with these potent new issues.

The Whig feud reached the breaking point over the Compromise of 1850. Radical Whigs backed Seward's policy of opposition to the Compromise; conservatives stood behind President Fillmore's efforts for sectional reconciliation. The struggle in Washington triggered a contest for control of the Whig party in New York, and this fight reached its climax at the state convention in September, 1850. Ably managed by Weed, the radicals succeeded in keeping the reins of the state organization.[3] Led by Granger, a large group of conservatives stormed out of the convention. The color of Granger's hair inspired the political sobriquet which subsequently denoted this portion of the Whig party—the Silver Grays.

The forces operating upon the New York Whig party took their toll. The canvass of 1851 started the downward slide. Whigs elected few state officers, lost control of the vital Canal Board, so necessary because of the patronage it provided, and forfeited their majority in the senate; only the assembly remained in Whig hands. The election of the following year proved disastrous, not only in New York but nationally as well. At the state level, Whigs failed to secure a single office, and gave up their ascendancy in the assembly. From the high point of thirty-two Whig Congressmen in 1848, the total dropped to seventeen in 1850 and ten in 1852. The national result was even more alarming. Presidential nominee Winfield Scott carried only four states. Many Southern Whigs deserted him and voted for Franklin

Pierce. They feared that if the Mexican war hero were elected, he would fall under the influence of Seward and Weed. The Silver Grays abandoned the party's nominee for the same reason.

To many Whigs, the campaign of 1852 signalized the death of their party as a national organization. Sectional tensions, they claimed, had overcome loyalties forged for nearly a generation. In New York, Whiggery survived and even managed to carry the 1853 election with a plurality. It did so because of the Hard Shell-Soft Shell split. But this respite could not hide the crippled condition of the party.

By 1854, both major parties in New York were in a condition of crisis. The second American party system depended upon the exclusion of slavery from political debate. When this condition could no longer be maintained, a hardening of sectional lines ensued.[4] The growing tension in the national parties was transmitted to the state organizations; in New York, it magnified internal dissensions within each party and made unity impossible. Other problems operated to exert pressure on the old structure. The obsolescence of the issues which had formerly helped to define political parties made it easier to abandon past alignments. The demand for temperance legislation and nativist discriminations against foreigners and Catholics brought havoc to existing groupings. At any time a powerful jolt could destroy the whole structure and pave the way for a political revolution.

1

The General Situation

At a time when the major parties were least able to cope with disruptive forces, they were subjected to major strains. The combined impact of the Kansas-Nebraska bill, the growth of the temperance movement, and the rise of a militant nativism destroyed the existing two party system and prepared the way for new alignments. To understand the transformations of parties in the Empire State, it is necessary to consider the origins of these disruptions, their interrelationship with each other, and their effect upon New Yorkers.

On January 4, 1854, Senator Stephen A. Douglas of Illinois introduced his bill for the organization of the Kansas-Nebraska territory. Although the bill underwent several changes before it explicitly repealed the Missouri Compromise, Douglas' first version had already accomplished this feat. The New York *Evening Post* spotlighted this fact a day later when it printed its key passage: When the Nebraska territories were "admitted as a State or States, the said territory or any portion of the same, shall be received into the Union *with or without slavery,* as their constitution may prescribe at the time of admission. . . ." [1] (my italics) Suddenly, the thirty year agreement which had forbidden slavery north of latitude 36°30' in the Louisiana Purchase stood in danger. When President Pierce appeared to support the bill, the tocsin sounded throughout the North.

Many historians have speculated on the reasons for Douglas' action.[2] Whatever his motives, the effect of his action was unmistakable: The delicate sectional balance achieved after the Compromise of 1850 received a devastating blow. Tension within the national parties reached the breaking point; the repercussions of this strain were immediately felt in New York, where the political situation was thrown into chaos.

The Northern response in opposition to the Kansas-Nebraska bill was almost unanimous. It constituted a remarkable example of a democratic mass movement. Citizens outraged by the news from Washington organized public protests to vent their indignation. Hundreds of meetings throughout the Northern states lent truth to Douglas' famous remark that he could ride from Boston to Chicago by the light of his burning effigies. These assemblies revealed the people's faith in their democratic institutions and in the efficacy of peaceful dissent. They also helped to seal the fate of the decaying major parties. Calls for these meetings sought to embrace all men "without distinction of party." This spontaneous exhibition of anti-Nebraska feeling provided the foundation for the future Republican party.

New York had its full share of public remonstrance. The roll call of upstate towns and cities hosting these gatherings read like a gazetteer of the state—Rochester, Lockport, Skaneateles, Oswegatchie, Penn Yan, Baldwinsville, Auburn, Albion, Cherry Valley, Hornellsville, Randolph, Albany, Oswego. The columns of the New York *Evening Post* and the New York *Tribune* were filled with numerous short notices of these proceedings. The legislature reflected the general indignation by passing resolutions condemning the bill, and instructing the state's congressmen to oppose it.[3]

There was no better indicator of the pervasiveness of wrath than New York City's strong reaction against the Nebraska bill. A center of conservatism in the state, the city had a long history of hostility to abolitionists and free soilers. This feeling was jointly rooted in the lucrative mercantile relationship the port enjoyed with the South, and the Irish laborers' often violent hatred of free Negroes. This powerful though incongruous alliance between wealthy merchants and poor wage earners had long placed a damper on antislavery agitation.

The unified front of capital and labor seemed to break down over the Nebraska bill. Pillars of the business community, previously distinguished as zealous proponents of the Compromise of 1850, took a leading role to defeat Douglas' measure. Commenting on the appearance of well-known conservatives at a protest meeting, the New York *Evening Post* observed that it took "a strong sense of injury to engage these men in a controversy on a subject concerning which they so earnestly desire that the agitation shall cease."[4]

The humbler citizens of New York staged their own meetings. John P. Hale of New Hampshire, the presidential candidate of the Free Democrats in 1852, addressed a gathering of "mechanics." He urged working men to preserve their heritage in Nebraska by preventing its loss to slave labor. The crowd responded enthusiastically to Hale's impassioned speech.[5] Only the Irish refused to participate in the protest movement.[6]

Although it would be an exaggeration to say that the intensely partisan newspaper press of the state reacted to Douglas' bill "without distinction of party," it, nevertheless, displayed an amazing unity. The New York *Tribune,* since its inception a scathing critic of the "peculiar institution," led the attack among the Whig papers. Judging from the substantial increase in its subscription list, the *Tribune's* vitriolic editorials expressed the opinions of a great number of New Yorkers and Northwesterners.[7] The Albany *Evening Journal* added the influential voice of Thurlow Weed, thereby setting the pattern for most Whig papers throughout the state.

The conservative Whig press of New York City followed in the wake of the merchants. Henry J. Raymond brought his New York *Times* into opposition the moment the final text of the Nebraska bill became available. He declared that passage of the measure would destroy the last vestige of Northern confidence in the South. Other generally cautious journals, like the New York *Commercial Advertiser* and the New York *Courier and Enquirer,* expressed themselves in similar terms. Newspapers with Silver Gray, anti-Seward leanings were also indignant. James and Erastus Brooks, editors of the pro-Fillmore New York *Express,* attacked the New York *Journal of Commerce,* one of the few papers defending Douglas. Upstate journals, like the Buffalo *Commercial Advertiser* (Fillmore's organ) and the Albany *State Register,* followed the lead of the *Express.*[8]

Before Douglas had proceeded with his bill he had secured the written endorsement of President Pierce.[9] This fact did not deter the Soft Shell Democratic press from condemning the whole scheme. The New York *Evening Post,* edited by William Cullen Bryant and John Bigelow, bitterly attacked Douglas and his adherents.[10] The Albany *Atlas,* generally considered the spokesman for Secretary of State William L. Marcy and the organ of the Softs, soon found itself involved in acrimonious exchanges with Pierce's Washington *Union.*[11] One of the *Atlas'* editors, Henry H. Van Dyck, wrote Marcy that a recent tour throughout the state had convinced him that "the feeling against repeal of the Missouri Compromise is nearly unanimous." Heman J. Redfield, the recently confirmed Collector of the Port of New York, reported his mortification at the position taken by the city presses of the state, mentioning specifically the New York *Evening Post,* the Albany *Atlas,* and the Buffalo Republic. He intimated the necessity for purchasing a new paper in New York City to represent the Administration.[12] This confrontation between Soft Shell organs and the President boded ill for the future of the Democratic party in New York.

A few papers resisted the tide and supported the Nebraska bill. The greatest number adhered to the Hard Shell Democratic faction, which consisted of politicians most sympathetic with the Southern point of view.[13] The New York *Journal of Commerce,* reflecting the sentiments of the most conservative merchants, also endorsed Repeal. It considered the commotion in the North as unnecessary and stirred up by demagogues; slavery, it averred, could never take root in Kansas because of the inhospitable climate.[14]

The Protestant clergy greatly strengthened the anti-Nebraska cause. Northern clergymen agreed that the repeal of the Missouri Compromise involved a moral as well as a political question; consequently, it demanded their attention. By taking prominent roles at protest meetings, ministers added significantly to the strain on the old party system. Henry Ward Beecher was only too glad to oblige an invitation to speak, and at a Brooklyn meeting the crowd enjoined clergymen in the audience to take places on the speaker's dais.[15]

The mixture of antislavery agitation and religion in New York was not new. New Englanders, who had migrated to central and western New York in great numbers during the early part of the nineteenth century, dominated that area. They left homes and farms behind, but they carried their religious idealism with them. The 1820's and 1830's witnessed a remarkable outpouring of crusading zeal, giving the name of "Burned-over-region" or "infected district" to that portion of the state settled by New Englanders. Sparked by such spellbinding evangelical ministers as Charles Grandison Finney, Theodore Dwight Weld, and the latter's thirty disciples, the people had been aroused to a high pitch of antislavery excitement. These men had preached that opposition to human bondage was incumbent upon truly pious men and women. The large number of anti-Nebraska protests revealed that this feeling was still powerful.[16]

The Nebraska struggle in Congress lasted for nearly six months. By dramatizing the issues involved, this extended conflict intensified the strain on the existing political order. The bill passed in the Senate on March 4, 1854, but not before the upper chamber had witnessed one of the most acrimonious debates in its history.[17] William H.

Seward delivered a blistering attack, while the conservative Hamilton Fish, New York's other Whig Senator, silently opposed the measure. With passage by the Senate, attention focused on the House. Here, the bill experienced fluctuating fortunes, alternately encouraging its foes and then casting them into despair. The press denounced the efforts of Douglas' floor manager, Congressman William A. Richardson of Illinois, to rush the bill through the House without debate in the Committeee of the Whole. They rejoiced when his plan failed. Throughout the protracted legislative battle, a belief prevailed that Congress would respond to the protest movement —hence, the consequent emphasis on public meetings and petitions. Seward communicated to Weed, Thomas Hart Benton's opinion that the bill could be killed if enough demonstrations revealed its unpopularity.[18]

Spring elections in New Hampshire, Connecticut, and Rhode Island added to the drama. President Pierce's native state was first, and it accurately revealed public opinion. The Democrats suffered a sharp setback. Thurlow Weed, heartened by the result, wrote that "Nebraska has received a black eye if not a bloody nose in New Hampshire." He believed that if Connecticut followed suit, the bill could not pass. The New York *Tribune* defied the House to pass the bill in the wake of the New Hampshire election. Democratic defeats in Connecticut and Rhode Island reinforced the pattern set in the first New England state.[19]

Ignoring these signs of Northern opposition, Douglas and Pierce rallied their supporters. Stymied in the Committee of the Whole from March 21 to May 8, their bill suddenly moved from eighteenth to first on the agenda. The New York *Tribune,* pleading for more time, argued that Northern "mis-representatives" who aided Nebraska were not only false to their constituents but also to their professed ruling principle: "The men who are forcing the Nebraska question in the face of the popular demonstrations against it everywhere are guilty of treason against the very fundamental principle of popular sovereignty." This logic failed to persuade. After several stormy debates, capped by a thirty-six hour session, the House passed it on May 22, 1854 by a vote of 110 to 100.[20]

The composition of the final division merits closer attention. Taking into account paired votes, and all who were absent but subsequently indicated how they would have voted, the bill passed by 115 to 104. Northern Democrats divided equally, 44 for, and 44 against; Southern Democrats, 57 for, and 2 against. Northern Whigs voted none for,

and 45 against; Southern Whigs, 14 for, and 7 against. The six Free
Soilers voted in the negative. New York's delegation stood 23 against,
and 10 for. All nine Whigs were opposed; they were joined by
thirteen Democrats and one Free Soiler. Ten Democrats voted to
sustain the bill, and half of these came from New York City.[21]

This vote destroyed the second American party system. Northern
and Southern Whigs, dividing along clear sectional lines, administered
the *coup de grâce* to their national organization. If the equal division
of Northern Democrats is contrasted with the unanimity of their
Southern brethren, it is apparent that the Democrats, too, had sustained
a powerful blow.

In Washington, men were aware that the political situation had
undergone a revolution. Observing the debate in the House, Preston
King, a former Barnburner Congressman from St. Lawrence county,
reported that caucuses were being held "on both sides in which the
members meet as they are for and against the measure without other
distinction of party." He noted that "as yet the demolition of party
lines is confined to the repeal of the compromise—but the conversa-
tion and opinion is pretty common and general—that past lines of
party division will be obliterated with the Missouri line—if this bill
passes."[22]

Nebraska added a powerful new ingredient into the confusion of
New York politics, but its long range impact remained uncertain. Men
had declared their opposition to Nebraska, joined protest meetings,
and flooded Congress with petitions. What would they do next? Would
they go beyond protest and take affirmative action? Would they seek
to reverse the repeal of the Missouri Compromise? Would they form
a new party for this purpose? Or, would they gradually forget the
whole matter, grow complacent, and shift their attention to other
issues? This last possibility loomed as a real danger to antislavery
politicians. The Republican party was by no means inevitable, granting
even the widespread and deeply felt wrath of the North. It must be
remembered that Nebraska was not the only disruptive force operating
upon the party system. The nativist and the temperance movements
had also played a role in destroying the old political framework; the
advocates of these causes would participate in the establishment
of any new partisan alignments. In 1854, no one could have predicted
with certitude which issue would emerge as the paramount concern
of the nation, or how many different parties would finally be
established.

The temperance movement had deep roots in New York's history.
Like the antislavery cause, it derived its chief support in the Burned-

over-region and its transplanted New Englanders. Evangelists, preaching during the 1820's and 1830's, included liquor along with slavery among the sins requiring eradication. The two evils were linked together by a logic which declared unremitting hostility to all kinds of human bondage—whether to a human or to an alcoholic master.[23] Neal Dow of Portland, Maine, the leader of the temperance movement, testified to the fellowship between the workers in these two crusades:

> The prohibitory movement received invaluable assistance from the distinctively anti-slavery element. . . . Most of the leaders in each reform were interested and active in both, exerting their influence to make the efforts for one contribute to the development of the other. . . .[24]

During the first four decades of the nineteenth century, temperance advocates had refused to consider prohibitory legislation as a proper means of securing their goal. Confident in the ultimate success of their cause, they relied entirely on argument and example to make converts. Neal Dow changed this strategy when he formed the Maine Temperance Union in 1837. He warned his associates that persuasion alone could not secure their object and that legislation would be necessary. He finally obtained his long sought goal, when on June 2, 1851, the Maine legislature passed a bill forbidding the manufacture or sale of intoxicating liquor within the state. This measure, subsequently known as the "Maine Law," became the model for similar prohibition movements in other states.[25]

State Senator Myron H. Clark led the prohibitionist forces in the New York legislature.[26] He represented the twenty-ninth district, which included Ontario and Livingston counties, an area deeply influenced by the religious idealism of New England immigrants. In 1852, Clark introduced a bill to suppress drinking houses and tippling shops, but it made little progress. Undaunted, restrictionists tried again the following year, this time imitating the provisions of the Maine Law. The senate approved this measure by a vote of 17 to 13; however, the assembly killed it by the small margin of 2 votes.

Encouraged by their near success, Maine Law advocates entered confidently into the fall campaign to capture the 1854 legislature. They followed the strategy of endorsing candidates from the two major parties rather than risk defeat as a separate organization. Their plan worked: Although the canvass of 1853 appeared as a strong Whig victory, it concealed the victor's dependence on temperance support.

When the legislature convened in 1854, Clark insisted that promises made during the campaign be kept. The senate passed a prohibition bill by a two-thirds majority, and two weeks later the assembly concurred by a vote of 78 to 42. In late March, however, Governor Horatio Seymour vetoed the bill. During the canvass of 1852, Seymour had hinted that he would approve a prohibitory law; but he refused to sign the measure set before him, because he deemed it unconstitutional.

The Governor's action aggravated the liquor question. Vowing to continue the struggle, temperance advocates began to concentrate their energies on the gubernatorial campaign of 1854. Nebraska now had a powerful new rival for the attention of the electorate.

In addition to its tie with antislavery feeling, the temperance cause was also allied to another strong movement—nativism. Among the motives influencing prohibitionists, there existed the desire to strike a blow at immigrants, especially the Irish Catholics, who were allegedly so fond of liquor. Although deeply resented by the foreign-born, agitation for the Maine Law represented only an oblique way of demonstrating nativist sentiment. At this time latent intolerance had given rise to a powerful new organization dedicated to discriminatory policies.

Mutual hostility between Catholics and Protestants was a heritage brought over from Great Britain. New Englanders whose Puritan ancestors had fled their mother country because they considered the Anglican church tainted with "Romanism" were particularly responsive to anti-Catholic agitation. Since by the mid-nineteenth century over one-half of New Yorkers claimed descent from New Englanders, the state was a potential seed ground for anti-Catholic bigotry.[27]

The migration of three million immigrants to the United States during the decade 1846-1855, of whom a great many were Catholic Germans and Irish, aggravated the preexisting tendency toward religious intolerance. The relative percentages of immigrants to native-born inhabitants in both the city and state of New York, had their greatest increase in this ten year period. In 1854, 7.52 percent of the state's population had been born abroad; by 1855, this total had risen to 18.54 percent. In 1845, 16.14 percent of the city's population had been born abroad; by 1855, this figure had increased to 36.93 percent.[28]

A portion of the crusading spirit which New Yorkers possessed in such abundance manifested itself in a desire to purify the nation from vestiges of privilege or "aristocracy." This aim appeared threatened by the new immigrant wave. The devotion of Catholics to a religious hierarchy with a foreign sovereign at its pinnacle seemed incompatible with Democratic institutions.[29] The newcomers' religion was not the only reason for animosity. The Irish, in particular, were excoriated for their poverty, clanishness, and alleged riotous behavior. All these factors combined to foster doubt in their suitability for American citizenship.

The Irish, however, had no doubts about their right to equality. Their eagerness sharpened by centuries of oppression in their native land, they were determined to exercise all their prerogatives. Wealthy Whig merchants, accustomed to the political control and the choice offices of New York City, were outraged when the Irish failed to show them deference. Hibernians expected rewards for their partisan zeal, and they obtained many plums in the city as well as the state. Disappointed office seekers played a major role in nativist agitation.

The accumulated grievances of New York City's native-born crystallized into the American-Republican movement of 1844-1845. Appealing for aid from the native American rank and file of both parties, this organization charged the Democratic and the Whig leadership with pandering to naturalized citizens. It nominated a Whig, James Harper, a book publisher and a strong temperance advocate, for mayor in the April, 1844 election. Conservative Whigs sensed the trend and aided his campaign. Emboldened by Harper's victory, they urged a fusion ticket with the American-Republicans for the fall election. This, they argued, would insure the success of the Henry Clay-Theodore Frelinghuysen ticket by riding the crest of nativist excitement.[30]

Upstate Whigs led by the Seward, Weed, Greeley partnership had grave doubts about this course of action. They were reluctant to abandon their hope that they might eventually gain the support of naturalized citizens, a policy inaugurated when Seward made his proposal to subsidize parochial school education with state funds. Moreover, they perceived that nativism was a two-edged sword; the conservative Whigs who sought to wield it were not only eager to cut down the Democrats, but might also turn it against Seward and his friends. Furthermore, it was feared that a nativist coalition, while politically advantageous in New York City, could wreck the party's chances in the state and the nation. Whigs would be accused of intolerance against Roman Catholics and lose thousands of votes.

Perhaps the urgency of carrying New York for Clay, and the prospect of gaining a large number of Democratic votes, overcame Seward's anxieties, for he consented to a Whig and American-Republican fusion ticket. Even Horace Greeley agreed to this policy. The coalition secured the success of the American-Republican candidates, but it did not help Clay. Democrats split their ticket, supporting the fusionists in local contests and returning to their own party's nominee for President, James K. Polk.

The result confirmed Seward's premonitions. Now certain that prejudice polluted the progressive image which he had striven to give the Whig party, and that fusion had defeated Clay, he turned to eradicate the nativist menace. The following year, the Whigs withdrew their support from the American-Republicans, and Harper's bid for re-election failed. Although the party lingered on for two more years, its strength was broken by the Whig defection.

These events influenced the reactions of Whig politicians toward the Know-Nothing movement of the 1850's. Seward, Weed, and Greeley refused to consider any affiliation with nativists. Many conservative Whigs, however, were angered by this decision; they had found anti-Catholic bigotry a powerful weapon against the Democrats and the Irish. This resentment widened the breach between the emergent radical and Silver Gray factions. The conservatives' alienation worsened when Seward supported the anti-Rent movement, but reached the breaking point over the militant antislavery stand of the Auburn statesman. Silver Grays looked back to the events of 1844-1845, and perceived that a nativist organization might be re-tooled into an engine of destruction for their former ally.

Political nativism failed to reach full stride in the 1840's, but organizations established in this decade paved the way for the Know-Nothings of the 1850's. In 1844, a secret fraternal society known as the Order of United Americans (or O.U.A.) appeared in New York City. Most of its original organizers were businessmen. This group, dedicating itself to nativist objectives, had a rapid growth and by 1851 it had fifty-three chapters.[31]

When the Order engaged in politics, it reflected the views of its most influential members, conservative Whigs. In 1848, it opposed Seward's elevation to the United States Senate, and two years later participated in efforts to build support for the Compromise of 1850. This last activity unveiled an important new element in the developing nativist creed—a devotion to the Union. This combination of anti-Catholicism, Unionism, and clandestine activity captured the imagination of Silver Gray Whigs. Here, was a weapon tailored to their needs; if used carefully, it could thwart both abolitionism and Catholicism, deliver a crushing blow to Seward and his allies, and elevate conservatives to a position of power.

The reluctance of the O.U.A. to support Daniel Webster for President in 1852 caused many Silver Grays to gravitate toward a new organization, the Order of the Star Spangled Banner, which became better known as the Know-Nothings. Founded in the spring of 1850, this society also emphasized the need for secrecy. It sought to influence the nominations of the two major parties by endorsing only native-born citizens for office. To prevent dissension, it eschewed the divisive issues of slavery and temperance. Almost defunct by 1852, it acquired a new lease on life from the infusion of new blood.

Differences between the O.U.A. influx and the original members of the Star Spangled Banner group sapped its strength until these were resolved with the formation of the Grand Council on May 11, 1854. James W. Barker assumed the presidency of the Council as his reward for conciliating the rival factions. Barker, a wealthy dry goods merchant and a former Whig, earned recognition as an opponent of Seward when he joined the campaign of New York City business-men to promote acceptance of the Compromise of 1850.

Barker quickly demonstrated his capacity, for the Know-Nothings enjoyed a phenomenal growth under his leadership. The Order spread rapidly throughout the state, but this failed to satisfy its leaders, whose ambitions were national. They had long harbored the dream of a new conservative party which would replace the Seward-tainted Whig organization. They took a long stride toward their objective with the establishment of the first National Grand Council on June 14, 1854. Barker was also selected president of this body. New York City nativism, strengthened by the pro-Union attitudes and political experience of the Silver Grays, would soon spread.

The remarkable appeal of Know-Nothingism was a product of many factors. Two recent events contributed to its expansion. The visit of the Papal Nuncio, Archbishop Gaetano Bedini, charged with the task of settling disputes regarding church property, aroused bitter resentment. President Pierce's appointment of James Campbell of Pennsylvania, a Catholic, as Postmaster General also aroused fears. Age-old religious prejudice combined with concern over the country's capacity to absorb so many newcomers made its contribution. The uniqueness of the organization, the opportunity for camaraderie, and the paraphernalia of exotic rituals, grips, and passwords enticed many.[32] A fear that the slavery issue must be quieted lest it break up the Union motivated conservative Know-Nothings in the North and the South.

Another element in nativist strength was its integral relationship with other evangelical reform movements. It is noteworthy that the American-Republicans, although desiring to expand their power throughout the state, were unsuccessful in northern, central, and western New York. Why did upstate men react so differently a decade later? Certainly, the superior organization of the Know-Nothings combined with their missionary zeal played an important role, but we must also remember the simultaneous growth of the antislavery and temperance movements in 1854. These, and nativism were often looked upon as common causes, and, in the estimation of their adherents, they shared a common enemy. Many believed that before they could restrict slavery they must first overcome Irish immigrant opposition.[33]

The effect of the Kansas-Nebraska Act and the temperance and nativist movements was to further disrupt the already decadent party system. The national Whig organization dissolved under the strain and the national Democratic party was damaged. The repercussions of these events left the New York political situation in chaos. Allegiance to both Whig and Democratic parties had been weakened. Anti-Nebraska protests inspired an attempt to build a new fusion party. Nativists launched the Know-Nothing organization, which made rapid progress across the nation. Temperance advocates eagerly pressed their demands and threatened to form their own political organization. These three causes competed with one another for the attention of the electorate.

It is essential for an understanding of the political revolution in New York during the years 1854-1856 to appreciate the integral relationship among antislavery, temperance, and nativist emotions. All three of these crusades appealed to the descendants of New England farmers in the Burned-over-region. Protestant evangelicalism had taken deep root in this area and had made it the center of crusading zeal in the state. Voters in the "infected district" soon confronted the problem of a choice among the three movements. Western and central New York became the critical battleground in the struggle to establish a paramount political issue and a dominant political party. Politicians were caught in this whirlpool of religious idealism. We now turn to their perplexities and their decisions.

2

The Softs

The Kansas-Nebraska bill presented New York Soft Shells with an immediate crisis. The reopening of the slavery controversy threatened to destroy the fragile alliance between Barnburners and moderate Hunkers which had been based upon the finality of the Compromise of 1850. Many Barnburners had joined the Free Soilers in 1848, to seek revenge against the Southern wing of the Democratic party and its Northern allies. There were others, however, who had bolted because of their sincere antislavery views. These, had reluctantly joined the Soft Shell amalgam, but they eagerly looked for some way to revive the defiant spirit of 1848. Douglas' measure afforded them the opportunity for which they had waited. Other dilemmas confronted the Softs. How could they convince Southern Democrats of their loyalty to the national party if they failed to aid the Nebraska bill? How could they maintain control over the President's patronage unless they backed his policy? If they did support this new course, how then could they hold the allegiance of an electorate hostile to the Nebraska scheme?

The Soft Shells experienced a period of anxious uncertainty when the news reached them of Douglas' proposal. One vital matter—the President's attitude toward the measure—remained in doubt. Tammany Hall politician, Lorenzo B. Shepard, asked the Softs' political chieftain, Secretary of State William L. Marcy, for enlightenment on this subject. George W. Newell, a close associate of the Secretary for many years, was also confused. "We are in a fog here," he acknowledged, "as everybody seems to be, what the Nebraska business means—what Douglas is driving at—whether the administration acts on compulsion or *con amore*."[1]

17

As it became clear that the Administration would accord its warmest support to Douglas, premonitions of disaster dominated the Secretary of State's mail. One Soft considered the bill a complete mistake. He did not hold congressional compromises sacrosanct; in fact, he believed non-interference in territorial affairs the best rule. His objections were of a practical nature: Nebraska was "ill-timed, unnecessary, the motive too palpable, and the success too uncertain." Another politician expressed a common attitude of doom: "I go for it against my own convictions of its wisdom, because I believe the Administration is committed to it, but in doing so, I can not shut my eyes to the consequences that is [sic] sure to follow."[2]

The Soft Shell press revealed the severe strain unleashed upon the party. Editors were torn between loyalty for the Administration and the mood of the people. Isaac Butts, the editor of the Rochester Union, expressed the dismay of his fellow journalists. He regretted the Administration's support of Douglas, for it had chosen a weak position. It had "offended its friends and exposed itself to the jeers of its enemies." Butts had been forced into opposition, because he knew that Nebraska would "be regarded as an insult by a large portion of the North—not abolitionist or free soilers; and that it would be regarded as a breach of faith pledged in 1820 and 1852 and hence lead to renewed divisions and sectional parties."[3]

The Albany Atlas was the most important paper to revolt against the new policy. Arguing that long-standing compromises should not be altered by a temporary majority, it deplored the unnecessary reopening of slavery agitation by unscrupulous politicians. The President's paper, the Washington Union, promptly attacked this editorial and threatened to expel from the party any Democrat who stood in the way of the Nebraska bill.[4]

The matter did not end here. Smarting from their rebuke, the editors of the Atlas published a new assault on Nebraska. They ridiculed the Union's view that the bill fulfilled the Compromise of 1850, and the Baltimore Platform of 1852, and that it would quiet agitation. They averred that nothing in the Compromise of 1850 sought to override the Missouri line, as the latter applied to the Nebraska territory; and the fact that agitation had not been silenced was painfully apparent. The Atlas urged Congress to recede from this dangerous ground and to adopt the territorial bill of 1853 which had kept the Missouri Compromise intact.[5]

Newell attempted to soothe Marcy's anxiety that this latest outburst was a signal for a general Soft Shell rebellion against the Administration. It was nothing as fundamental as that. It merely reflected "a sort of vague apprehension of the *crushing* process and a feeling that a certain self-respect demands the appearance of dissent from what it has always opposed and what it claims to be hostile to the Compromise and the platform."[6] The fear of being crushed out of the party derived from the Union's assertion that the Nebraska bill would constitute a test of Democratic orthodoxy. Newell hoped that the President's newspaper could be made to temper its remarks in the future; it could better influence the Northern mind, if it displayed greater calm and dispassion. He believed, moreover, that the less responsibility the Administration had for the abrogation of the Missouri Compromise, the better.[7]

A change in the *Union's* management failed to mollify this dispute. In early March, the paper did backtrack from a strict Nebraska test; it announced that the President would not regard Democrats who differed on details of the bill as party enemies. With the passage of Douglas' bill in late May, however, the *Union* reverted to its former position. It now maintained that the law's approval by a majority of Democrats made it party policy. The Albany *Atlas* rejected this interpretation and charged that the law owed "its vitality to the votes of Southern *Whigs* and northern mis-representatives without whose concurrence it could not have been forced on the country."[8]

The *Atlas-Union* blowup demonstrated the strained relationship between New York Soft Shells and the national party. Democrats throughout the country, but especially in the South, had not forgotten the Barnburner bolt of 1848.

Professor Roy F. Nichols has shown that Southern insistence for repeal of the Missouri Compromise was partly designed as a loyalty test for former free soilers. Professor Eric Foner has revealed the Barnburners' resentment against similar tests in the past; they believed that Southern pressures for proslavery concessions damaged them with their own antislavery constituents.[9] Thus, it is not surprising that the Albany *Atlas* and most Soft papers reacted to the Nebraska bill with such hostility; they accurately reflected the attitudes of Radical Democrats who regarded Douglas' measure as another unreasonable demand from the Southern wing of the party.

The Nebraska bill placed prominent Softs in an unenviable position. This is best illustrated by considering the dilemma of Secretary of State Marcy. Marcy never had an opportunity to offer an opinion on Nebraska before the President gave his written endorsement to Douglas. If he had, he would certainly have objected. It required little of the Secretary's political sagacity to realize that repeal of the Missouri Compromise would create havoc in the Northern states.[10] But confronted with a *fait accompli,* he had either to resign or to accommodate himself to this new policy. He chose the latter.[11]

The Soft Shells' rebelliousness put Marcy into a difficult situation. He was trapped between his obligation to the President and the opposition of his followers at home. He knew, also, that he must not offend Southern Democrats, who scrutinized his every move. Marcy's dilemma of selecting two New York newspapers for the publication of official documents illustrated the awkwardness of his position. He wrote Governor Horatio Seymour that he had intended to confer this boon upon the Albany *Atlas* and the Utica *Observer,* but the situation had "changed since the opening of this Pandora's box—the Nebraska question." The Secretary feared that the *Atlas* had aroused the suspicion that it was a free soil journal which, masked for a time, had now come into the open. His endorsement of it, Marcy believed, would impair his strength in the Cabinet and receive a sinister interpretation in every part of the Union. He asked Seymour to suggest "two papers which had been at least silent on the subject." Marcy desired to avoid the charge of free soilism but was "unwilling to do an act which will look like making the support of that bill a test of democracy." But the Soft press had become so hostile to Nebraska that Seymour could not help Marcy's quest.[12]

The matter of greatest importance to the Secretary of State and to other Soft Shell leaders was the maintenance of the Hunker-Barnburner alliance which constituted their faction. Radical Democrats had acquiesced in the Compromise of 1850, and the Baltimore Platform of 1852, as the price for returning to the party. But would they accept the Nebraska bill—a measure antithetical to the Wilmot Proviso which they had once espoused, or would they rally around discontented free soilers once again?

The Softs' apprehensions focused upon the former leader of the Radical Democrats, John Van Buren. Known as "Prince John" by his contemporaries, Van Buren derived his power from the combination of his illustrious parentage, his flamboyant personality, and his oratorical ability. In 1847 and 1848, he had led the Barnburner defection from the Democratic party and the alliance with the Free Soilers at Buffalo. Since 1849, when he supported a joint ticket of Barnburners and Hunkers, he had followed a conciliatory course. Although he acknowledged his dissatisfaction with the Fugitive Slave Law, he had urged acquiescence in the Compromise of 1850 and the

Baltimore Platform. Van Buren's power had been eclipsed by former Hunkers in the Soft Shell faction, especially Marcy and Seymour; they feared that he might use Nebraska as an excuse to lead a new free soil crusade.

These anxieties owed more to the nervousness of the Softs than to any overt threat from the ex-President's son. Newell informed Marcy that Van Buren had expressed his discontent with Douglas' scheme, and of his intention to speak at a protest meeting in New York City. But Newell was not overly alarmed, for he observed his mild tone. A series of letters between Van Buren and an ex-Senator from Alabama, Jeremiah Clemens, were also distinguished by their moderation. John A. Dix, a prominent Barnburner politician and the Free Soil candidate for governor in 1848, had even felt compelled to defend his friend against Benton's charge that Van Buren had shown insufficient zeal in opposition to Nebraska.[13]

Despite "Prince John's" lack of menace, the Tammany Hall friends of Secretary Marcy took precautions that they would control any utterance from the Democratic General Committee on the Nebraska question. They also sought to follow the Secretary's counsel to avoid any precipitate declaration of policy lest it freeze Democrats into irreconcilable positions. John Cochrane, who enjoyed the lucrative position of Surveyor of the Port of New York, assured Marcy that he could control the General Committee. He would postpone action for the present, but when the Committee did speak out, it would pursue "a course of action that not only shall not embarrass but that shall confirm the Democratic Party." Cochrane's associate Lorenzo B. Shepard did not know what Van Buren planned, but he was confident that his supporters were "in a very lean minority." He believed that more Barnburners would follow his lead than the free soil leader's. Shepard requested Marcy's ideas on proper resolutions for adoption by the General Committee. He thought they could be passed nearly unanimously; he would try to secure this result by keeping adverse members of the Committee away.[14]

The Democratic General Committee met on February 2, 1854, and approved resolutions praising the Pierce Administration and the Nebraska bill. The New York *Evening Post* promptly denounced these declarations as "feeble, cowardly, indirect, and circumlocutory." Their timorous style, the *Post* declared, reflected their author's awareness that he spoke for Washington and not the people. Unruffled by this attack, Shepard sought to mollify the Barnburners. He reported to Marcy that he was doing all he could to quiet feeling, though Van

Buren, he was told, was doing all he could to blow it up. He predicted success, nevertheless, for "the cooler Barnburners here approve what we've done and if he [John Van Buren] makes a fight, I think we'll satisfy you that he has not any strength here."[15]

These exertions to keep the shining knight of the Radical Democracy from leading a new bolt were expended on a man who no longer had the stomach for political warfare. Van Buren confided his thoughts to the Secretary of State to prevent misrepresentation of his position. He acknowledged that he had opposed Marcy's selection for the Cabinet (he had favored John A. Dix), but the Secretary's just and honorable treatment of the Barnburners had reconciled him to his appointment. He believed that Pierce was ill-advised to have allowed a renewal of the slavery excitement. The great question of his Administration, Van Buren had hoped, would "be *'stealing'*—not stealing *negroes* but money. . . ." He admitted that the Radical Democrats would oppose the Nebraska bill, and he hoped that Marcy would not urge them to vote for it. But so long as the Secretary dealt fairly with them, he would have their support. He desired Marcy, moreover, to take any stand on the Nebraska question that would sustain him in the Cabinet. Thus, Van Buren served notice that he was prepared to put up only a mild resistance *within* the party rather than lead a new revolt.[16]

"Prince John's" decision to pay only lip service to the free soil cause relieved the immediate pressure on Soft Shell federal office-holders, but it did not solve the problem of keeping the Barnburners loyal. There were many other Democrats determined to resist the expansion of slavery. Such leaders as Preston King, John Bigelow, and William Cullen Bryant carefully bided their time before calling Radical Democrats to the abandoned standard of 1848.

The vital support, which Tammany Democrats provided the Administration on the Nebraska question, was threatened when a smoldering dispute over patronage flamed into an open revolt with the appointment of John McKeon as the United States District Attorney for the Southern District of New York. Because McKeon had openly professed to have voted the Hard Shell ticket in 1853, his selection enraged Lorenzo B. Shepard who had coveted the post for himself. Secretary Marcy, who was in receipt of angry letters from Tammany Hall, suffered the keenest embarrassment. He was caught between his loyalties to the President and his New York City associates.[17]

The Secretary explained to Seymour why the President had appointed McKeon. Marcy believed he had a fair chance to secure Shepard's selection before the news broke that Seymour had offered a judgeship to Gilbert Dean, an anti-Nebraska Soft Congressman. This antagonized Pierce, and he resolved to grant no more favors to the Softs. Marcy feared that the President had been greatly misled about New York politics. He had pressed his advocacy of Shepard— and more particularly his opposition to McKeon—very far, perhaps too far. He was uncertain what the consequences would be, but at the present moment he was "as deeply mortified as a man can be. . . ." This disclosure enraged Seymour who threatened a public denunciation of the President.[18]

McKeon's appointment led to a brief rebellion against Pierce. The Democratic General Committee, which had previously endorsed the Nebraska bill, now adopted a resolution sponsored by Fernando Wood which declared the new District Attorney an unfaithful Democrat; it also criticized the President for fomenting dissension within the party. At the urging of Cochrane, Tammany rescinded its censure, but the narrow margin of victory reflected the depth of discontent.[19]

The Kansas-Nebraska Act drove a deep wedge into the Soft Shell organization. By reopening agitation over slavery, Douglas' measure underlined differences which divided Barnburners from moderate Hunkers and jeopardized the delicate harmony then existing. The Radical Democrats' resentment against this new test of party loyalty was only partially restrained by federal officeholders. Although John Van Buren had abandoned his commitment to the free soil cause, others were ready to take up the struggle. Problems over patronage also afflicted the Softs, and these difficulties worsened with the Nebraska bill. In this crisis, it seemed that only one powerful force held the Softs together—the remarkably resilient bond of Democratic party loyalty. It remained to be seen whether this bond could withstand the prodigious strains exerted upon it.

3

The Hards

New York Hard Shells were a threat to the harmony of the state and national Democratic parties. For over a decade, bitter factionalism between Barnburners and Hunkers, and then between Hard Shells and Soft Shells, had sapped the strength of the state organization. Disgruntled by their failure to secure the choicest plums of federal patronage, the Hards (also known as Adamantines) were eager to ruin the Pierce Administration and its favorites, the Softs— and if necessary, the Democratic party. By dragging their quarrel into national politics, they added significantly to the tense political climate.

The Hard Shells had determined upon a rule or ruin policy even before the introduction of the Kansas-Nebraska bill. Heedless of the delicate harmony established by the Democratic party after the Compromise of 1850, they seized upon the most potent weapon at hand—the charge of free soilism and abolitionism. Their organ, the Albany *Argus,* printed incessant attacks: "They [the Softs] know they can do more damage to the country and get better places for themselves by pretending (just at present) to be democrats, rather than abolitionists. And so in this way the paradox of praising abolitionists —just a little, and professing democracy—a very great deal,—is entirely explained."[1] The Softs felt vulnerable to these charges because of the preponderance of Barnburners in their ranks, and made every effort to discredit them.

The Hards tried to maneuver their rivals into a damaging position with respect to the slavery question. An instance of this type of harassment occurred during the spring of 1853. By introducing resolutions in the state legislature calling for the endorsement of the Baltimore Platform of 1852, the Adamantines sought to embarrass Barnburners opposed to its approval of the Fugitive Slave Law.

24

Secretary of State Marcy feared that this move would harm both himself and the Softs unless the Radical Democrats went along. Consequently, he counselled that, like it or not, the resolutions must pass: "The radicals must not prove impracticable; for if they do, they will lose everything and the *hards* will gain their object . . . the radicals must go unflinchingly for the Baltimore resolutions. . . ." The Barn-burners' compliance with his wishes relieved Marcy's anxiety. He retaliated by setting his own snare; he forced his detractors to vote on a resolution approving the state and national administrations.[2]

This skirmish and similar encounters had a definite audience in mind—the Southern wing of the Democratic party. If they were to replace the Softs as the dominant faction in New York, the Hards knew that Southern help was essential. Sympathetic Senators could aid them by refusing to confirm Pierce's Soft Shell appointees, thereby forcing him to revise his patronage policies. Higher stakes were also involved. Because of the two-thirds majority required for the party's presidential nomination, anyone who had dreams of this office, and there were several among both Hards and Softs—including Secretary Marcy, Governor Horatio Seymour, and Daniel S. Dickinson—must have the support of Southern Democrats; therefore, no aspirant could afford even the suspicion that he was opposed to the Baltimore Plat-form.

Arriving in Washington for the opening of the Thirty-third Congress in December 1853, Hard Shell Congressmen tested to see if their efforts to create friction between Southern Democrats and the Administration had succeeded. They were disappointed. Marcy informed Seymour of the Hards' astonishment and chagrin at their impotence within the party caucus. They had expected "to find the Cabinet tottering but soon ascertained that it was firmly seated." He accused the Adamantines of sending Edwin Croswell, an editor of the Albany *Argus,* southward

> with full power to go as the members from that section wished provided they would recognize and reward the Hards for their present efforts to *save* the Union, but the South did not feel disposed to acknowledge the value of their faithful services and bore very complaisantly the re-proaches of ingratitude.

Marcy concluded that "the *hards* are here very generally regarded as a *faction* having for their object the elevation of Dickinson. I have not heard of a single Southern member of Congress who sympathizes with them."[3]

The Hards' frustration increased when they entreated the House of Representatives to investigate the dismissal of Greene C. Bronson, an Adamantine stalwart, formerly the Collector of the Port of New York. This move, a transparent ploy to elicit sympathy, failed. The House denied their request by a vote of 104 to 65. This incident revealed the strength of Democratic opposition to the President: Twenty-eight Congressmen from New York and other states, who called themselves National Democrats, voted against the Administration.[4]

On January 17, 1854, Francis Cutting, a New York City Adamantine, expressed the Hards' resentment on the House floor. Delving into the preceding decade of his state's history, he sought to demonstrate the continuity between the Soft Shells and the 1848 supporters of Martin Van Buren, and the Hard Shells and the 1848 followers of Lewis Cass. He complained that the treacherous Softs were richly rewarded by the Administration, while the faithful Hards were left empty-handed. With his characteristic earthiness, the notorious Mike Walsh—gang leader, drunkard, and workingmens' advocate—also castigated the President.[5]

Theodore B. Westbrook, a freshman Congressman from Kingston, delivered the major rebuttal for the Softs. He denied any direct line of descent between the Barnburner-Hunker factions of 1848 and the present division. He enumerated the names of well-known Softs who had supported Cass in 1848, and of prominent Hards who had been Free Soilers at that time. He defended his political associates against allegations of hostility toward Southern rights: When the Hards bolted from the 1853 state convention and thus inaugurated the split, the majority of remaining delegates "were men who [had] stood up for the South. . . ." Moreover, they adopted resolutions that were "as broad and as national as national can be. . . ." Westbrook charged that the real reason for dissidence was simply that President Pierce had called Governor Marcy to his Cabinet and not Daniel S. Dickinson.[6]

These departures into partisan history failed to undermine support for the Administration. Representative William R. Smith of Alabama criticized the Hards for their selfish factionalism and compared the Hard-Soft controversy to the Lilliputians' war over which end to break an egg.[7] No Southern member rose to dispute Smith or to praise the Adamantines. This result confirmed Marcy's appraisal that the Hards would receive no solace from the South, which considered them merely as disappointed office seekers.

How this intransigence to recognize their claims infuriated the Hards is seen in a remarkable letter from Daniel S. Dickinson to a

Southern friend, just prior to the election of 1860. In this long epistle, Dickinson lamented the consistent failure of the South to support her true friends, the National Democrats of the North. He began with New York's split delegation of Barnburners and Hunkers at the Baltimore convention in 1848. The former professed free soilism while the latter stood on the national platform. But through the votes of Southerners, both delegations were treated equally. This was an early and fatal blow, according to Dickinson, for it gave life and perpetuity to free soil heresies and their advocates.

Dickinson then gave his version of the Hard-Soft split: "General Pierce had been elected, and although elected as a 'Hard' or National man, he early took the 'free-soilers' into favor and ultimately removed the few 'Hards' he had appointed and gave the entire patronage of his administration to the 'free-soilers' and 'Softs.' " When the "Hards appealed to their Southern friends for aid," they "received neither encouragement, support or sympathy. . . ." In 1853, the two factions separated at the Syracuse state convention. Again, the Hards appealed for Southern support but met with rebuff. Dickinson went on to describe later instances of disappointment, but what has been outlined here is sufficient to appreciate his bitterness toward Southern Democrats.[8]

Douglas' Kansas-Nebraska bill was useful for the embattled Hard Shells, for here was an opportunity to expose their rivals' free soilism. So fortuitous did this measure seem, that some speculated whether the Hards were partially responsible for its introduction. The seasoned political observer and historian, Jabez D. Hammond, believed that the idea of repealing the Missouri Compromise originated with the Hards for the double purpose of gaining the support of the slave-holding states, and of exposing the Softs to them. It was obvious to Hammond that if the Softs went for Kansas-Nebraska, they would disgrace themselves with their constituents.[9]

Subsequent historical research has failed to uncover any direct evidence of Hard Shell collusion with Douglas. There remains, however, the intriguing possibility that Pierce's political troubles in New York persuaded him to support Nebraska. Angered by his failure to secure the French Mission, James Gordon Bennett, the owner of the New York *Herald,* had turned his editorial wrath against Pierce and aided the Hards. He offered a large reward for the President's "Scarlet Letter," in which it was claimed, he had endorsed Van Buren in 1848. Upset by this and other charges of free soilism, Pierce tried to vindicate himself. He may have imagined that Soft endorsement of the bill would remove any lingering Southern doubts about himself and his New York friends. Seward first interpreted the bill in these terms—as a maneuver by Pierce to deprive the Hard Shells of ammunition.[10]

Perceiving their chance, the Hards redoubled their efforts to ingratiate themselves with Southern Democrats and embarrass the Softs. The Albany *Argus* immediately announced its agreement with the principle of popular sovereignty or non-intervention, whereby territorial settlers would decide the status of slavery for themselves. Shortly thereafter, prestigious Adamantines declared themselves in favor of repealing the Missouri Compromise. Dickinson set a pattern by his early support; Charles O'Conor, whom Pierce had removed from his post as United States District Attorney, followed; Bronson renounced an earlier position opposed to slavery extension, thus falling into line with other Hards. By February 14, 1854, thirty-seven Adamantine newspapers supported Repeal.[11]

After announcing their support for the Nebraska bill, the Adamantines opened their batteries upon the Softs. They were confident that this time they possessed an issue which would smoke out the anti-slavery leanings of their rivals. A friend of the Secretary of State informed him that the Hards in Sullivan and Dutchess counties were exultant. At last, they believed, they had cornered the President; he would now have to dismiss a part or even all of his Cabinet or be set aside himself.[12]

The hostility of the Soft press to Nebraska has been described. This "insubordination" delighted the Adamantines, for it seemed to confirm what they had long been saying. The Albany *Argus* incessantly attacked its chief rival, the Albany *Atlas*. It had this comment when the *Atlas* came out against repeal of the Missouri Compromise: "The *Atlas,* which has so long maintained a position of armed neutrality between the camps of Baltimore [the Democratic convention of 1852] and Buffalo [the Free Soil convention of 1848] has renewed its adhesion to the latter." The Hard Shell organ hoped that "the rottenness of the root upon which the Administration leaned. . . is evident to disinterested observers abroad, as at home." The *Argus* even tendered an olive branch to the President:

> And when the Administration, which has forgotten their [the Hard Shell's] proven heroism and devotion in the past, shall turn from later favorites with disgust and dismay, it may find in the national democracy of New York, a band of men whose unbought support it might have earlier secured, had it not imagined the need of purchasing it from others.[13]

Since this overture received no response, the *Argus* continued its war with Pierce and his newspaper, the Washington *Union*. It ridiculed the *Union's* presentation of two pro-Nebraska editorials as exemplary of general Democratic opinion, while ignoring the condemnations from the Soft Shell press. To illustrate its point, the *Argus* prepared its own synopsis of printed opinion. It could find but two Soft journals advocating Nebraska, while counting twenty-six in opposition. In contrast, all National Democratic papers supported it. The *Argus* dared the *Union* to copy its list and "show the South the *complexion* of the men into whose hands every appointment has been surrendered [and] upon whom the title of 'Administration party' has been conferred. . . ."[14]

Although delighted by the discomfiture of their political enemies, National Democrats were uncertain what course to pursue. Edmund Burke, editor of the New Hampshire *Reporter* and the arch-enemy of the President, counselled a policy of opposition to Nebraska unless two conditions were met: Either Pierce repudiated the free soil faction of the party or Southern Democrats abandoned the Administration and allied themselves with Northern National Democrats. If neither of these contingencies occurred, Burke advised his political associates to kill the bill.[15]

New York Hards were also in a quandary. They had committed themselves in favor of the Nebraska bill, yet they hesitated to render aid to the Administration. Animosity finally governed their actions; they could not resist the temptation to vex the President. Their great *coup* was the successful advocacy of extended discussion on Nebraska in the House's Committee of the Whole. Francis Cutting proposed this procedure on March 21, 1854. This motion threatened the bill's future; if it carried, it would place the measure at the bottom of the calendar; and to bring it up for a vote would require nearly twenty roll calls. The Administration had hoped to avoid this pitfall and had exerted considerable pressure to prevent it. Cutting's initiative, however, emboldened other Representatives who wanted further consideration on so momentous an issue, and the motion passed by a vote of 110 to 95. This result encouraged anti-Nebraska forces throughout the North.[16]

In the speech defending his motion, Cutting alluded to several objectionable points in the Senate bill, matters which required further scrutiny. His high-minded scruples were hardly taken seriously by many members; they judged them a smoke screen designed to kill the bill. John C. Breckinridge of Kentucky accused Cutting of hypocrisy. The New Yorker rose to defend himself, and a bitter exchange followed. Breckinridge took especial umbrage at a remark that he had acted dishonorably and had been "skulking" about his chair. Rumors spread of an imminent duel. The mediation of friends, however, resolved the quarrel without bloodshed.[17]

Although Cutting emerged from this encounter physically unscathed, his own and his party's political fortunes sank to a new low. George E. Baker, who was at this time compiling an edition of Seward's speeches, informed the Senator that Cutting was "the most wretched man in the House—he can neither advance or [sic] retreat without annihilation." After a short period of indecision, the Albany *Argus* approved the Congressman's stand, and the Hard Shell State Committee commended his opposition to executive dictation.[18]

Despite their approval of Cutting's obstructionism, Adamantine leaders urged their followers to support Nebraska on the final vote. Five Hard Shell Congressmen disobeyed these appeals. They published a joint letter to their constituents in which they assailed the reopening of the slavery controversy. They had been elected on the Baltimore Platform which had closed this subject forever, and they meant to be faithful to it even though the President was not. Citing as additional evidence the Gadsden Purchase and designs to annex Cuba, they accused Pierce of striving to create a sectional party with himself at its head.[19]

Other prominent Hard Shells also opposed the decision to support the Nebraska bill. James A. Cooley, the Adamantines' candidate for controller in 1853, was so angry that he presided at an anti-Nebraska meeting. Newell wrote Marcy that rebellion in Hard ranks was widespread, and that if the New York *Evening Post* and the Albany *Atlas* would forbear a little in their opposition to Douglas, the Hard Shells would come around to this position too. James T. Brady, the Hards' nominee for attorney general in 1853, also dissented. He had always assumed his faction's dedication to insuring the full constitutional rights of the South, but he had never imagined that it would "give the slightest sanction to any device for extending Slavery, or permit the least diminution of any right which belongs to the North."[20]

Thus, the Nebraska bill was the final straw to many politicians hitherto known for defending the South. They could no longer persist with self-respect, even though many of their colleagues were steadfast. They resigned from their faction and were adrift, the first of a growing number who could no longer find satisfaction within their old parties. Many of these would find the blandishments of Know-Nothingism irresistible.

When the Hard Shell state convention assembled on July 12, 1854, the Adamantines proved faithful to their name. Without flinching, they adopted a resolution approving the Nebraska Act. They applauded the doctrine of congressional non-intervention into territorial affairs, and even maintained that Dickinson had originated this idea when he introduced two resolutions into the United States Senate on December 14, 1847. The Hards now proceeded to criticize the President for "his unwarrantable interference with our local politics . . . and his unjustifiable and undisguised use of his patronage to control our State elections. . . ." Their final resolution condemned "unmanly and dishonest coalitions"—that is, the Hunker-Barnburner alliance of Soft Shells—which "lead only to tricks and struggles for ascendancy between the discordant interests which have bargained to coalesce. . . ."[21]

After adopting these resolutions, the convention nominated its slate. Ignoring Bronson's refusal to run for governor, it chose him by acclamation. The former Collector's candidacy was another act of defiance of the President. The ticket was otherwise undistinguished. Its task completed, the convention adjourned.[22]

New York Hard Shells represented a threat to the unity of the Democratic party. Unscrupulous, often cynical, and totally devoid of principles, they were in politics solely for the spoils of office. When the Hard Shell state convention endorsed the Nebraska Act in defiance of the popular outcry from dozens of public protests, it outraged many old Democrats. These were attracted to new alignments. In the process of carrying out a remorseless campaign against the Softs, the Adamantines reopened the old wounds of 1848 and helped to undermine the unity of the national party. Despite the Hard Shells' willingness to follow Southern initiatives, they met repeated rebuffs. These snubs led to an obstructionist policy with regard to the Nebraska bill which only worsened their alienation. Eager to latch onto a movement with the prospect of success, the desperate Hards were an unsettling influence on the entire party system.

4

The Saratoga Convention

The political upheaval caused by the Kansas-Nebraska Act manifested itself in many ways; the most important and enduring result was the formation of the Republican party. In several Northern and mid-Western states, anti-Nebraska feeling crystallized into movements to hold conventions "without distinction of party." By early July of 1854, such meetings had taken place in Vermont, Ohio, Indiana, Michigan, and Wisconsin. The principal feature of these gatherings was the selection of a fusion ticket for the campaign of 1854. The name increasingly used to denote these new political organizations was "Republican." The success of Republicanism in other states inspired free soilers to strive for fusion in New York. Their efforts added to the turbulent political situation in the Empire State. New York Whigs experienced this new strain most acutely. Torn by incompatible loyalties to the national Whig party and the free soil cause, threatened by defections from Know-Nothings and temperance advocates, confronted by a bewilderingly complex canvass, the Whig party in New York was in a state of crisis. Groping his way in the transformed political climate of 1854, Thurlow Weed struggled to keep himself and his party in power.

The Nebraska Act had the same effect on New York Whigs that it had on the Democrats; it intensified already existing divisions within the party. A strained relationship between conservative and radical Whigs had existed for more than a decade. During this period, many conservatives had joined the Silver Grays' war against the Seward-Weed organization. By reopening the subject about which Whigs differed most heatedly—the slavery issue—Douglas' measure threatened to destroy what remained of Whig unity.

The introduction of the Kansas-Nebraska bill elated radical Whigs. As agitation in the North mushroomed, they perceived an opportunity to cast off their status as a minority party and rise to state and national power. George W. Patterson, an influential Whig from Chautauqua county, wrote his long time friend Thurlow Weed that he was confident Douglas' bill would become law and that the Whigs would reap the benefits. "Let them go their length," he counselled, "and if Seward don't [sic] make more out of its passage, than those who favor it, then I am no judge of the 'signs of the times.' " Another Seward supporter was even more emphatic. He informed Weed that "the Nebraska Bill kills *Pierce* and *Douglas* dead as 'Hell.' " Horace Greeley came to believe that if things were handled right, the entire North would turn against the Democrats.[1]

It appears that Seward also appreciated the opportunities presented by the Nebraska bill. In fact, the Senator may have been so intrigued by these possibilities that he could not resist the temptation to help their realization. Appearing to follow a course of strong opposition to Douglas' scheme, he delivered several speeches which were widely hailed by anti-Nebraska men; and he urged Weed to promote public demonstrations and legislative resolutions. But evidence has come to light which suggests that the New Yorker may have played a far more complex role. He later told both Charles Francis Adams and Montgomery Blair that it was he who had initially suggested the explicit repeal of the Missouri Compromise to Whig Senators Archibald Dixon of Kentucky and James C. Jones of Tennessee. Dixon later offered this amendment to Douglas' first bill, and the Little Giant, under Southern pressure, accepted it.[2]

If Seward did indeed adopt this course, his motivation is unclear and open to speculation. Two points appear certain: He wished to make the bill obnoxious to New Yorkers and cripple the Northern Democrats; and at this time, as we shall see, he opposed disbanding the national Whig party and participating in a fusion movement with antislavery Democrats. Perhaps he believed that a crisis within Whig ranks would foster his personal ambition. He might then emerge as a compromise figure between the North and the South and go to the White House as the candidate of the united Whig party.[3] Such a strategy would be consistent with Seward's subsequent attempts at reconciliation during the secession crisis of 1860-1861.

Unlike the radicals in their party, conservative Whigs saw nothing bright in the Nebraska controversy. They viewed it as an unmitigated disaster. Former Governor Washington Hunt accurately expressed the attitude of conservatives: "The attempt to disturb the Missouri Compromise is audacious and atrocious. I regret this new agitation in all its aspects. It will prove more dangerous than the conflicts of 1820 or 1850." New York's wealthy and urbane junior Senator, Hamilton Fish, did all he could to prevent passage. He submitted to Weed his own draft of anti-Nebraska resolutions which he believed preferable to those already before the state legislature. He warned that swift action was essential to make wavering Congressmen aware of the indignation of their constituents. One Whig, who described himself as "old fashioned," professed to believe in the Union and the Compromises of 1820 and 1850, and the South's existing rights over slavery. But he feared that Douglas and the Democrats would drive him from this position into the arms of the abolitionists.[4]

The major reason for the conservatives' despair was their apprehension that the Nebraska crisis would destroy the Whig party as a national organization. They believed that an alliance of the more substantial citizens in both the North and the South was essential for the prosperity and the very continuance of the Union. The national party had received a strong blow in the election of 1852 when many Southerners deserted Winfield Scott to vote for Pierce. Greeley had declared the party dead soon after the canvass and many agreed with his verdict. Despite the erosion of mutual trust, the party had held together, and because of bickering among the dominant Democrats, elected some of its local candidates. Conservatives in both sections gained confidence and hoped that the old alliance could be patched up in 1856. The Nebraska bill seemed to destroy these hopes.

Thurlow Weed was at heart a conservative, although closely allied with Seward and the radical wing of the party. He had no desire to sever ties with Southern Whigs and organize along strictly Northern lines. Quite the contrary is true; the Albany politician's joy at the discomfiture of New York Democrats was tempered by his concern for the national Whig organization. "This Nebraska business will entirely denationalize the Whig Party," he lamented to Fish. "I cannot see how or where good can come out of it—If Southern Whigs would have been sustained at Home in going against it, we would have [been] well." Weed made several vain appeals in his Albany *Evening Journal* for Southern Whigs to eschew the Nebraska bill.[5]

Although radical and conservative Whigs differed about the implications of the Nebraska Act, the former, considering it an opportunity to be exploited, and the latter, a catastrophe to be remedied, both groups looked upon it in terms of its effect upon the Whig party. The initiative for forming the Republican party in New York did not come from the Whigs, but from Free Soilers or Free Democrats. Rather than welcoming Free Democratic efforts for fusion, most Whigs conceived them as serious threats, which they were determined to thwart. The ensuing conflict between opponents and proponents of fusion added significantly to the tense political situation in the state.

The Whigs' determination to maintain their party intact was challenged when a call appeared for a state convention "without distinction of party" to be held at Saratoga Springs on August 16, 1854; New York seemed to be following those states which had pioneered the Republican movement. The call specified that a mass meeting in each county would choose five delegates from each assembly district. It is noteworthy that the formation of a new state ticket was not mentioned as a subject for consideration.[6] Despite this omission, Free Democrats had precisely this goal in mind. Before we consider the struggle between Whigs and Free Democrats at Saratoga, we must investigate the motives of both.

After its initial campaign in 1848, the fortunes of the Free Soil party declined. The large Barnburner contingent which had swelled its ranks returned to the Democratic fold in 1849. The Compromise of 1850 struck another blow. Gamaliel Bailey—the editor of the *National Era,* the Free Soilers' organ in Washington—issued a call for a "National Convention of Freemen" to oppose the Compromise, but it went unheeded. By late 1850, the name "Free Soil" had fallen into disuse, and the remaining small group of zealots called themselves the Free Democratic party.[7]

For the presidential campaign of 1852, the Free Democrats waged a vigorous campaign. Their platform denounced the Compromise of 1850, especially the Fugitive Slave Act, which the Whig and Democratic national conventions had endorsed. With John P. Hale, the former Senator from New Hampshire as their standard-bearer, the Free Democrats garnered about one-half of their vote in 1848. Their greatest loss came in New York, where they obtained 25,000 votes compared to the 120,000 they had received during Martin Van Buren's candidacy. It nevertheless, was a good showing. A party commanding this many votes could not be disregarded in the closely contested elections of the Empire State; the lure of these ballots was a constant force on politicians seeking to construct winning coalitions.

The Kansas-Nebraska Act provided the opportunity for which Free Democrats had been waiting. The precarious sectional peace that had prevailed under the Compromise of 1850 was broken; old party loyalties were crumbling; thousands of Whigs and Democrats were experimenting with new political allegiances. The constant warning of Free Democrats that the "slaveocracy" was an unappeasable, aggressive force seemed warranted. Under these changed circumstances, the dream which had sustained loyal Free Democrats in the discouraging years from 1849-1853—the formation of a broad coalition opposed to the extension of slavery—appeared realizable.

The *National Era* played a prominent role in advocating the creation of this amalgam. Immediately after the House passed Douglas' bill, the *Era* urged the eighty anti-Nebraska Congressmen from the free states—Democrats, Whigs, and Free Democrats—to call "upon the people to disregard obsolete issues, old prejudices, mere party names, and rally as one man for the re-establishment of liberty and the overthrow of the Slave power. Never mind your parties, gentlemen. 'Let the dead bury their dead.' "[8]

The New York Free Democratic party had been ineffective in the 1853 election; the division between Democrats had reduced its leverage over the Whigs. Encouraged by the uproar against the Nebraska Act, the Free Democrats sought to align New York with those states which had already established a branch of the Republican party.[9] Focusing their efforts on the forthcoming Saratoga convention, they wanted it to form a fusion ticket and not merely to denounce Douglas and Pierce.

Free Democrats played an active role in county mass meetings to select delegates to Saratoga. They had two objects in mind: the adoption of resolutions calling for nominations and the election of Free Democrats as delegates. John P. Hale delivered a two hour oration at both Rome and Oneida. Another Free Democratic hero, David Wilmot of Pennsylvania, spoke in Chemung county. His efforts succeeded; the assemblage adopted the following resolution: "*Resolved,* That we will support no nominee, of any party, unless that party is entirely separated from the *Southern wing* of either of the old Whig or Democratic parties." The citizens of Madison county passed a similar declaration. As the convention date approached, the New York Times' editor, Henry J. Raymond, reported to Weed that he had "found Joseph Blunt and John Jay busy in preparing resolutions, delegates & c. for the Saratoga Convention. Both are anxious for nominations."[10]

The enthusiasm of the Free Democrats for a fusion ticket at Saratoga finally came to be shared by Horace Greeley. The crusading editor of the New York *Tribune* had not always believed that a new organization was possible in his home state. Greeley abruptly changed his mind, however, once Douglas' bill had been enacted. He was now certain that the people were not only ready but demanded a union of all those hostile to Nebraska. The *Tribune* carefully watched and highly praised fusion conventions in other states. Pleased with the name "Republican"—which the Jackson, Michigan meeting (July 6, 1854) had given to its new fusion party, the editor thought this title would "be very generally adopted."[11]

Greeley devised a bold political course which he believed would further the antislavery and temperance causes, and secure the governorship for himself. Linking the two issues was the essential component of his strategy. "I like the two questions together," he wrote to his friend, Schuyler Colfax. "My first concern is to deserve victory, and I know we do that on the new platform." [12]

Greeley expected his strategy and industry to be rewarded by the gubernatorial nomination at Saratoga. Despite his formidable talents and success as a journalist, he harbored a burning ambition for elective office. He had labored long and hard in support of others' advancement. Now he would collect those debts and force his friends, especially Seward and Weed, to acknowledge his contributions and award him his rightful prize.[13]

The Free Democrats' and Greeley's efforts to promote fusion in New York put considerable pressure on Seward. Although the Senator's motives during the Nebraska controversy are cloudy, it is clear that he had no desire to disband the Whig party. Rather than welcoming Free Democratic overtures for fusion, he sought to avoid them. From Washington, he wrote to Weed that he was "plagued to death with letters asking advice about disbanding and reorganizing. . . ." "The Free Soilers here are engaging in schemes for nominating Col. Benton and dissolving the Whig party. We are to hear all manner of absurdities practiced, and there are not less than half a dozen parties coming to negotiate with me as if I was a vender of votes." Seward hoped that he could avoid saying anything indiscreet.[14]

Particularly embarrassing was Greeley's request that Seward draft a statement proposing a union of all parties against Nebraska. "How would such an address look, signed by me? How would it look signed by others and not by me?" he asked Weed. The Senator implored his friend to help him by writing a strong appeal for the people "to look away from Washington and settle these things practically at home. I shall forbear at all costs."[15]

By studying the actions of Thurlow Weed in 1854, one can best appreciate the stresses brought to bear upon the Whig party. Weed shared Seward's reluctance to abandon old party ties. He had attempted to hold the national Whig organization together during the Nebraska struggle in the Congress; it was not easy for him to adjust to the permanent loss of the Southern wing of his party. Perhaps he still clung to the hope that a reconciliation could somehow be affected. But Weed was a political realist, and he began to take hesitant steps in the direction of new alignments. By the summer of 1854, he crossed party lines to endorse the anti-Nebraska Soft Shell, Reuben E. Fenton of Chautauqua, for re-election to the House. He gave his approval to the Jackson, Michigan meeting which established the Republican party in that state and urged Whigs to cooperate in the movement. He praised three-hundred New Englanders bound for Kansas as "noble men" engaged in a "holy crusade."[16]

Despite this movement toward a broader coalition, Weed resolutely refused to disband the Whig party in New York. He declared that the Northern Whig party, by its unanimous opposition to Douglas, had demonstrated that it was the party of freedom and deserved the support of all anti-Nebraska men. Fusion was only justifiable in areas where the party was weak (as in most of the mid-West); where the Whigs were strong, they should remain a distinct entity. From three decades of experience, Weed realized that a state-wide party could not be built rapidly. To abandon a smooth functioning machine for a new and untried organization was always dangerous. In 1854, political experimentation seemed more than ever fraught with peril. The rise of Know-Nothingism posed a formidable threat to New York Whigs and especially to Seward's re-election to the Senate. The Albany leader felt that any further confusion could only benefit his arch-enemies, the Silver Grays.[17]

Weed took a number of steps to insure that the Saratoga meeting would not make nominations. He accepted Washington Hunt's suggestion to see that the Whig State Committee issue a call for a convention, in advance of the Saratoga gathering. This would signalize Whig intentions to act independently. Weed, however, also had more aggressive action in mind. He informed Patterson that he "did not like the movement [Saratoga] and can not now see any good that it will do. But we ought to have Friends in it—to guard against mischief." Weed's will was carried out by his lieutenants as they filtered into the county mass meetings which chose delegates to Saratoga. At one such public assembly—significantly held at Auburn, the village where Seward made his home—the Whigs were observed to be violently opposed to a resolution recommending the organization of an independent party. An associate of the Albany leader reported that the Albion convocation was controlled by abolitionists, Free Democrats, and Softs, pushed on by a few Silver Grays—all of whom ardently desired the dismemberment of the Whig party. Although they could not prevent a resolution calling for a fusion ticket, the Sewardites did succeed in choosing two delegates of the "right stamp." Whigs in Monroe, Genesee, Livingston, Erie, and Niagara counties encountered fewer difficulties and reported everything under control.[18]

Weed's most difficult task was to convince Greeley to abandon his own plans. It is not exactly clear how this was done. He must have appealed for aid in thwarting the nativist conspiracy against Seward, generating in Greeley's mind his own fear that if nominations were made at Saratoga, he would be powerless to prevent a Silver Gray-Know-Nothing takeover of the Whig convention of September 20. It is also possible that Weed hinted—or Greeley thought he hinted—at the editor's nomination for some state-wide office, most probably lieutenant governor. In any event, Greeley agreed to cooperate with Weed, but not without the severest misgivings. He revealed his despair to his confidant, Colfax:

> We shall have no nomination at Saratoga and alas, no fusion at all, which will do harm in all the "fusion" states. It will tell heavily against us that we carry all the states Whig that we can, and go "fusion" where we can do no better. Schuyler, this won't work, and you'll find it so.[19]

Representatives of the entire spectrum of New York politics—Hard and Soft Shells, Free Democrats, Seward and Silver Gray Whigs, temperance advocates, Know-Nothings, and abolitionists—arrived at Saratoga by August 16, 1854.[20] They came from all but three counties. Horace Greeley reported as chairman of the committee on resolutions. He read statements condemning the Nebraska Act and the doctrine of popular sovereignty, affirming the right of Congress to prohibit slavery in the territories, opposing the admission of any new slave states into the Union, and declaring that free labor could never compete with a slave system.

It was the last resolution which precipitated the crucial question of a fusion party with its own state ticket:

Resolved, That we heartily approve the course of the freemen of Connecticut, Vermont, Iowa, Ohio, Indiana, Wisconsin, and Michigan, postponing or disregarding their minor differences of opinion or preference, and acting together cordially and trustingly in the sacred cause of freedom, of free labor and free soil, and we commend their spirit to the freemen of this and other states, exhorting each to renounce his party whenever that party proves unfaithful to human freedom.

Before a vote could be taken on this declaration, E. F. Bullard of Saratoga, a former Hard Shell, moved an amendment to follow the example of the previously mentioned states by nominating a state ticket made up of all political organizations. He said the "convention was a scrap book of all parties, and it must act true to the cause." Great confusion greeted this proposal. Despite the hubbub, a vote was called on the amendment and an attempt made to count the yeas and nays. It was defeated.

Several delegates now insisted on being heard to urge reconsideration. One speaker warned the convention that if it did not do its duty, the people would; he hinted at a bolt. A Free Democrat from Genesee county pleaded that it was time for the North to remove the South's black flag from the Capitol. He wanted the meeting to serve its true function, which was an oven to bake doughfaces. Leonard Gibbs of Washington county, a professed abolitionist, warned the delegates to beware of both major parties, for they were false to freedom. He urged unity of action among men of all parties in a common cause against slavery.

During this flurry of appeals, repeated cries were heard for Preston King to address the meeting. As a Congressman representing St. Lawrence and Herkimer counties, King had been an early supporter of the Wilmot Proviso and had played a prominent role in the bolt of 1847-1848. He had drifted back to the Democratic party following the Compromise of 1850, but he had done so reluctantly. The Nebraska bill stirred him into activity. He addressed public meetings and wrote privately to former Barnburners to gather support against the measure. At this time, he was trying to start a presidential boom for Thomas Hart Benton, who had voted against Nebraska. By the late summer of 1854, it was apparent to many that King had assumed the leadership of the free soil Democrats—the position which John Van Buren had relinquished.[21]

If the Free Democrats expected King to give a powerful boost to their pleas, they were disappointed. He argued that the great mass of the people was not prepared to receive a new slate from the convention. It was true, he declared, that all parties were rotten and required outside pressure to hold them together. Yet the time was not ripe for a new organization; it would be inundated by the unprecedented complexities of this election year. Quite unintentionally, King had done Weed and Seward a great favor. Just as sentiment was warming up for reconsideration of the nominations question, he had dampened this enthusiasm. Thus developed a unity of opinion on the forthcoming campaign which would lay the basis for future cooperation.

The convention finally decided to postpone the decision on an independent ticket until September 26, 1854, when it would reconvene at Auburn. The political situation would be clearer then; both the Soft Shells and the Whigs would have held their state conventions. Henry J. Raymond, arguing that by delaying its deliberations the meeting could exercise greater pressure on the other parties' platforms and candidates, espoused this solution. This, he said, was the proper task of the present assembly and not the creation of a new organization.

Although this course did not please the abolitionists and the Free Democrats, the Whigs, who were in control, pressed for adjournment. A Know-Nothing delegate tried to discuss a resolution pledging the convention "to support no man or measure who will subject us to a foreign hierarchy." It was significant that this attempt to divert attention from the slavery to the nativist issue was unsuccessful. The delegates refused to consider the resolution and adjourned.

The Saratoga convention climaxed several months of struggle between Free Democrats and Whigs throughout the state. Although divided among themselves, radical and conservative Whigs united under Weed's leadership and thwarted the aggressive Free Democratic campaign to establish the Republican party in the Empire State. Weed's behavior revealed the pressures exerted upon him and other Whigs. He sympathized with the conservatives in his party and viewed the Nebraska bill as a disaster. A Whig for over twenty years, he could not easily accept the idea of his party's dissolution, but he was opposed to the extension of slavery and had said so on many occasions. Also, it could not be denied that the sectional vote by Northern and Southern Whigs on the Nebraska bill had given a blow to the national Whig organization. As a practical politician, Weed recognized that he had to make adjustments, and he made some gestures toward a new alignment. When confronted with the Free Democrats' demand for immediate fusion, however, he resisted their attempts. His basic conservatism played a part in this decision; perhaps he shared the hope of other conservatives that the national

Whig party could be revived. But his most pressing reason for opposing fusion was a practical one, his belief that it would further disrupt the political situation. More turmoil, he felt, could only aid his most bitter opponents, the Silver Gray-Know-Nothings, and result in Seward's defeat for re-election in 1855. Weed knew that his problems were not over; he would soon have to confront a powerful challenge from the nativists for control of his party.

5

The Softs Acquiesce in Nebraska

The Soft Shells' prospects for the election of 1854 looked dim. Their unity was threatened by ex-Barnburners outraged by Douglas' measure; their newspapers antagonized the Administration by heaping abuse on the Nebraska bill; discontented Tammanyites had carried strident resolutions against the President's patronage policies; the Hard Shells continued to spurn overtures for reconciliation. Could the Softs overcome these problems? Could they maintain unity and make a respectable showing in the coming canvass? The answers to these questions were of critical importance for the future of the Democratic party in New York.

The Softs' principal dilemma was to formulate a position on the Nebraska issue acceptable to the dissidents in their own ranks, their constituents, and the President. The immediate problem was to persuade Radical Democrats who had opposed the *bill* to acquiesce in the *law*. Secretary Marcy had labored to keep this path open by opposing any test of Democratic orthodoxy while the bill was before Congress. He had urged that Nebraska's adversaries be treated indulgently and suffer no penalties, cautioning his political lieutenants against peremptory behavior, lest this alienate those who could subsequently be drawn back to the party. The Secretary of State grasped that the only way for his party to weather the Nebraska storm was through an *ex post facto* reconciliation.[1]

It remained to convince the President that he must relieve the pressure on Northern Democrats, that he could not demand active support for his Nebraska policy, and that he must be content with acquiescence. That Pierce had reluctantly come to this conclusion seemed apparent from the resolutions adopted by the "Softs" in his native New Hampshire. These statements, widely believed to have

43

been penned in Washington, expressed no direct approval of Nebraska; they merely accepted the *status quo*. The pragmatic effect of this position did not escape notice. The New York *Evening Post* stated: "Not to condemn it is to approve of it. Everyone feels that the New Hampshire resolutions were intended to obtain by indirection what could be construed into an approval of the Nebraska bill." The *Post* quoted from the Washington *Union* to show that the Administration took this view of the matter.[2]

The action of New Hampshire offered the prospect of imitation in other Northern states, and New York Democrats warned Secretary Marcy that unless they obtained a similar privilege, they could not hope to avoid a bolt. The Collector of the Port, Heman J. Redfield, made his plea in this candid letter:

> As to the resolutions—We can *acquiesce in* but *not approve* Nebraska. I saw [Henry H.] Van Dyck [an editor] of the Atlas yesterday. He says that we *can acquiesce* and keep together—but if more is attempted we may divide—in which case, *between you and I,* the administration will be in *very small minority. I have* no hesitation in approving fully the principle contained in the late territorial bills and many others would do likewise—But I should not like to call a *division* upon the question in the State Convention and it ought not to be invited on. Will acquiescence satisfy our friends at Washington?

After this appeal went to Washington, the Albany *Atlas* began to editorialize for the policy of letting bygones be bygones; it urged the forthcoming Soft Shell convention to condemn the Nebraska bill but *not* to ask its repeal.[3]

The Democratic State Committee announced that the forthcoming convention would take place at Syracuse on September 6, 1854. Some of the local meetings to select representatives for the Syracuse convention went off smoothly; the rural postmaster, generally the party leader in his area, engineered the selection of pro-Nebraska delegates. New York City's Tammany delegation consisted of an almost solid block of custom house and post office appointees and their associates. However, in other counties Barnburners resisted the federal office-holders' attempt to control the proceedings. In several cases the insurgents succeeded in choosing delegates and passed strong resolutions against the repeal of the Missouri Compromise.[4]

The dominant note, however, of most pre-convention meetings was reconciliation. Politicians eagerly sought to smooth over differences, even at the price of embracing opposites simultaneously. The Softs in Chautauqua passed one resolution praising the President, and another lauding their anti-Nebraska Congressman, Reuben R. Fenton. A declaration adopted in Yates county eulogized the Pierce Administration, supported the Missouri Compromise and the Wilmot Proviso, and denounced the Nebraska Act in the same sentence. In Geneva, Judge Chester Loomis tried to censure the President, but the meeting could not agree on any statement. Loomis refused an offer of a nomination for the assembly; he would not accept an honor from men afraid to declare their principles.[5] These efforts to relieve the tensions caused by the Nebraska Act revealed the desire of most Softs to hold their faction together.

As the Syracuse convention approached, Administration supporters feared they would have difficulty controlling it. The Batavia *Democrat,* Collector Redfield's organ, believed Preston King and other free soilers would be seduced by the blandishments held out by the Whigs at Saratoga. The Oswego *Palladium* and the Westchester *Gazette* also noted the anxieties of the custom house. Distressed by the large number of anti-Nebraskaites in the Buffalo delegation, one Soft expressed his opinion that there would be "too many *prominent ultra free-soilers* in the Convention, to pass such resolutions as might be desirable, or to make such a platform as Seymour can run on."[6]

A day before the Syracuse convention assembled, two caucuses designed to test the views of the delegates revealed a strong anti-Nebraska attitude. John Cochrane attempted to assuage this feeling by opposing any party test on the issue; the past position of each delegate would be forgotten provided he acceded to the repeal of the Missouri Compromise and did not advocate its restoration. Despite a similar effort at conciliation at the other caucus, Captain Isaiah Rynders, Cochrane's assistant as Surveyor of the Port, encountered heavy resistance. When it adjourned, he gathered his supporters, who pledged to walk out if anti-Nebraska resolutions passed. The Captain could be seen lobbying with groups of rural delegates for the rest of the day.[7]

The convention convened on a steamy hot day in which the mercury rose to a temperature of ninety-eight degrees in the shade.[8] A proposal to seek reconciliation with the Hard Shells by offering to split the ticket with them went down to defeat. The committee on resolutions then announced that it wished to make two reports. The majority supported the following resolution:

> *Resolved,* That we consider the introduction of the clause in the Nebraska and Kansas bill repealing the Missouri Compromise as *inexpedient and unnecessary,* but we are opposed to any agitation having in

view the restoration of that line, or tending to promote any sectional controversy in relation thereto: And we congratulate the country that the results to grow out of that measure are likely to prove beneficial to the people of the territories. . . . (my italics)

Abijah Mann, Jr., of Queens county, then read the minority declaration:

> *Resolved,* As the sense of this convention representing the democracy of the state, that we *unqualifiedly disapprove* of the repeal, by the present Congress, of the section of the act, commonly known as the Missouri Compromise. . . . (my italics)

This set the stage for a confrontation between King and Cochrane, the champions of the rival positions.

King had carefully considered what action he would take with Democrats who shared his indignation about Nebraska.[9] At the Saratoga convention, he had opposed the formation of a fusion ticket, much to the regret of Free Democrats but to the delight of Weed and Seward. He was now present at Syracuse to make a last effort to save his party from Southern domination. Taking the floor amidst cheers to concur with the minority resolution, he warned that a veiled approval of the Nebraska Act would abandon the Democracy to the cause of slavery expansionism which would be repudiated by the people. He acknowledged that party discipline required adherence to the majority of the convention, but he could not give such an assurance on a question of so much importance.

Cochrane immediately rose to deny the charge that his position surrendered the Barnburners' objectives and replaced them with proslavery principles. He had not forsaken the credo of "free-soil, free speech and free men" when he embraced a then ancient Democratic doctrine of the right of all men, whether in a state or territory, to govern themselves. It was this right, Cochrane declared, that was the true "higher law" and the foundation of all our institutions. The Surveyor reiterated his opposition to the expansion of slavery and his belief that Kansas and Nebraska would be free states.

The chairman, William H. Ludlow, called for a division on the question, and the convention defeated the minority resolution by a vote of 245 to 149. Over one-hundred delegates failed to vote. Abstention must have appealed to many of them as a compromise between self-respect and self-preservation.

Abijah Mann, Jr., tried to offer amendments to the resolution just adopted, but the chairman ruled them out of order. Undaunted by this check, Mann demanded that Governor Seymour's views on the

Nebraska Act be made known to the convention before he was considered for renomination. Again, his proposal was ruled out of order.[10] These arbitrary decisions by the presiding officer aggravated the anger of delegates who had sought a strong condemnation of Repeal. Preston King now rose, declared he could no longer work with the convention, and walked out. This served as a signal for a general exodus. The New York *Evening Post's* correspondent estimated the number of bolters to have been over one-hundred. The Albany *Atlas* disputed this figure, however, maintaining that few had walked out and that some had returned.[11]

With this disruption over, the remaining Softs renominated Horatio Seymour for governor and chose William H. Ludlow, the chairman of the convention, for lieutenant governor. By supporting Seymour, they presented a challenge to the prohibitionists. The Maine Law had rapidly become an important issue in the coming election.

These results destroyed the hopes of those Democrats who had desired and anticipated a re-enactment of the events of 1847-1848. The New York *Evening Post* called the Syracuse resolutions "spiritless and cowardly," and "wholly inadequate as they were to express the views of the great majority of those who were represented in that convention." The Administration had received a mild rebuke instead of the broadside it deserved.[12] Other old Barnburner papers expressed their disappointment in similar terms.[13]

The *National Era's* aim to unite all those opposed to Repeal into a new party suffered a setback. Although the Democrats in New Hampshire, Vermont, Maine, and Pennsylvania had succumbed to the Administration, the *Era* had hoped that the Barnburners would show their old defiance. Gamaliel Bailey, the editor of the *Era,* sarcastically wrote:

> They [the Softs] would blow hot and cold with the same breath; they would ride two horses traveling in opposite directions; they would enact contradictions, serve God and the Devil, please the People and Franklin Pierce. So the Soft Convention met—a softer one never assembled—and the game of double dealing began.[14]

The New York *Tribune* was not disappointed, because it had expected such a result. However, Greeley believed the Softs had lost "their golden moment." Had they spurned the yoke of the federal officeholders and nominated Preston King for governor on an anti-Nebraska platform, they would have been swept into power. The editor also could not resist the temptation to scorn the Softs' Nebraska resolution. Was there "ever a more sniveling, twaddling, ropedancer balancing proposition?" he asked. This declaration, he predicted, would seal the fate of its proponents; they would be reduced to a powerless faction, abandoned by the thousands who once supported them.[15]

Why did the Soft Shells give up "their golden moment" and follow the lead of Tammany Hall at this critical juncture? The answer, like the answer to all questions of human motivation, is complex.

Certainly, the desire to retain the Administration's patronage played the dominant role with New York City politicians; the thought of relinquishing the custom house and the post office to the Hard Shells was too painful. Tammany Congressmen who voted for the Nebraska bill expected their rewards. In fact, Collector Redfield complained about the overbearing arrogance of William A. Walker and Peter Rowe; he had been compelled to inform them that there were limits to their influence in regard to appointments.[16]

At this time, as throughout most of its history, Tammany Hall was not the meeting place of the genteel, the squeamish, or the weak. The Wigwam, as Tammany was affectionately called, boasted a well-stocked bar and a host of rough-and-ready politicians, equally adept at wielding brassknuckles and in formulating resolutions. The activities of Isaiah Rynders at the Syracuse convention have been described. Additional to his duties as Deputy Collector, Rynders led the notorious Empire Club, a band of toughs famous for their street fighting abilities. William M. Tweed had begun his rise to the top by serving a term in Congress where he voted for the Nebraska bill. The young John Kelly had just secured the Soft nomination to oppose the Hard's Mike Walsh for a seat in the national legislature. Fernando Wood prepared to run for his first term as Mayor of New York City against the leader of the national Know-Nothing party, James W. Barker. In spite of a reputation already dubious, Daniel Sickles had recently been appointed Secretary to James Buchanan, the United States ambassador to Great Britain.

Despite its frank love for the spoils of office, Tammany Hall did represent the views, and in its way, looked after the needs of its constituents, largely impoverished Irish immigrants. The Wigwam responded to the Hibernians' fear of free Negro competition and consistently opposed any agitation with a remote tinge of abolitionism, and it classified the anti-Nebraska movement in that category. It also led the party against the nativist menace. On June 21, 1854, the Democratic General Committee adopted resolutions against any attempt to limit the rights of adopted citizens, and the chief feature of the Softs' Fourth of July celebration was Lorenzo Shepard's attack on Know-Nothingism. It should be noted, that although the Syracuse convention hedged on the Nebraska issue, it took an unequivocal position against religious and anti-foreign bigotry.[17]

Why did the great mass of rural delegates, many of them former Barnburners, follow Tammany Hall's leadership? For some, the tie of party was the crucial factor. Ironically, the Barnburners' bolt strengthened rather than weakened their loyalty to the Democracy. Many never had any real heart in the Free Soil party and had entered its ranks because of their fidelity to the Van Burens. They were relieved to have been able to return to their familiar alliances and set themselves against any new revolts.[18]

Some antislavery Democrats easily convinced themselves that substitution of Douglas' squatter sovereignty doctrine for the Missouri Compromise did not constitute grounds for leaving the party. They reasoned that no irretrievable damage had been done; Kansas would in all probability enter the Union as a free state. So why inflame a situation from which only the Whigs could benefit?[19] Samuel J. Tilden, an ex-Barnburner himself and an opponent of Nebraska, accurately described the state of feeling among the great majority of his old colleagues:

> The general disposition among those most dissatisfied with the course of things at Washington is disgust; indifference, in some cases individual opposition, in many independent personal action; but very little towards organized, affirmative movement. They expect the Democratic party to be broken down for the time. They expect the folly of its leaders to inure to the benefit of the Whigs . . . Most will expect the Democratic party to rise again, purified, and to resuming relations with it. I know of none —tho' doubtless there are such individuals—who intend permanent union with the Whigs. I know of few who would undertake the formation of a new party outside of existing organizations. The body of those who went with us in 1848 will continue within the organization in which they have since acted.[20]

At this point, only a few Barnburners who were dedicated to preventing the spread of slavery could not live with the Softs' actions. Those who followed Preston King from the Syracuse convention were the vanguard of their party in the new Republican organization.

Another reason for the Radical Democrats' reluctance to enter a fusion movement was their distrust of Whiggery and their hatred of nativism. The Albany *Atlas* presumed that the Know-Nothings would overwhelm the Seward-Weed organization at the Whig state convention. It warned Democrats to beware of a party which professed devotion to human freedom but was gangrened by bigotry. Moreover, the intolerant behavior of the Whigs at the Saratoga anti-Nebraska convention alienated many Democrats who considered joining them.[21]

Thus, the Soft Shells decided to submit to the Administration and to Southern Democrats, and to spurn fusion. This was a crucial choice and determined the future course of the party. Desire for patronage, optimism concerning Kansas' and Nebraska's eventual freedom, and fear of being submerged within a Whig party tainted by Know-Nothingism, played a part in this decision. These reasons seem inadequate, however, to completely explain the Softs' actions, and one is encouraged to speculate about another motive, the motive of party loyalty, which although more difficult to assess, probably outweighed all other factors. To Democrats who had participated in the political battles of the Jacksonian era, the party was held in deep reverence. Perhaps it is not too much to say that party affiliation was an important part of a man's identity, that it was a tie that transcended reason, and that consequently, it could not be easily shed. When we assume this powerful devotion, we can better understand the remarkable resilience of the Democratic party. Although the Kansas-Nebraska Act antagonized many former Barnburners, most of them remained loyal. As Tilden correctly observed, the great majority of them believed the Democratic party would be purified. In 1854, they allowed their hopes to blind them to the fact that the Softs had capitulated to Southern demands. Durable as were the bonds uniting the Democratic party, they were not unbreakable; and as the crisis of the party system continued, more and more Democrats would cut loose from the organization.

6

Political Wizardry

With the disintegration of the party system, politicians were forced to deal with a turbulent and uncertain environment. The eclipse of old landmarks—the familiar questions of tariff, monetary policy, and internal improvements—made the situation especially difficult. Gauging the relative strengths of the new issues—Nebraska, temperance, and nativism—became essential for political survival. Thurlow Weed felt the pressures of this upheaval most acutely. He confronted a series of challenges which endangered his party's existence. At the Saratoga anti-Nebraska convention, he had thwarted the Free Democrats' attempt to dissolve the Whig organization and to establish a Republican party in New York. However, his problems were far from over. He had yet to grapple with temperance advocates and Silver Gray-Know-Nothings; these posed an even greater menace to his leadership. How Weed fought against these threats to the unity of his party provides an example of a consummate politician's response to the crisis of 1854. It also reveals the important role which political manipulators played in shaping the course of events.

Governor Seymour's veto of New York's version of the Maine Law brought the temperance issue into prominence. The Governor's action restored an old dilemma for Weed; he had hoped that enactment of this measure would have removed this troublesome question from politics. Personally, Weed considered temperance agitation as a dangerous nuisance inspired by fanatical reformers, whom he had always held in contempt. But as the Whig leader, he knew that this question had created a dangerous situation within his party. Whigs in the central and western sections of the state overwhelmingly supported prohibition while conservatives, especially in New York City, generally opposed it. Party ties had become so weak that both groups threatened to cut loose from their old organization unless they had their way.[1]

Seymour's motives for the veto cannot be known with certainty. His message declared the bill unconstitutional, "unjust and oppressive in its character and subversive of well settled principles of legislation."[2] As might be expected, prohibitionists were unimpressed with his reasoning, and they roundly criticized him for it. Horace Greeley charged the Governor with a maneuver designed to shore up his own and his party's political fortunes by securing the support of the liquor dealers. Agreeing with this analysis, Weed wrote Patterson that Seymour had "made a desperate plunge on the grounds, I suppose, that he had nothing to lose."[3]

Whether idealism or politics or a mixture of the two influenced Seymour's decision, the effect of his action cannot be disputed: it made temperance an important issue in the forthcoming election. Washington Hunt, who was in Albany following the veto, informed Hamilton Fish that "the Maine Law was about as prominent a topic there, as Nebraska at Washington . . . There is no denying that Seymour's veto gives him an active and positive force, it makes him somewhat formidable as a candidate. . . ."[4]

Almost at once, the anti-Nebraska movement, which had absorbed so much of the energies of religious idealists in the Burned-over-region, was overshadowed. Temperance organizations immediately declared that they would renew the struggle and that they would not allow their cause to be subordinated to any other; moreover, they announced that if the Whigs would not cooperate, they were prepared to form their own party. One group, the Friends of Temperance, insisted on the primacy of the liquor question and pledged itself "to disregard in the coming political contest all party-ties and partisan associations, and cast our votes for none but men pledged to enact a prohibitory law." Public meetings in central and western New York echoed this demand. In Allegany county, prohibitionists urged that support for the Saratoga anti-Nebraska convention be contingent on a resolution favoring the Maine Law. This proposal created a furor as many considered it irrelevant, but it passed.[5]

A day after the veto, Greeley rallied the temperance forces for a final battle: "If we must have the controversy over again, and under a form calculated to render it more sharp and bitter, why so be it. We are ready for the contest whenever and wherever it must be waged." Frowning upon a suggestion to adjourn the liquor question and concentrate on the Nebraska issue, he argued that this action would not bring as many German-Americans into the antislavery coalition as its advocates claimed; before the election they would be corrupted by custom house politicians in the grog shops of the city.[6]

Although the resurgence of temperance agitation exerted a great strain on the New York Whig party, to Thurlow Weed the growth of Know-Nothingism in the rural areas of the state was even more alarming. The American-Republican movement of 1844-1845 had been isolated in New York City.[7] Logically enough, nativist sentiment had always been strongest in cities and towns where the great majority of Catholic immigrants settled. But in 1854, the countryside, which was overwhelmingly American-born and Protestant, was suddenly seized with xenophobic hysteria, and Know-Nothing lodges were formed everywhere, especially in central and western New York, the center of Whig power.

Know-Nothing expansionism posed a powerful threat to Weed's control over the Whig state convention, scheduled to assemble at Syracuse on September 20. The reason for this was simply the difficulty of knowing whether a formerly faithful Whig had given his allegiance to the Order, and was now pledged to betray his old comrades. None could be absolutely depended upon, and all depended on the strength of the personal friendships which Weed had established during his long career.

County meetings to select delegates often witnessed battles for domination between Sewardites and Silver Grays, who were in league with the Know-Nothings. Weed received varying reports of success and failure from his lieutenants. At Little Falls, the nativists took a caucus entirely out of the hands of loyal Whigs and elected their own delegates. The situation was reversed at Albion; despite a thorough effort by the Silver Grays, the Sewardites remained in control. As the convention approached, Weed was worried. "I don't see how we are to get through the convention safely," he wrote to Patterson. "The breakers ahead cause serious apprehensions."[8]

The efforts of Daniel Ullman, a New York City lawyer and a prominent Silver Gray, to secure the gubernatorial nomination complicated the maneuverings that preceded the Whig convention. His activities also illustrated the problems which politicians faced as they sought to navigate a future for themselves in a new political environment. Ullman's desire for office and his repeated rebuffs from the Sewardites had driven him into the Know-Nothing organization sometime in 1853.[9] His latest scheme was to present himself as a compromise candidate, who would be acceptable to all groups. Some of his partisans, assuming the name of "The New York Central Whig Association," sent out a circular letter to a wide spectrum of Whigs throughout the state asking for support. They maintained that Ullman deserved the nomination because of his past political sacrifices, his fidelity to all cherished Whig principles, and his determined opposition to the Nebraska bill.[10]

Ullman's prospects did not look encouraging. He heard that despite great efforts, Weed's followers, who were deeply entrenched in county politics, had triumphed. Those Know-Nothings who felt that they had succeeded in local caucuses were not optimistic either. One campaigner believed that the Order had carried the state, "but many of those who are delegates are green in politics and I fear may be out generalled." The failure of Silver Grays and Know-Nothings to concentrate their support upon one candidate handicapped their efforts. Even with the Whig convention only a few days away, pleas for concerted action went unheeded.[11]

Judging it his only chance, Ullman authorized his manager to confer with Weed and see if the boss could be induced to back him as the least objectionable Silver Gray. Weed, however, would have nothing to do with this overture; he had been too often betrayed by the conservatives in his party to trust them now. He knew that his old enemies provided the organizational skill which made the Know-Nothings a success, and that this movement had been "invented to kill Seward and his friends." Moreover, he interpreted this last minute appeal as a sign that Ullman knew he would be beaten.[12]

Even an opportunist like Daniel Ullman found it difficult to measure the strength of the new issues. That he was a Know-Nothing, and that his circular declared hostility to the Nebraska bill was well-known. Significantly, he had omitted his position on the liquor question. Apparently judging this matter too dangerous, he had adopted a wait-and-see attitude. To his surprise, he discovered that most of his potential backers in the central and western sections of the state made their support contingent upon his willingness to sign a Maine Law. Confronted with the intensity of prohibition feeling, he gave in and promised to sign a bill should it pass the legislature. This last moment conversion only underlined his previous failure to speak out. His assessment of the dominant issue of the canvass had been wrong, and one of his campaigners feared that it had been fatal: "I gather from various sources . . . the importance of having candidates of well known Maine Law proclivities. I shall feel mad and mortified if such a *dirty question* should be made instrumental in defeating us, and yet it looks a little like it."[13]

Weed, hoping that the extraordinary political confusion would subside, refused to make any premature decision regarding the governorship. There is evidence to suggest that prior to the veto of the Maine Law he had toyed with the idea of nominating Seward and replacing him in the Senate with Washington Hunt. Whether this notion ever became a serious purpose is not known, but it was quickly abandoned because of the liquor question. The temperance men detested Seward; they roundly condemned his Washington dinner parties which were known to feature the finest wines and liquors. Appreciating this fact, Weed sought to stifle any further conjecture about his friend's candidacy.[14]

The boss then considered his close associate, George W. Patterson. But Patterson, too, was not held in esteem by temperance organizations, which refused to support anyone unless he was absolutely reliable. If they were not satisfied, they threatened to nominate their own candidate. Moreover, as a loyal Sewardite, Patterson was an anathema to the Know-Nothings and would be a perfect target for them.[15]

As the clamor for a Maine Law grew, the appeal of state senator Myron H. Clark of Canandaigua became irresistible. Besides his role as leader of the prohibition forces in the legislature, Clark had other valuable attributes: He was "a true reliable ardent Seward man" and a member of a Know-Nothing lodge. Daniel Ullman's partisans also considered him their strongest adversary. They presumed that Weed would choose that Know-Nothing whom he could best manage, and the senator was generally considered as a man of only moderate abilities. These predictions turned out to be correct; shortly before the convention, Weed consulted with Clark and found his views satisfactory.[16]

An unusually large number of aspirants for the governorship appeared at the Whig convention in Syracuse. The Hard and Soft Shell division in Democratic ranks made the nomination especially attractive, and those hitherto known for their magnanimity in yielding such honors to others now insisted that their reward was due. Several distinguished Whigs were in the field—Elbridge G. Spaulding, Levi Harris, Henry J. Raymond, George W. Patterson, and Washington Hunt. Each hoped that Weed would favor him. Also present were the followers of several Silver Gray-Know-Nothing candidates, including Daniel Ullman; but an attempt to focus support on a single nativist failed. None of the candidates agreed to withdraw. On the first two ballots, no one had a clear majority. On the third roll call, Clark's vote started to climb, revealing him as the second choice of many delegates, and he finally received the nomination.[17]

The delegates chose Henry J. Raymond, the ambitious editor of the New York *Times,* for lieutenant governor. Weed, trying to balance his ticket by adding a candidate who would appeal to conservatives, engineered his selection. Horace Greeley, who had also sought the nomination, bitterly resented the choice of his rival—whom he dubbed the "little villain." He could barely contain his anger, and he never forgave Weed or Seward. He had no other choice than to stand behind the ticket, but the political partnership of these three Whigs, which had endured for over fourteen years, would soon be over.[18]

The keynote of the Whig platform was caution. Although it concentrated on attacking the Nebraska Act and its perpetrators, the convention revealed that it was in no mood for sweeping antislavery proposals; a modest declaration for repeal of the Fugitive Slave Act was hissed down and its advocate forced to withdraw it.[19] The platform was worded to satisfy conservatives who were eager to denounce Repeal, but had no wish to alienate the South. They wanted to keep the door open for an eventual reconciliation between the Northern and Southern wings of the party.

As a result of Weed's management, the Sewardites now possessed a ticket and a program which had appeal to many Whigs who were tempted by new political paths. Such diverse groups as temperance advocates, nativists, conservatives, and anti-Nebraskaites could still adhere to their old organization. It remained to be seen whether this "package" which Weed had concocted would have sufficient cohesive power to hold his party together.

During the proceedings of his own convention, Weed was mindful of its effect upon the reconvened anti-Nebraska and the temperance meetings, scheduled to assemble at Auburn a few days later. One of his major aims was to prevent these bodies from making separate nominations. He wrote Patterson that "unless we hit right the Auburn Conventions will act."[20]

In the closing days of September, Auburn was the site of feverish political activity as no less than three conventions were to meet in as many days—the Free Democratic on September 25, the adjourned Saratoga anti-Nebraska on September 26, and the temperance on September 27. The choice of a common location afforded many delegates the opportunity to attend all three.[21]

Several Free Democrats had fought an uphill battle to steer the Saratoga anti-Nebraska convention toward fusion. Although this hope had been frustrated, they had not given up. They assembled at Auburn to make another attempt to establish the Republican party in New York. When the Free Democratic convention met, it was divided between those who urged acceptance of the Whig nominations, and those who wanted to hold out for a new fusion party. Those holding the latter view, however, greatly predominated. John P. Hale urged the more popular course; he cautioned his party to avoid a recurrence of 1848, when it had been used merely to whip adversaries and then discarded. The majority finally adopted the following resolution, offered by Judge Robert Snow of Madison county, to serve as a clear manifesto of its purpose:

> *Resolved,* That while this Convention cannot completely officiate with either of the political organizations or adopt the tickets nominated by them, we are ready and willing to co-operate with the true friends of freedom of all parties in this and other states by the formation of a Republican organization, and the nomination of a Republican ticket, composed of men who have abandoned, or are ready to abandon the existing political organization of this state.

The delegates agreed not to make a separate nomination at that time, but to adjourn until they knew the results of the anti-Nebraska meeting. Following these decisions, many Free Democrats proceeded across town to that convention, which was beginning its opening session.

The reconvened anti-Nebraska convention proved to be as thoroughly in the grip of the Whigs as its predecessor at Saratoga. Weed's agents had done their work well. They successfully reversed the previous agreement to vote by assembly districts and substituted a system of individual voting. Free Democrats considered this a breach of trust, for many district delegations had entrusted their vote to one delegate who had undertaken the journey to Auburn.[22]

Although thrown off balance by this maneuver, several Free Democrats would not give up. For the second time that day, Judge Snow introduced a resolution for a Republican ticket. John P. Hale advocated it, pleading with the Whigs to place a Democrat on the ballot, thus creating a genuine fusion. The hopes of Free Democrats rested on the following strategy: They agreed to accept the Whig nominee for governor, Myron H. Clark, provided that Bradford R. Wood, a former Wilmot Proviso Congressman and free soil Democrat, was substituted for Henry Raymond as the candidate for lieutenant governor. Their attempt failed; the vote was 127 for Raymond, 84 for Wood. As the roll call went against them, some of the fusionists left the hall.

The convention then nominated the entire Whig ticket, adopted a series of resolutions condemning the 1852 Baltimore platforms of both major parties, the Nebraska Act, the Fugitive Slave Law, and called for an assembly of delegates from the free states to nominate presidential and vice-presidential candidates. The remaining delegates, however, had been unnerved by the bolt, and in the closing moments of the proceedings, they passed a proposal by a Free Democrat, identified as Dr. J. E. Snodgrass, that the standing state committee be called the Republican organization.[23] Thus, at the last instant, the Whigs offered an olive branch to Hale's followers; the Republican party of New York existed in name if not in substance.

The seceders met at the courthouse that afternoon. They roundly condemned Whig chicanery and defiantly nominated the fusion slate of Clark and Wood. They issued a statement declaring their independence from old parties and their fellowship with Republicans in other states. The Free Democratic convention endorsed this stand when it reassembled that evening; it renamed its standing organization, the Republican State Central Committee.

On the following day, the state temperance convention also met at Auburn. It followed the same pattern as the anti-Nebraska meeting; indeed, it contained almost the same personnel, demonstrating the fact that reformers who opposed slavery's expansion were also active in temperance circles. Some were dissatisfied with Raymond because of his former hostility to liquor legislation, but Clark's name at the head of the ticket, plus assurances from Raymond that he had experienced a conversion on the Maine Law, reconciled them to the Whig ticket. A small group of die-hards, many of whom had been previously identified as Free Democrats and abolitionists, tried to replace Raymond with Wood but failed.

With the state temperance convention's endorsement of his candidates, Thurlow Weed had achieved all of his major objectives. Although caught in the turbulence of a political revolution, Weed had successfully neutralized the stresses on his party and steered it into a safe position. He had disarmed the threats to his leadership from Free Democrats and Silver Gray-Know-Nothings, and had harnessed the temperance movement for his own purposes. He had formulated a ticket and a platform which appealed to many who had severed old party ties and adopted new causes—to such diverse groups as temperance advocates, nativists, conservatives, and anti-Nebraskaites. Here, certainly, was an example of political wizardry. Yet, Weed's brilliant performance was only a holding action. He had played a very cautious hand in 1854, seeking to shore up the Whig organization rather than strike out on new paths. His primary motive was to secure the reelection of Seward to the Senate, but his basic conservatism also played an important part in his decision. As the party system continued to deteriorate, Weed, however, was forced to abandon his cherished party and enter a new alignment.

7

An Indecisive Election

The election of 1854 revealed the effects of the disruptive forces exerted on New York's party system. A chaotic political situation existed. Four distinct tickets were nominated. Traditional party lines were blurred. The new issues of Nebraska, temperance, and nativism had displaced the old issues. The election further weakened past party alignments; and it thereby prepared the way for the emergence of new political loyalties.

By the end of September, 1854, three separate tickets were in the field—the Soft Shell, the Hard Shell, and the Whig. One other would shortly add to the confusion—the Know-Nothing. Outmaneuvered by Thurlow Weed in their bid to gain control of the Whig party, the Silver Grays now turned to the nativist organization which they had carefully nurtured.

The meeting of the New York Grand Council, scheduled to begin on October 5, 1854, proved to be stormy as adherents of every political stripe tried to manipulate it for their own purposes. The past policy of the Order had been to select candidates from other parties rather than nominate its own, and several delegates, presumably Sewardites, urged that Myron H. Clark be endorsed. However, Silver Gray Whigs, who were in firm control, squelched this move and pushed through the nomination of Daniel Ullman for governor. The Know-Nothings formed a completely new slate for the other state offices and chose James W. Barker, the president of the Council, to oppose Tammany's Fernando Wood in the New York City mayoralty race. These events caused a bolt by those opposed to the creation of a separate ticket. The seceders, subsequently known as "Know-Somethings" or "Choctaws," included a number of antislavery men who wanted an explicit denunciation of the Nebraska Act.[1] The Grand Council refused to adopt any platform, thus leaving the position of its candidates on the Nebraska and temperance issues in doubt.

The Know-Nothings now found it necessary to derogate the credentials of the Whigs' gubernatorial nominee who claimed to be a member of the Order. Clark, like many other Sewardites, had joined the secret organization for his own protection and to establish some control over it. Weed deemed Clark's membership an asset, because he wanted to give a nativist tinge to the ticket. In any case, the Ethan Allen Council No. 133 located in Clark's town of Canandaigua, printed a circular accusing him of being a member of a spurious lodge, whose purpose was to subvert the genuine chapter for the advantage of William H. Seward.[2] The Whigs in turn spread the rumor that Ullman was not really a native American, but a foreigner born in Calcutta of German-Jewish parents. Horace Greeley seized upon this "exposé" and dubbed the nativists "Hindoos." This title stuck and caused the Know-Nothings considerable embarrassment.[3]

Ironically, the Silver Grays within the Know-Nothing organization had to remain as unobtrusive as possible, because they were held in particular disrepute in central and western New York, where they had a reputation for acquiescence in the demands of the South. When Ullman sought to call a meeting of prestigious Silver Grays to endorse his candidacy, Know-Nothing organizers in Sewardite strongholds warned him against this move. They feared that nativists with strong anti-Nebraska feelings would abandon the ticket if they suspected Silver Gray influence. They argued that to maintain the Know-Nothings' zeal at a high pitch, it was necessary for the members to believe that their movement was unsullied by discredited politicians.[4]

Silver Grays took the advice of their organizers; they remained in the background while affording as much help to the nativist slate as they could. No Silver Gray newspaper formally endorsed the Know-Nothing ticket. Greeley bitterly denounced these journals' practice of "displaying the Whig State ticket ostentatiously at the mast-head and all the time doing their best to defeat it by every kind of sneaking disparagement or open detraction." The Albany *Argus* made a similar observation, noting that the editorial policy of the Buffalo *Commercial Advertiser* (Fillmore's organ) was totally at odds with the Whig candidates it professed to support.[5] This policy of the Silver Grays helps to explain the initial success of Know-Nothingism in the Burned-over-region. At first, the conservative leadership of the Order managed to keep its pro-Southern views hidden. Subsequently, when conceal-ment became impossible, nativist strength went into a rapid decline.

Ullman's strategy for the campaign was succinctly expressed by a friend who urged him "not to write any letters, to keep dark and 'Know Nothing.'" To secure the Whig nomination he had been prepared to go on record against Nebraska and in favor of a prohibitory liquor law. Since these admissions were never made public —they were contained in a letter for the exclusive use of his managers—there was no need to retract them.[6] Ullman decided to take his cue from the Grand Council, which had been silent on all other matters in order to give urgency to the nativist issue. He knew, moreover, that Nebraska and temperance were dangerous subjects and that a definite position on them would alienate many voters. He deemed it best to act in the mysterious manner which so delighted the members of the Order, and let his lieutenants drop hints where they would do the most good.[7] Consequently, he refused to answer requests that he clarify his views on these questions.

The Know-Nothings' great efforts to organize new lodges achieved remarkable success. Particularly heartening to Ullman was the encouraging news from central and western New York, hitherto known for its vigorous antislavery, pro-temperance sentiment and loyalty to the Seward-Weed machine. A correspondent from Rochester informed him "that the district which used to be called by the Albany Regency, the 'infected district,' is at this moment very badly infected with Know-Nothingism." Writing from what he called the "sink hole of Sewardism in the State," an organizer reported that "he addressed the Council in Rome last night. We were at it until midnight and a more enthusiastic set of fellows you never saw—they will give Ullman a good vote there." L. L. Pratt, the Silver Gray editor of the Fredonia *Advertiser,* rejoiced:

> Old Chautauque, once the home of Seward, now the residence of one of his principal sattelites [*sic*] Ex Lt. Gov. Patterson, and a district until now supposed to be under the control of the viceroy Weed will give you and your associates a considerable majority over the Clark or any other ticket.[8]

After the Soft Shells had chosen their ticket and announced their platform, it seemed that they had only the remotest chance of success, but gradually their prospects improved. Governor Seymour had been renominated, but it was by no means certain that he would run. He bitterly resented the President; his recommendations for appointments had been repeatedly snubbed, and the McKeon affair had brought him to the point of open rebellion.[9] He succinctly expressed his opinion of Pierce as "a fool who aspires to be a knave." Although he had not made his views public, Seymour approved of the Nebraska bill and assured Senator Douglas that his measure was not responsible for the divided condition of New York Democrats. The real cause was the President's patronage policy which had abolitionized the party by infusing new life into the free soil faction; the recipients of this bounty had shown their gratitude by going "into full operation vigorously and effectively against the Bill."[10]

The Governor's refusal to run for re-election alarmed Soft Shell leaders. The equivocal Nebraska resolution had cost them the support of those Barnburners who agreed with Preston King, and Know-Nothingism had also made inroads into their ranks. It seemed that the only chance of recouping these losses was to attract Whig and Hard Shell votes on the liquor issue. Since Seymour could generate more anti-Maine Law enthusiasm than any other candidate, many Softs entreated him to change his mind.[11]

Before Seymour would reconsider and enter the canvass which he judged would "be bitter beyond all precedent," he wanted assurances that he could rely on the President's support. Although not pleased with the Soft Shells in New York, Pierce could not permit their total destruction and promised his full cooperation. He had a trusted postal official sent to New York to expedite Seymour's wishes on appointments. The Governor believed that the proper postmasters could influence a great number of votes and help repair the disorganization of the party. Swift recuperative action was imperative, and he explained why: "There will be many whigs who will be discontented with the proceedings of their convention. They will take ground in favor of the opposition ticket which they deem the strongest. We must create the hope that our ticket can be elected to call forth any efforts."[12]

In his speech accepting the nomination, Seymour revealed that his campaign would emphasize the liquor issue and ignore Nebraska and nativism. Such an approach had its perils. Collector Redfield feared that the Governor would be decried as the rum candidate: "The difficulty will be in separating him, in the public eye from the liquor *interest* and making an issue upon the principle involved in the veto message." The Soft Shell organ, the Albany *Atlas,* realized its responsibility for elevating the level of the campaign; and it launched into long philosophical discussions with such titles as "Individual Liberty, the True Foundation of Political Freedom," in which it argued that prohibiting alcohol would lead to greater tyrannies and end by depriving the citizen "of all the most sacred safeguards of his

person and property." A meeting, however, held at Tammany Hall
to ratify Seymour's nomination was more prosaic. The speakers and
the audience fulminated against the Maine Law, saying nothing about
any other topic, and then adjourned to the bar for liquid refresh-
ments.[13] The Governor's motive was apparent to shrewd politicians
at the Wigwam. It would draw attention away from the slavery question and thus help to ease the strains which the Nebraska Act had
caused. Tammanyites were more than willing to toast such a policy.

The willingness of temperance advocates to abandon political
loyalties had put heavy pressure upon the old parties. But, it should
be noted that opponents of the Maine Law were also ready to abandon
party ties to further their cause. Liquor interests, from distillers to
local merchants, realized the danger to their livelihoods, and, disregarding former political preferences, they made heavy contributions
to the Softs. In Steuben county, a group of liquor dealers pledged
themselves to spare no effort in electing Seymour. The chairman
and one-third of the members of the organization were Whigs. The
Softs expected considerable aid from the Liquor Merchants' Committee of New York City which contained several prominent Whigs,
who could reputedly sway large numbers of ballots. The body predicted
that forty to fifty thousand voters would change their political allegiance and support the Softs. Know-Nothing businessmen also forgot
their oaths. "By—I would like to vote for Ullman, but I must take
care of No. 1 and vote for Seymour," was the comment of one store-
keeper.[14] Consumers were also drawn to the Softs. A surprising
number of laborers who enjoyed their beer and ale, and gentlemen
who relished their wine with dinner, were willing to relinquish old
political affiliations. For these people, the menace to their pleasure
appeared more immediate and important than either loyalty to party
or the threats of slavery expansion, foreigners, and Catholicism.

The Hard Shells' campaign never attracted much attention. The
Hards were the only party to endorse unequivocally the Nebraska Act,
an action which made them most unpopular. Their gubernatorial
nominee, Greene C. Bronson, wrote a series of public letters on the
temperance question in which he tried to take a middle ground
position between Seymour and Clark by favoring a more stringent
licensing law.[15] His efforts, however, to gain anti-Maine Law support
were ineffective, because Seymour, as the stronger candidate, had
preempted this source.

The Softs entreated the Adamantines to abandon their unsuccessful
campaign and join them. These appeals had some success in local

contests where the desire to be sheriff or judge overcame old pre-judices, and an agreement was reached to share offices. Weed, Seward, and Greeley always expected a more extensive deal to be imminent, but Hard Shell leaders refused to countenance any cooperation on state or congressional tickets.[16] They were playing a desperate game of rule or ruin and their repeated failures intensified their ambition. It might be expected that the Know-Nothings would be the bene-ficiaries of this situation, and the results satisfied their hopes.[17]

In defense against the Know-Nothings' and Soft Shells' attempts to emphasize one issue in order to break up the Whig party, Thurlow Weed had constructed a composite platform which he hoped would hold his organization together. A firm, yet moderate anti-Nebraska and antislavery position, a strong temperance candidate, and a hint of nativism emerged as the campaign formula. Yet, not even Weed's wizardry could prevent many former Whigs from breaking party ties.

The first component of the platform came under attack after the Saratoga-Auburn conventions had endorsed the Whig nominees. Did the candidates' acceptance of this support imply that they now stood upon the aggressive platform of these conventions, which had re-pudiated the Whig's Baltimore Platform of 1852, urged the repeal of the Fugitive Slave Law, and gone so far as to recommend the creation of a new sectional party? This question worried conservative Whigs, and their concern was reflected in two New York City papers which claimed to be their spokesmen, James Watson Webb's *Courier and Enquirer* and Robert H. West's *Commercial Advertiser.* Henry Raymond attempted to quiet the fears of the conservative mercantile community by denying that he or any other candidate had abandoned his party's platform.[18] Despite these assurances, the question was never conclusively settled.

By endorsing the prohibitionist cause, Weed knew that he had alienated a number of conservatives. Washington Hunt informed him that more were lost than had been anticipated: "They are ready to sacrifice party, country and everything, sooner than be deprived of the [bottle?] and too many of them are against us." The Whigs sus-tained other losses among German-Americans who revolted against the "cold water apostle, Myron H. Clark" and declared themselves "absolved from all party obligations during the present canvass. . . ." Weed was also aware of the liquor dealers' extraordinary efforts in Seymour's behalf.[19] Weed accepted these tidings without too much alarm. Relying on his gambler's instinct and his long experience with the ebb and flow of popular passions, he was hoping that temperance feeling had reached its peak and would carry everything before it.

The greatest threats facing the Whig party were not dissatisfied conservatives, German-Americans, or liquor dealers, but the Know-Nothings. As the campaign progressed, Weed was appalled to discover the extent of their strength in once safe Whig areas. Reports poured in from central and western New York that his lieutenants had never experienced such rough going. "There never was a time when party ties seemed of so little account," wrote Hunt. "The new questions have destroyed party discipline, and many staunch old Whigs are floating off they don't know where." Defections by Whigs hitherto known for their fidelity were common. "I have never seen the time before when our best Whigs could not be relied upon," reported one campaigner. To protect themselves, many loyal Sewardites were forced to join the Know-Nothings. Weed encouraged this practice; he would fight treachery with more treachery. Greeley was upset that the party's leader had resorted to the tactics of his enemies:

> Some of those he [Weed] relies on are red-mouthed Know-Nothings, going their whole length for the Order and having its regular nomination. This is just the most scoundrelly canvass that I was ever engaged in. I feel a crawling all over on account of it.[20]

The Know-Somethings or Choctaws, those who had bolted from the Grand Council when it made separate nominations, were also a factor in the election. Although no definite evidence exists to implicate either Seward or Weed in the bolt, it is probable that they played an important role. Using loyal Whigs who had infiltrated the Order was too tempting an idea to resist; a rival organization might expose the anti-temperance, pro-Southern Silver Gray leadership of the parent body and help break it up.[21] The results of the Know-Something convention, which assembled at Utica on October 26, suggest Whig influence. Several delegates tried to divert some of the reformist energy then concentrating in nativist hysteria into antislavery and prohibitionist channels. Although the Choctaws refused to endorse any of the candidates already in the field, one Know-Nothing in Utica wrote that "they no doubt understand to vote and work for Mr. Clark."[22]

The results of the election for the national legislature were soon apparent, and they indicated that New York had joined other Northern states in administering a severe rebuke to the Democratic party for its Nebraska policy. In 1852, a united Democracy could claim about two-thirds of the state's thirty-three Congressmen, but in 1854, not a single Hard Shell was elected and only two Softs. One of the latter was Francis E. Spinner from Preston King's district (encompassing Herkimer and St. Lawrence counties), and he was staunchly anti-Nebraska. The only Congressman-elect whom the Administration could claim as friendly to its territorial policy was the young and ambitious Tammanyite, John Kelly, who had launched his long career by defeating the popular Hard Shell, Mike Walsh, by 21 votes in an Irish district. Approximately fifteen successful candidates received the Know-Nothings' endorsement, but these, though of varied political antecedents, were all opposed to Douglas. The remainder of those elected were Sewardites whose attitudes toward Nebraska were never in doubt.[23]

The result of the state canvass remained in doubt for nearly two weeks because of an extremely close vote. At first, to everyone's astonishment, it seemed that Ullman would win as he piled up an early lead. As more returns came in, however, the contest narrowed to a struggle between Clark and Seymour. It stayed this way for days, one or the other candidate taking the lead as some report was added or discredited. Most newspapers despaired of sifting through the conflicting data and waited for the official canvassers to deliver the verdict. When finally counted, the vote stood as follows: Clark, 156,804; Seymour, 156,495; Ullman, 122,282; Bronson, 33,850. Clark's plurality over Seymour was only 309 votes.[24]

The Whig state ticket had squeezed through by the narrowest of margins. Weed's gamble that temperance would be the pivotal issue of the campaign paid off; fervent prohibitionists did not trust the Know-Nothings' hints that Ullman would sign a Maine Law and went heavily for Clark. The newly elected legislature was also a cause for satisfaction; it contained a preponderance of Whigs, although it remained to be seen how many of them would vote for Seward's return to the Senate.

These successes, however, could not disguise the fact that the Whig party had been badly battered. Most alarming to the Sewardites was the size of the Know-Nothing vote. "Who would have believed that K.N. fanaticism was so extensive and so well organized," wrote George E. Baker to Seward.[25] A glance at the returns confirmed the Whigs' worst fears; areas of their greatest strength in central and western New York returned pluralities, and in some cases, majorities for the secret Order.[26] The extent of their loss may be illustrated by examining the balloting in Chautauqua and Cattaraugus. These counties had been among the few to give majorities for Winfield Scott in 1852, but in 1854, they delivered 50.51 percent and 51.44 percent of their vote respectively to Daniel Ullman. In the congressional race, a coalition of the Soft, W. P. Angel, and the Whig, George W. Patterson, in support of Reuben R. Fenton's re-election, failed to prevent the victory of the Know-Nothing candidate, Francis S. Edwards.[27] These results and other similar cases cast a shadow over the future of the Whig party.

Another casualty of the Whig victory was the political partnership of Weed, Seward, and Greeley. The *Tribune's* editor had soon regretted his acquiescence in Weed's plan to thwart fusion in New York; the nomination of Raymond and Weed's cooperation with Know-Nothings had alienated him even more. As the canvass progressed and it appeared that a Whig victory was doubtful, Greeley could no longer restrain his anger. He charged that if New York failed to show a popular majority against Douglas of at least one hundred thousand, it would be the fault of selfish Whig politicians who refused to follow the will of the people. On the eve of the election, he acknowledged his premonitions of disaster, and the result seemed to confirm his fears; from November 7 to 18, the *Tribune* predicted Seymour's victory. It was during this period that Greeley wrote to Seward his famous letter, declaring that henceforth he would act as an independent agent.[28]

The Know-Nothings and the Silver Grays were delighted with the outcome, despite their loss. Ullman received numerous congratulatory messages for his large vote; some of his partisans believed that two more weeks of campaigning would have brought success. The nativists, judging the canvass a harbinger of subsequent triumphs, exuded confidence in the future. The leader of the original Silver Gray bolt, Francis Granger, assumed that victory was near:

> The more I examine the late election and see how completely this abolition fusion tribe are routed in almost everyone of their former strongholds, the stronger is my conviction that discreet and firm, unwavering action now, will secure a victory.

Another politician immediately thought of the presidential campaign of 1856, and he envisioned a sweep of "at least twenty-five states." Nothing was impossible, he asserted, provided we avail "ourselves of the resistless Know-Nothing element."[29]

The Soft Shells were dismayed by their congressional defeats but buoyed by their strong vote on the state ticket. They could not escape the revulsion against Nebraska and shared the fate of their party throughout the North. However, Seymour's strategy of focusing his campaign on the liquor question almost succeeded. The Governor maintained that he was satisfied with the result and so were other Soft politicians who believed that the party had stood up remarkably well, considering Hard Shell factionalism, Barnburner defections, and Administration bungling with which it had to contend.[30]

The Softs discovered several aspects in the outcome which gave them confidence that they would return to power. The victory of Fernando Wood over James W. Barker in New York City's mayoralty race showed that the Know-Nothings could be beaten; it also strengthened the bonds which tied adopted citizens to the Democratic party. But most important was their feeling that the coalitions against them could not be maintained. They shared Douglas' view that the Democracy had only sustained a temporary loss and accepted his admonition to "be of good cheer . . . Though the skies are partially overcast, the clouds are passing away."[31]

It had not escaped notice that the combined Soft and Hard Shell vote would have resulted in an easy victory. Moreover, the Adamantines had lost considerable ground. Their gubernatorial candidate obtained 33,850 votes compared to 99,835 for the head of the ticket in the preceding year; this represented a loss of nearly two-thirds. Even more damaging than this sharp decline, however, were the indications that Hard Shell ballots had gone directly to the Know-Nothings. A supporter of Seymour wrote the Governor that it would "be a difficult matter for them [the Hards] to maintain a respectable organization after the general desertion of their ticket in all parts of the state and the suspiciously small vote in the places where Dickinson has influence."[32] It would not be easy for the Adamantines to disprove charges of conspiring with the nativists, and it seemed that their bid to convince the South that they were the reliable Democrats of New York had failed. In view of these facts, some Soft Shell politicians predicted that within a short time the so-called National Democrats would come trooping back to beg forgiveness.

The election of 1854 clearly demonstrated that an upheaval was taking place in American politics. The effects of the great strain placed on the party system by the Nebraska Act, the temperance movement, and the Know-Nothing crusade were apparent. The national Whig party, which had existed in weakened condition ever since the canvass of 1852, was moribund. Northern and Southern Whigs were politically adrift and drawn to other alignments. The national Democratic party, too, had sustained severe losses. Only two years before it had elected a President by a great majority and achieved preponderance in the national legislature; now it confronted a hostile North and an anti-Nebraska majority in Congress.

In New York, the state parties were also victims of the forces destroying the party system. The Softs could not escape the opprobrium attached to the Nebraska Act and suffered a crushing defeat in the congressional elections. Aided by vast sums of money from the liquor interest, they made a good showing in the gubernatorial race; however, resistance to the Maine Law was hardly a traditional Democratic issue and certainly a poor basis on which to build a party. Because of an explicit endorsement of the Nebraska Act, the Hards lost two-thirds of their former voting strength. Hards and Softs were still unreconciled, each faction competing for Southern support. This feud taxed even the remarkable resilience of the Democratic party; a growing number of old Jacksonians were attracted to nativist and anti-Nebraska coalitions.

Under the able management of Thurlow Weed, New York Whigs had won a nominal victory in the state contest. But this success could not hide the widening fissures in the Whig party. The election of Myron H. Clark was more a temperance than a Whig triumph. Silver Gray-Know-Nothings had lured thousands of old Whigs into the secret Order. Nativist strength was growing in the "infected district" of central and western New York. Free Democrats continued to agitate for the breakup of the Whig organization and alliance with the Republican party in other states.

Although a political revolution was in progress, its course was not immediately apparent. The election of 1854 acted like a crucible —it helped to melt down old political loyalties—but it was inconclusive. Because the religious idealism of citizens in the vitally important Burned-over-region had been diverted into different channels, neither a dominant party nor a paramount issue had emerged. More time was needed before the upheaval could work itself out and reveal the shape of the future.

8

The Know-Nothings and Slavery

In their efforts to build the Know-Nothing party—or as they preferred to call it, the American party—the New York Silver Grays had tried to avoid the slavery issue at all costs, lest their organization fall victim to the same pressures racking the Seward-Whig and Democratic parties. They predicated their strategy upon making nativist goals paramount. This policy had been followed by the New York Know-Nothing Grand Council in the campaign of 1854, when it refused to make a statement regarding any other issue. However, in 1855, silence became impossible. Sectional feeling began to divide the Know-Nothings and threatened to destroy the hopes of the Silver Grays.

The impending selection of a United States Senator by the New York legislature on February 6, 1855 attracted wide attention. This would be a crucial confrontation between nativists and Whigs, and both sides exerted themselves to the utmost. Know-Nothings throughout the nation eagerly waited to see if Seward would be defeated; his humiliation could give a powerful boost to the secret Order all over the Union.

One of the consequences of the disruption of the party system was the great uncertainty in politics. This fact was clearly demonstrated in the New York senatorial contest. The Whigs appeared to have an impressive majority in the assembly. The *Whig Almanac* listed its composition as follows: "Whigs of all sorts, 82; Softs of all grades, 26; Hards, 16; Maine Law Independents, 3; Vacancy, 1; Total, 128." However, these figures did not reveal the true picture as the *Almanac* observed: "Know-Nothings are sprinkled miscellaneously among Whigs, Hards and Softs; and exactly how many there are of these gentry in the Assembly Nobody knows."[1] The operations of the secret Order had cast doubt upon the party affiliation of practically every legislator. Thus, the re-election of Seward depended on the fidelity of the ostensible Whig majority.

During this period of political crisis, critical choices had to be made. Many politicians felt themselves pulled simultaneously in two directions. Old party connections were still strong. Yet, with the breakdown in the party system, politicians were forced to make adjustments. These were not always painless decisions and often caused considerable personal distress. Caught between the old and the new politics were approximately thirty Whig assemblymen from rural areas, who had been elected with Know-Nothing backing. Should they follow their oaths to the Order and vote against Seward or should they break them? Tremendous pressure would be brought to bear to influence them.

Know-Nothing leaders exerted every effort to defeat Seward. Silver Gray newspapers, which had ostensibly supported the Whig ticket in 1854, vigorously attacked their old foe. Emphasizing his reputed pandering to Catholics, they pointed to his proposal for public support of parochial schools as evidence. Meanwhile, the Order tried to keep its representatives in the assembly faithful to their anti-Seward pledges. One nativist believed that the ruling consideration with thirty-two Whig-Know-Nothings would be concern for their reputations in their rural districts. Although great pressure would be exerted by Weed, what they were certain to fear most was the "stain of perjury on their souls" and the consequent loss of trust among their neighbors. The legislators received letters warning them not to violate their oaths lest they be burned in effigy and shunned in their home towns.[2]

Thurlow Weed had been working hard to secure his friend's re-election; all other considerations during the preceding canvass had been subordinated to this objective. The boss did not relax after his 1854 victory. He used Governor Clark's patronage power to make promises to those most receptive to this kind of persuasion. There is evidence to suggest that, pledging Whig votes for a Maine Law in return for backing Seward, he came to an understanding with temperance forces. He struck a similar bargain with antislavery nativists who wanted legislation ending the control of Roman Catholic bishops over their churches' property and giving it to elected members of the congregation.[3]

Two events prior to the senatorial vote revealed that Weed's strategy had been successful. The Whig caucus gave Seward the preponderant majority of 74 of 80 ballots, and DeWitt C. Littlejohn of Oswego—a politician whom the Know-Nothings had singled out for defeat because of his betrayal—was elected speaker of the assembly. These results caused an acrimonious debate in both legislative chambers between those who had abjured the Order and those who had remained faithful to it. Littlejohn, for example, admitted that he had joined the secret organization because of a sincere apprehension of the foreign vote menace, but he had found the remedy worse than the disease. He denounced the despotic structure of the Know-Nothings which resembled the hierarchy of their reputed enemy, the Catholic church; it gave to one man, James W. Barker, an arbitrary power similar to that exercised by the Pope of Rome. Loyal Know-Nothings angrily accused the turncoats of trampling on sacred oaths, and the galleries, largely filled with nativist partisans, became unruly. Pandemonium broke out on several occasions during these exchanges, and the Chair remonstrated with members, and threatened the removal of visitors.[4]

The balloting for United States Senator was anticlimactic; Seward was re-elected by 69 of a possible 128 votes. The opposition divided its strength among several candidates, and none of them ever posed a serious threat to the front runner. Acknowledging his debt to Weed, the Senator wrote a brief note to his friend in Albany. He expressed his deep gratitude and "amazement at the magnitude and complexity of the dangers through which you have conducted our shattered bark and the wonderful sagacity and skill with which you have saved us all from so imminent a wreck."[5]

Weed's management was not the only reason, nor even the most important reason for the result. The legislators from the Burned-over-region who disregarded their oaths were not persuaded by any combination of threats, cajolery, and blandishments. They were following the dictates of their conscience and making a shrewd political gamble at the same time. Loyalty to old friends and political colleagues asserted itself and played an important part in their decision; the Whig party, like the Democratic party, still possessed considerable resilience. They had joined the Order when it was spreading, but they had soon learned to despise it and saw that its strength would not last. They knew that their constituents' indignation over Seward's fondness for alcoholic beverages and his advocacy of publicly supported Catholic schools was at variance with their admiration for his eloquent denunciations of the slave power. The politicians who voted for the Senator staked their futures upon the judgement that opposition to the slaveholders would become the most powerful and enduring issue.

Several Silver Grays tried to disparage the importance of Seward's return to the Senate as only a temporary setback to "Sam"—a commonly used sobriquet for the Know-Nothings. Since they attributed their defeat to treachery rather than to any weakening in nativist sentiments, they hoped to repair their organization; they predicted that no amount of skulduggery could prevent their triumph in the next election.[6]

In retrospect, it is clear that Seward's victory was a disaster for the nativists. Several politicians perceived this fact; they predicted that future historians would date the beginning of Know-Nothing decline with the vote in the New York legislature. One astute observer of many political wars, the historian Jabez Hammond—who was in his seventies at the time—made this assessment. He wrote to Seward that the nativists would gradually fade out of existence. Some Whigs assumed that the public exposure given to the Order's practices had shocked people into the realization that they had been lured into an authoritarian organization in their zeal to perfect American democracy.[7]

Because the New York senatorial contest demonstrated the difficulty of subordinating the slavery question to the anti-Catholic and anti-foreign issues, it hampered the plans of the Silver Gray Whigs who had seized upon the Know-Nothing movement as a vehicle for their own aims. Although they generally sympathized with nativist objectives, they judged these secondary to the creation of a national conservative party which would play down the slavery issue, and consign to oblivion the free soilers and abolitionists of the North and the fire eaters and secessionists of the South. Seward was opposed not so much for his past pro-Catholic stand as for his present menace to union.

Although Seward's triumph disappointed Know-Nothings throughout the country, its impact was greatest in the South. The spectacle of so many New York nativists casting their votes for a prominent antislavery politician demoralized Southern Know-Nothings. Nativists below the Mason-Dixon line had begged New York leaders to exert every effort to defeat the Senator. "It will hurt us greatly in our part of the Country if he [Seward] should be elected by 'Know-Nothing' votes," wrote Kenneth Rayner, a former North Carolina Whig, now a nativist. "For God's sake, have him defeated, if possible."[8]

The outcome in New York had an important effect on the Virginia gubernatorial election of May 24, 1855, which was a crucial test of the Know-Nothings' capacity to establish a viable national party.

In general, the nativists were confident of success during the campaign. Their optimism was not even lessened by the Democrats' nomination of Henry A. Wise, a politician renowned for his stump speaking ability. To achieve victory, however, it was essential to convince Virginia Whigs that the Know-Nothings had inherited their old party's conservative principles without its antislavery propensities. Thus, Virginia members of the secret Order were looking forward to Seward's defeat; it would belie Wise's charge that they were only abolitionists in disguise. "We are advancing gloriously now," wrote one campaigner. "But arm us with this anti abolition fact, and we will bear down all opposition. The effect in all the South, too, will be prodigious."[9]

Adding to the impact of Seward's victory on the Virginia election was the action of the Massachusetts Know-Nothing Grand Council. This body, under the leadership of Henry Wilson, adopted resolutions hostile to slavery and its expansion, and the New Hampshire Grand Council swiftly followed suit. These proceedings placed great pressure on New Yorkers to hold up the Northern wing of the party. Rayner wrote that the two New England states had discouraged the Order in the South, and he greatly feared the consequences on the Virginia election. He appealed for aid: "Conservative action on the part of N. York can put all right. Your state is now the great Break-Water, as it were, to preserve us against the floods and tides of mischievous agitation." However, it was too late to offset the effect of these events —Virginia Whigs were now throroughly alarmed by the "ghost of Abolitionism stalking among the Councils at the North"—and Wise scored an impressive victory.[10]

The Virginia election cast a shadow over the National Grand Council, which was scheduled to assemble in Philadelphia during the middle of June. Many Know-Nothings in both sections agreed with New York Silver Grays that the only chance for the Order to survive was for the Council to ignore the slavery issue and declare the primacy of the foreign and Catholic questions.[11] This view did not prevail, for extremists on both sides wanted to force a showdown. Southern representatives demanded the inclusion of Article XII in the platform. This plank endorsed the principle underlying the Nebraska Act; it denied the power of Congress to determine the status of slavery in the territories or to exclude any state from admission into the Union, because its constitution did or did not recognize the institution of slavery.

The inclusion of Article XII in the party's platform caused a bolt by every Northern delegation except New York. The seceders went to Cincinnati to participate in a national Know-Something convention, which had been scheduled to compete with the Philadelphia meeting. Choctaws from the Empire State played an important role in this assembly. The united convention adopted a platform which combined a mild nativism with a firm opposition to the extension of slavery.[12]

The disastrous outcome of the Philadelphia convention intensified a split in the New York Order which had festered for a long time and had sapped its effectiveness. Internal rivalries, especially between the forces of James W. Barker and Daniel Ullman, had weakened the Know-Nothings' attempt to control the Whig convention of 1854 and to defeat Seward the following year.[13] Barker had dominated his state's representatives at the National Grand Council and was responsible for its position as the only Northern delegation that refused to bolt. One member from New York had tried to propose a substitute for Article XII which he felt would have been less objectionable to Northerners and would certainly have passed, but Barker, closing off debate, had moved the previous question.[14] This high-handed behavior had enraged his enemies, and a struggle began for control of the State Council which would have to pass on the Philadelphia proceedings.

Barker's opponents believed that Article XII would ruin the party in New York and urged its repudiation. "With the Slavery Clause in the platform I very much doubt whether a single County in the state can be carried whereas if it had been omitted the state would have been perfectly secure," wrote one dissident. Another nativist concurred: "That 12th article introduced into the platform at Philadelphia must come out forthwith in this State or we are lost . . . Our delegates to that convention entirely mistook and misrepresented four fifths of this state. . . ." Some predicted that Southern intransigence would provoke a counter reaction. "Had the South been willing to make mutual concession with the North, for the purpose of harmonizing the party—we could have submitted to a little pro-slavery," was the view of an upstate Know-Nothing, who feared now "that nothing short of the restoration of the Missouri Compromise will satisfy the Northern sentiment." A friend pleaded with Daniel Ullman to prevent him from publicly denouncing the Philadelphia platform: "If you continue to encourage the idea of revolt you can't repair the injury after a short time. Weed evidently wants us to shake in the wind and then he has a point from which to assail us."[15]

Know-Nothing leaders in central and western New York, where antislavery sentiment was strongest, had great difficulty controlling the membership. Francis S. Edwards, the newly elected Congressman from Chautauqua and Cattaraugus counties, found it necessary to sponsor a set of resolutions which gave a "harmless dose of anti-slavery" to the councils in his region. James R. Thompson, a prominent Rochester Silver Gray, opposed this deviation from the national platform. Arguing that repudiation of Article XII would destroy the "nationality" of the New York party, he warned that "the moment you break your nationality you are broken and beaten and Weed knows that right well." Thompson still believed that the only way to prevent the antislavery issue from engulfing the party was to insist on the primacy of the nativist cause. Consequently, he advocated the following resolution at his Rochester council:

> . . . we condemn *now* as we *have* ever done the repeal of the Missouri Compromise as a breach of national faith and a base design of northern and southern demagogues to divide the American people . . . and thereby defeat forever the only opportunity which Americans will ever have of taking the helm and divesting our national and state administrations of the foreigner and Catholic influences which now disgrace the Country.

Another organizer reported substantial success with a similar approach in Ontario county:

> Now in reference to the members of the Order, many of them do not like the twelfth article, but we take the position that we are not to be driven from our great object if there be something that does not precisely suit us.[16]

The meeting of New York's State Council, held at Binghamton at the end of August, resulted in a struggle between the Barker faction, largely the New York City and the Brooklyn delegations, and the representatives of upstate nativists. The former fought for the endorsement of the entire Philadelphia platform, while the latter demanded the omission of Article XII and its replacement by a statement more in accord with the anti-Nebraska sentiments of their constituents. By the time of the meeting, even James R. Thompson, who had formerly opposed tinkering with the platform, felt that some action was necessary to prevent his party from forfeiting its excellent prospects. He reasoned that elections had already been held in the South, and that the New York Order must now look out for itself.[17]

The Binghamton convention rejected the extreme Southern orientation of the Barker faction and refused to accept Article XII. Nevertheless, the Silver Gray leadership still made a feeble attempt to uphold their policy of subordinating the slavery question, and one resolution declared foreigners and Catholics the foremost menace to the nation.

However, the rest of the platform contradicted this statement by concentrating almost entirely on the slavery issue. The convention took the position that slavery was a local and not a national issue, that regional differences of opinion on the subject were natural and permissible, and that these should not divide members of the American party. The delegates then satisfied antislavery nativists by condemning the Nebraska Act and its perpetrators. Although the platform did not demand restoration of the Missouri Compromise, it resolved that repeal should not result in territorial advantages for slavery.[18]

Try as they might, the New York Silver Grays could not overcome the slavery dilemma and avoid the sectional tensions which had engulfed the Whig and Democratic parties. Nor could they escape from the fact that the "peculiar institution" had become the paramount issue before the nation. Thousands of nativists in the Burned-over-region would vote the Know-Nothing ticket only if they believed it was also an antislavery ticket. Silver Gray leaders were forced to accommodate anti-Nebraska sentiment, even at the cost of diverging from the national platform. This decision eventually proved disastrous; to Southerners, there was no such thing as a "harmless dose of anti-slavery." Repercussions of the Philadelphia debacle were immediately felt in New York, where they intensified old dissensions and reduced the party's effectiveness. Ironically at a time when the long range future of both the national and state parties looked bleak, the New York organization was in its heyday and appeared on the threshold of its first electoral triumph. Years of patient effort had brought it to the peak of its power. From then on, its path would be one of rapid decline.

9

Fusion

In 1854, the Whigs had resisted the attempts of Free Democrats to establish a branch of the Republican party in the Empire State. The response of Seward and Weed to the political chaos of that year had been conservative; they had sought to shore up the Whig organization rather than participate in any fusion movement. By 1855, the forces disrupting the party system had not abated but had increased. The New York Whig party had been weakened by temperance advocates, Free Democrats, and Know-Nothings. The disbandment of the Whig organization throughout large parts of the country had dashed any rational hope for its revival. The election of 1854 revealed that the Republican party had made impressive gains in large portions of the Northwest and New England. The threat of armed hostilities in Kansas had added a new and dangerous strain on sectional relations. Clearly, the political revolution had reached a stage which made looking backward impossible. New York Whigs were forced to adapt to these pressures. They could no longer cling to the Whig party.

During the spring of 1855, New York Whigs continued to resist the Republican movement. Preston King, who was in Albany for several days in March, noted the absence of any general concurrence on political action; politicians devoted to particular men or cliques still dominated the scene. However, he did observe the existence of the "vague idea" that it was necessary for those who agreed on principles and measures to come together. "This last idea is gradually developing itself and growing more clear to the minds of all," he wrote. A month later, Jabez Hammond acknowledged his disappointment that a union of Radical Democrats and Seward Whigs would not take place. He believed the major obstacle to such action was "the love of office and its emoluments . . . The Democrats want *all* offices and so do the Whigs."[1]

The frustration of would-be fusionists disappeared in mid-July when newspapers printed calls for Whig and Republican conventions, both scheduled to assemble at Syracuse on September 26, 1855. The significance of this announcement was clear: it heralded the formation of the New York Republican party. Why did the Whig leadership reverse itself? The answer lies in happenings outside of the state and beyond the control of its politicians. The election of 1854 had brought the Republican party into prominence in the Northwest and in much of New England, while the Whig party in these areas had either been abandoned or existed as only a remnant. The intervention of pro-slavery Missourians in Kansas' elections on two occasions—the first in late December of 1854, and the second in early April of 1855—confirmed warnings that the territory was in danger and greatly strengthened the fusionists. By giving a new character to the political crisis, these developments exerted great pressure on New York Whigs and forced them to give up their organization.

The growing power of the Republican party and the ominous situation in Kansas convinced many New York Whigs that they could not afford to maintain a separate organization for very long. Besides, the election of 1854 had shown the Whigs to constitute a hopeless minority of the total vote, and it seemed that their only chance of securing a majority was through an amalgamation with free soil Democrats. Some politicians had foreseen this result after the canvass. One prominent Whig, after the victory of Myron H. Clark, acknowledged that his party would have to join the fusionists, if it were to retain its power. He believed that this could be accomplished in a way which would maintain control in the present leadership. By the summer of 1855, delay was no longer possible; Sewardites had either to enter the Republican movement or be crushed by it. Weed explained the reason for his conversion: "The necessity for getting in line with other states is imperative."[2]

Having made his decision, Weed skillfully effected a reconciliation with the Free Democrats whom he had spurned the previous year. Although they had been infuriated by Sewardite duplicity at the Saratoga and Auburn anti-Nebraska conventions of 1854 and had initially refused to support Henry Raymond for lieutenant governor, they had subsequently relented and had supported the entire Whig ticket. However, the Free Democrats let it be known that they would not make similar sacrifices in the future; if their aid was desired, they must be accorded a fair share of the spoils. Weed's overtures delighted Free Democratic leaders, and they issued an address recommending that energies be concentrated on the election of delegates to the Re-

publican convention. It alluded to certain ungenerous and unfair proceedings at Auburn, but expressed confidence that future efforts would
result in a genuine fusion.[3]

Since his major objective was to attract recruits from the Democratic
party, Weed had to find men with unimpeachable Democratic credentials who were willing to cooperate with him. For several months
a rapprochment had been going on between the Whig leadership and
Preston King. Although they had been bitter political opponents
during the Jacksonian period, the events following the repeal of the
Missouri Compromise had drawn them together. Although King had
bolted from the Soft Shell convention of 1854, he had refused to aid
the Free Democrats' attempt to launch the Republican party at Saratoga. Shortly thereafter, he had begun a correspondence with Seward.
At this time, King was disgusted with parties, conventions, and
political double-dealing. His solution for the nation's ills rested on
an overwhelming popular draft of Thomas Hart Benton for President;
he believed that the people would gladly jettison the whole corrupt
party system and respond with one voice to a man of proven integrity
and courage. However, Benton's defense of the Missouri "brigands,"
who voted illegally in Kansas, killed any hopes of his candidacy. King
was now receptive to overtures from the Whigs; in March of 1855,
Governor Clark appointed him to a commission investigating New
York City's harbor facilities.[4]

The next task was to work out the details of fusion. A difficulty
arose immediately because the Republican organization existed in
theory but not in fact. A month before the convention met, Horace
Greeley worried that the absence of county and district machinery
would prevent representation of many areas—even those most in
accord with Republican aims. Consequently, he urged his readers to
take independent action, to draw up a brief call for a district meeting,
and to induce their anti-Nebraska neighbors to sign it. He advocated
the selection of two delegates who represented "diverse by-gone
politics, if that be feasible."[5]

The process of fusion went smoothly. The two conventions at first
met separately. Each appointed committees of conference to work
out a basis for merger. Weed and King were the dominant figures in
these negotiations. After these preliminaries, the Whig delegates entered the Republican meeting hall, thereby formally surrendering their
organization. The Republican members cheered when they appeared
and accorded them the center seats. The platform adopted the typical
Republican position. It opposed the introduction of slavery into the

territories; condemned President Pierce's removal of Kansas' Governor, Andrew H. Reeder, who had frustrated the aims of proslavery settlers by refusing to issue commissions to fraudulently elected legislators; and praised the citizens of the free states who had migrated to the territory. One resolution denounced secret political associations, specifically naming the Know-Nothings, as inconsistent with the liberal principles of free government. Meeting in their own convention, the Know-Somethings of New York strengthened the fusion movement by endorsing the Republicans' nominees.[6]

The Syracuse conventions tried to give the impression that a true fusion had been achieved, that the product was not the old Whig party with a few Democrats placed up front for window dressing. An equal balance existed between former Whigs and Democrats on the Republican State Committee and on the state ticket, where five men from each of the old parties were nominated. Preston King, running for secretary of state, headed the slate. The second most desirable position, that of comptroller, went to the Whig incumbent, James M. Cook.[7]

Democrats admitted that they had been treated fairly. Abijah Mann, Jr., who had distinguished himself the year before as an insurgent leader during the Soft Shell convention, had coveted the comptroller's position, but he was content with his nomination for attorney general. He assured Weed that he recognized the equity of the result: "The arrangement was not only proper in itself but was made in entire good faith with my consent." Democrats could not expect to occupy the two most influential places, especially when they "could not bring a large force to its support." Mann added that John Bigelow, the co-editor of the New York *Evening Post,* and David Dudley Field, a once prominent Barnburner, were also satisfied.[8] Thus, a good beginning had been made by securing the confidence of Democrats that they would be treated justly by the overwhelming Whig majority in the new party.

Now that fusion had been accomplished, what course would the temperance forces take? Their efforts had been rewarded with the passage of a prohibition act in early April of 1855. The Democrats promptly charged that the Whigs had reluctantly fulfilled their part of the bargain which had returned Seward to the Senate. Much to their chagrin, however, the foes of alcohol discovered that it was one thing to pass such legislation and quite another to have it obeyed. The law was openly flouted in many areas, while local authorities looked in the other direction. Fernando Wood, the recently-elected mayor of New

York, added to his notoriety by refusing to enforce the measure. Temperance men naturally demanded strict adherence and expected their Whig allies to support them. However, Weed and other Seward-ites, who had been opposed to the reform from the beginning, turned down this request; they did not want to suffer the consequences of forcing compliance in hostile localities. Moreover, their efforts to secure harmony within the new Republican organization would be jeopardized; several prominent Democrats and Whigs who had crossed over into fusion ranks were well-known opponents of the Maine Law.[9]

By this time the Maine Law movement had ebbed considerably. For one thing, the accomplishment of its object had reduced the zeal of its supporters. But most important, their attention had been held by the slavery extension issue. Some fervent prohibitionists still in-sisted that enforcement should be the paramount concern of reformers. Two of these enthusiasts requested the removal of their names from the Republican convention call when that document made no direct reference to the temperance question, and stated that the restoration of the Missouri Compromise was the *only* political issue before the people. But the advocates of temperance often found their old audience in the Burned-over-region too busy raising money for "Beecher's bibles"—a popular expression for rifles to be sent to Kansas—to listen to their entreaties. Even Horace Greeley, who the year before had refused to subordinate the temperance cause, changed his mind and urged his readers to do likewise. He wrote that temperance was a local matter while the extension of slavery was of national im-portance. It was the latter concern, he declared, which was responsible for the abandonment of old parties.[10]

At the Syracuse fusionist conventions, a majority of the Republican delegates revealed again the close relationship between reform move-ments by demonstrating that antislavery men were also temperance advocates; they favored a plank in the platform demanding strict en-forcement. However, the Whigs would not tolerate it. The two meet-ings worked out a compromise: they demanded a fair trial for the prohibition law but made no commitment to any definite action.[11]

Attention now focused upon the state temperance convention, which assembled at Utica on October 3, 1855. There was some fear that this body might reject the Republican candidates and nominate its own ticket. These apprehensions proved unfounded; the Utica convention, though not happy with the fusionist proceedings, agreed to accept its state-wide nominees while urging the election of local temperance men.[12] By this action, anti-liquor zealots tacitly acknowledged the primacy of the slavery extension issue; they refused to draw off votes for their own slate and thereby weaken the impact of New York's demand for freedom in Kansas.

The formation of the New York Republican party left many conservative Sewardites in a dilemma. Although they had frequently differed with the liberal wing of the party, they had tried to cooperate with it. In this respect, they differed from the Silver Grays, who had declared war against Seward and Weed. Fusion, however, marked the line beyond which some would not venture. These conservatives were often cosmopolitans—well-educated, well-traveled, and of substantial means. Many were merchants and lawyers who had business ties with Southerners. Incensed by the Nebraska bill and the events in Kansas, they had participated in public meetings, sent petitions to Congress, and contributed to aid free state emigrants in the territory. They had, however, opposed any mention of disbanding the Whig party and had only disdain for the Republicans. One fundamental consideration dominated their motives: they believed that the establishment of a purely Northern party would lead to the end of the Union.

Hamilton Fish, Washington Hunt, and Robert A. West may serve as examples of conservatives who declined to follow their associates into Republican ranks. All three had attained prominence as Whigs: the first was then the junior United States Senator; the second had been governor from 1850-1852; the third was editor of the New York *Commercial Advertiser*. These men shared a common antipathy toward the extension of slavery, but they wished to pursue this campaign in a conservative manner. They also wanted to play down the slavery issue, both North and South. White men should end their constant bickering over the black man and return to the task of building the country. Hunt wrote a poignant letter to Weed in which he regretted that his sense of duty prevented him from joining his old friends. He gave his reason:

> In every proper way, I want to do right and prevent wrong on the slavery question, so far as we have any power over it. But you know I never could make it the sole object of my thoughts, to the exclusion of more practical concerns.

Fish also denounced the attempt "to make the slavery question the 'be all and end all' of political organization, and of political strife. . . ." West did not believe that Whigs could "be transferred unresistingly from their broad, tried national platform to this single plank of Abolitionism."[13]

Having made their decision to oppose fusion, it was necessary for Old Line or straight Whigs, as they came to be called, to determine their future action. There were three possible alternatives: to remain as Whigs, hoping that somehow their state organization and a national alliance could be patched up; to swallow their distaste for Know-Nothingism and join the nativist party; to embrace their traditional opponents, the Democrats. In 1855, all three of the men mentioned above decided to take the first course.

Several difficulties stood in the path of a successful revival of the Whig organization. One of these was the reluctance of former Sewardites to associate with their old enemies, the Silver Grays. Fish, for example, whose elevation to the Senate had been opposed by these in 1851, specifically cautioned against their inclusion. Hunt was also distressed that those who had done their best to destroy the party should now presume to be its saviors.[14] Moreover, it was feared that Silver Gray participation would weaken the movement by exposing it to the charge of being proslavery. An even greater handicap was the lack of party machinery, nearly all of which had remained loyal to Seward and Weed; Whig papers opposed to fusion had discredited themselves by rushing into Know-Nothingism. The most crushing problem, though, was this: to a substantial degree the success of the straight Whigs depended upon a similar resurgence in the South. Critics of the Old Liners effectively capitalized on this point, charging them with blindness to actual political conditions below the Mason-Dixon line. The New York *Tribune* argued that men like Washington Hunt engaged in wishful thinking when they appealed to conservative Southerners for help in repealing the Nebraska Act; there was hardly a politician or a newspaper in the South which dared to occupy such ground.[15]

A straight Whig state convention assembled in New York City on October 23, 1855. Hunt observed that a more desirable location would have been Utica or Syracuse, no doubt to avoid the inference that the meeting was the voice of cotton merchants. Upstate representatives from thirty-one counties did attend, but their mood was not encouraging. They generally reported that there was little opposition to fusion in their areas and that the rank and file of former Whigs had gone over to the Republicans. Robert A. West drafted a set of resolutions which condemned the formation of a sectional party, declared the Whig party to be still alive, and urged all true Whigs to vote against the Republicans. It remained for the convention to decide whether to nominate its own ticket. The Know-Nothings were fearful of this possibility, while the Republicans welcomed it; another conservative slate would draw away votes from the nativists. The Old Liners finally resolved not to enter the canvass with their own candidates; instead, they recommended that their adherents vote for those most in accord with Whig principles.[16]

Although many conservative Whigs agreed with the Old Liners, there were others who entered the Republican party because they had come to the conclusion that the aggressive tactics of the South necessitated active resistance. They judged the Whig organization moribund, and recoiled at the thought of joining either the Know-Nothings or the Democrats.

James Watson Webb, the editor of the New York *Courier and Enquirer,* was an important convert to this point of view. Webb had impeccable credentials as a conservative Whig, and his paper had faithfully reflected the opinions of the New York merchant class.[17] Less than a year before, the *Courier* had joined with the *Commercial Advertiser* in criticizing the Whig candidates for accepting the nomination of the Saratoga-Auburn anti-Nebraska conventions because that body had issued resolutions in favor of a Northern fusion party. Sympathizing with the demand for a change in the naturalization laws, he had considered joining the Know-Nothings, but their secrecy and proscriptive practices against Catholics had dampened his enthusiasm. Subsequent occurrences, especially the eruptions in Kansas and the Philadelphia Grand Council, had convinced him that cooperation with the South was no longer possible. Webb now took the lead in persuading his readers to become Republicans.[18] More powerful than his arguments, however, would be the course of events which forced more and more conservatives into the party they had always dreaded.

By 1855, the disruption of the second American party system brought about a transformation in New York politics. Ravaged by temperance men, Know-Nothings, and Free Democrats, the Whig party had surrendered its organization and joined fusionist ranks. The successes of the Republican movement in other states, and the threat of war in Kansas had applied additional pressure on New York Whigs and made their decision unavoidable. One favorable development for the New York Republican party was the reduction in temperance fervor. The religious idealism which had flowed into this cause had largely dried up as the slavery issue held the people's attention. But New York fusionists still confronted many difficulties. Not all Whigs had made the transition. Old Liners vowed hostility to the new party and tried to thwart its progress at every opportunity. Enormous problems of building an effective organization, and of harmonizing former political opponents existed. The Know-Nothings remained a formidable threat; yet, it appeared that they were losing their appeal. Although weak in 1855, the New York Republican party had been built upon a solid foundation, and it would grow rapidly.

10

The Hards and the Softs in 1855

In 1854, the New York Democratic party had suffered severe reverses. By 1855, its problems were compounded. The situation in Kansas made it increasingly difficult for the Softs to convince antislavery constituents that the Nebraska Act was innocuous. Angered by repeated failures to gain the upperhand over their rivals, Hard Shell leaders were cooperating with the Know-Nothings. The formation of the Republican party provided an alternative for the dissatisfied of both factions. These new pressures challenged the ties of loyalty which had held the Democratic party together.

After the election of 1854, many Softs had hoped that the reverse suffered by the Hards would convince them to abandon their tactics and seek alliance with their fellow Democrats. However, they again underestimated the tenacity of Daniel S. Dickinson and his followers. The Softs argued that no substantive difference separated the two factions on the slavery extension issue, while the Adamantines seized every opportunity to indict their opponents as abolitionists in disguise. Seeing that their wooing was of no avail, the Softs gave up conciliation and accused their antagonists of defecting to the Know-Nothings, a damaging charge in view of the large nativist vote in Hard Shell strongholds.[1]

Meeting in their state convention on August 23, 1855, the Hards reaffirmed the position they had taken on Nebraska: they praised the measure and set themselves against all efforts to repeal it.[2] Conspicuous by its absence was any reference to the interference of armed Missourians in Kansas' elections which had outraged the North. Attempting to belie the accusations of Know-Nothingism leveled against them, they condemned all secret political societies which dis-

87

criminated on the grounds of religion or place of origin. They also condemned the prohibitory liquor law and called for its repeal.

Dickinson and his allies now nominated a slate of delegates who would claim to represent the New York Democracy at the forthcoming national convention, which would meet in Cincinnati in June of 1856. Some National Democrats resisted this move; they argued that the convention had not been called for any such purpose and championed the right of each district to choose its own representatives. One opponent, observing that the majority thought it necessary to act immediately in order to secure good Dickinson men, asked pointed questions: "Why were these gentlemen afraid to trust the people? Was Mr. Dickinson so unpopular that the people would not select delegates favorable to him?" The lopsided vote of 88 to 19 squelched this revolt.

The Adamantines again disregarded their constituents' views on the slavery extension issue. Their platform was not written for New Yorkers, but for Southern Democrats and Northern doughfaces who would determine whether they or the Softs would be recognized at Cincinnati. The New York *Evening Post* charged them with a flagrant display of their subserviency to the South. Horatio Seymour appraised his opponents' convention as an unrepresentative body, carrying little weight in the state. He added that its purpose to act solely with reference to the Cincinnati convention was well understood. But Seymour acknowledged that the resolutions were shrewd and the selection of delegates was judicious. He concluded that they had "played their best card."[3]

Negotiations over the sale of the Albany *Argus,* the Hard Shell organ, shed more light on the relationship between the Adamantines and the Know-Nothings. After the canvass of 1854, James I. Johnson, one of the editors of the *Argus,* judged the National Democratic cause to be lost and desired to change his political allegiance. He was a man for hire, and both the Know-Nothings and the Soft Shells made their bid. According to one Know-Nothing who was involved in the bargaining, Dickinson advised Johnson to go over to the nativists. The former Senator admitted that he favored the Order and wanted it to succeed, but his position was such that he could assume no open stand. Edwin Croswell, another Hard Shell stalwart, expressed a similar opinion. Gideon J. Tucker, who owned a small share of the *Argus,* remained faithful to Dickinson. Forced to sell his interest in the paper, Tucker reminded Daniel Ullman that no definite offer had been made by his party. He wrote: "As I would greatly prefer that *they* [the Know-Nothings] should purchase the property, I am only acting in good faith when I intimate the absolute necessity of an offer, this week, in their behalf." The nativists' hesitancy benefited Soft Shell politicians who were determined to gain control of the *Argus,* and Seymour, backed up by Erastus Corning, John Stryker, and Secretary of State Marcy, made an attractive offer to Johnson which he accepted.[4] The Adamantines, despite their professions to the contrary, were quite willing to co-operate with the Know-Nothings provided it was done secretly so that their relations with the South would remain undisturbed.

The year 1855 was difficult for the Soft Shells. In addition to Hard Shell obstinacy, dissension over patronage still threatened to destroy the organization. A reconciliation had come about during the campaign of 1854, when the President had agreed to follow the advice of the state's party leadership, but the new year brought fresh difficulties. The most important case was that of Henry C. Miller, who was to be appointed Secretary to the Peruvian Legation. Opposition developed against his confirmation because of his anti-Nebraska activities. Seymour came to Miller's defense. He urged Senator Douglas to aid the nomination, for a rejection would create severe difficulties in New York. Seymour acknowledged that Miller had been a Free Soiler in 1848 and had been against Nebraska, "but when the scheme of a 'Northern Party' was started by Preston King and others he took decided grounds against it and supported the Democratic ticket last November with great zeal and ability." The ex-Governor pleaded for some appreciation of New York's special problems:

> We have so few in New York who can point to clear records that I have always contented myself with learning that men are 'right now' without looking into their past histories . . . I am very anxious our friends in New York should be taught to look forward and not backwards.

Despite a strong campaign in Miller's behalf, his name was withdrawn by President Pierce, who was afraid of antagonizing Southern Democrats. For several months after this episode, Secretary Marcy had to employ all his curative powers in order to reassure his friends.[5]

Assembling in Syracuse on August 29, 1855, the Soft Shell convention quickly agreed on such matters as the financial profligacy of the Whigs and the threat to democracy from both the Know-Nothings and the prohibitory law.[6] The meeting then came to loggerheads over the Kansas policy of the Administration. Tammanyites entrenched within the New York City Custom House and Post Office were present in force. Ably led by Lorenzo Shepard, they were determined to defend the President. They demanded endorsement of Pierce, approval of his actions in Kansas (including the removal of Governor Reeder), and an "unqualified approbation" of the doctrine of popular sovereignty and the Nebraska Act. A new crop of insurgents, who came primarily from the "infected district," put up an unexpectedly strong resistance against the officeholders and demanded the explicit condemnation of Nebraska and the Administration's conduct in Kansas. They pleaded with the convention to give them a platform which would satisfy their rural constituents, and refused to be swayed by warnings that their position would prevent the Softs from gaining recognition at the Cincinnati convention.

Since neither position was able to secure a majority, the delegates decided upon a compromise. This plan accepted the Nebraska Act as a *fait accompli,* but enjoined its strict enforcement. Although refusing to criticize the President for his conduct in Kansas, it did denounce the illegal interference of armed bands in that territory's elections. Just at the moment of the final vote, with feeling running high on both sides, John Van Buren dropped a bombshell. He proposed as an amendment, the so-called Corner Stone declaration of the 1848 Barnburner convention at Utica:

> *Resolved,* That while the Democracy of this State will faithfully adhere to all the compromises of the Constitution and maintain all the reserved rights of the States, they deem this an appropriate occasion to declare and repeat their fixed hostility to the extension of slavery into free territory.

Tammanyites knew that this statement could be interpreted as a reaffirmation of the Wilmot Proviso, pledging the Softs to resist actively the extension of slave territory, and they were afraid it would give the Hards victory at Cincinnati. But, thrown off balance by Van Buren's maneuver, they were powerless to halt the flood of popular enthusiasm which carried it.[7]

The Syracuse convention ended much like its predecessor in 1854. Once again, incompatible positions appeared in the platform: the delegates sought to soothe anti-Nebraska feeling with the Corner Stone declaration, but they refused to censure the President and Southern Democrats who had brought about the Kansas situation and continued to inflame it. This type of equivocation seemed to be the only method for smoothing over differences within the party caused by the slavery issue. Ambiguity could serve another function: it might keep antislavery constituents loyal without antagonizing Southern Democrats. This scheme, however, could also backfire; the Softs might lose voters alarmed about Kansas and also incur the hostility of their colleagues below the Mason-Dixon line.

Some Soft Shell leaders were satisfied with the outcome. Seymour confessed to a sense of relief that the convention had abstained from attacking the President; he did not interpret Van Buren's amendment as foisting the Wilmot Proviso on the party; in fact, Seymour was delighted that free soil trouble makers had been rebuffed. George W. Newell was also pleased. He judged the proceedings to be the best thing for the state and the Union, "if people would look at them calmly. But there are very many who will not do so nor let others."[8]

Newell was correct. The "balancing act" performed by the convention was now subjected to attacks from both the right and the left, from those who felt that it constituted a provocative challenge to Southern interests, and from those who believed that it had capitulated to "the lords of the lash."

Tammany Hall called a special meeting to give its own interpretation of Van Buren's amendment. According to a Tammany resolution, the Softs' profession of "fixed hostility to the extension of slavery into free territory" did not commit them to *oppose actively* the admission of new slave states. They had merely announced a preference or an "abstract opinion" which had no binding effect. Put bluntly, the Softs would acquiesce in the extension of slavery, even though they disapproved of it. Lorenzo Shepard did not think highly of this pronouncement, but he had sponsored it because the editors of the New York *Journal of Commerce* promised to support the Softs if they adopted it. "This acquisition of the Journal of Commerce is of very great importance," Shepard wrote to Marcy. "And whatever may be their reason for going with us and I am entirely ignorant of it, it is an ally very deserving of consideration."[9]

The motives of the *Journal* were not really difficult to fathom. The paper, which represented the most conservative members of the mercantile community, had come to the conclusion that a united Democracy was the only chance for thwarting the Republicans. After the Know-Nothing debacle in Virginia in May of 1855, it realized that the nativists could never win a presidential canvass, and began a campaign to convince its readers not to waste votes or money on the American party. The paper considered the straight Whig movement, led by the New York *Commercial Advertiser,* to be equally ineffectual. The *Journal* had endorsed the Hard Shells in 1854, but had grown increasingly dissatisfied with their selfish factionalism.[10] Thus, when Dickinson and his followers refused to unite with the Softs in 1855, the *Journal* turned to the latter. Before it would commit itself, however, it demanded the dilution of Van Buren's amendment.

On the slavery question, Tammany Hall had become the spokesman not only for Irish immigrants, but also for the merchant princes.

The support of the *Journal of Commerce* was offset by the defection of the New York *Evening Post*. Although in disagreement with the Soft Shell position for nearly two years, William Cullen Bryant and John Bigelow had not officially endorsed the fusionists. Their hesitancy was due to a deep distrust of Seward and Weed. But their dissatisfaction with the Soft convention of 1855, and the supplementary resolution of Tammany Hall, plus conciliatory gestures from the Whig leadership, overcame their reluctance. Unlike the brilliant lawyer Samuel J. Tilden, who had not only endorsed the Soft Shell proceedings but had accepted the Softs' nomination for attorney general, they refused to compromise.[11]

By 1855, the difficulties of the New York Democratic party were even greater than the year before. The Hard Shells rejected all proposals for reconciliation with the Softs and continued to pillory them as free soilers. Having divorced themselves from the opinions of their constituents, the Adamantines were willing to go to almost any lengths to gain Southern support. In the event, however, that they were again rebuffed, Dickinson and his colleagues had established connections with the Know-Nothings. In 1854, the Nebraska Act had threatened to divide the Softs; the most pressing problem had been holding antislavery Barnburners faithful to the party. The following year, the possibility of violence in Kansas made this task even more difficult. The Softs had also to satisfy the Administration and Southern Democrats, who suspected their loyalty to the national party. When confronted with incompatible demands from antislavery men and federal officeholders, a majority of delegates to the Syracuse convention equivocated in order to prevent the party from being torn apart. Evasion, however, had its limitations. By trying to please everyone, the Softs' platform pleased no one. Alarmed that Van Buren's resolution would be construed as a revival of the Barnburner movement, Tammany Hall Democrats demanded that it be watered down. Disgusted by the second refusal of a Soft convention to denounce the policy of the Administration, some Democrats from the Burned-over-region rebelled. In the past, Democratic loyalties had prevented them from bolting and following Preston King into the Republican camp. They were now ready to take this step. Subjected to these pressures, the resilience of the New York Democratic party showed signs of reaching the breaking point.

11

The Election of 1855

The New York election of 1854 had been indecisive—neither a paramount issue nor a dominant party had emerged out of the political chaos of that year. Politicians waged the campaign of 1855 with an energy entirely out of proportion to the minor state offices involved. They knew that much more was at stake—that the survival of their parties depended upon the result. Although the election failed to eliminate all the uncertainty which marked the previous contest, it clearly established one fact—that the slavery issue was the voters' foremost concern, and that both the temperance and nativist causes were of secondary importance. This basis for the supremacy of the Republican party in the Empire State had been established.

In 1855, the Know-Nothings in New York reached their greatest strength but they were soon shown to be fatally weak. They sought to repair their organization, expelling those who had voted for Seward during the senatorial struggle, and to increase the number of lodges. They maintained their momentum in the county and town elections, which were held during the winter and spring, and routed the Whigs in many districts.[1] However, nativism in the Empire State was seriously affected by the disorders in Kansas, the election in Virginia, and the disruption of the National Grand Council in Philadelphia. Hostility to slavery extension overshadowed everything at the State Council at Binghamton.

The Silver Grays were in a precarious situation during the campaign of 1855. Caught between the incompatible demands of New York and Southern Know-Nothings, they had been forced to accept the deletion of Article XII at the Binghamton convention, but they knew that this decision would not go unnoticed in the South. All efforts to avoid the sectional strains destroying the other national parties

93

had so far been abortive. The anti-foreign and anti-Catholic issues, which were to be the basis of a national conservative party, were being submerged by the slavery question. Desperately, the Silver Grays tried to reverse this process. James R. Thompson offered Daniel Ullman this advice for a speech:

> Dwell upon the fact that the Pro-slavery prejudices of the South are appealed to by demagogues to oppose the American party and that the Black Republicans of the North are led by men who have long slept with [Archbishop John] Hughes. Show that Seward and Pierce have a common interest in crushing out the American sentiment of the country—that one fights with certain weapons at the South, and the other with different weapons at the North, but they both fight under the Black flag of political Romanism.

He cautioned him against spending too much attention on the slavery issue:

> Go just far enough and then stop in denouncing the repeal . . . attempting to set up now for restoration of the Missouri line, makes the slavery issue *the* prominent issue. Be *careful* to speak to the *audience before you* and let them see and feel that *your heart* is in the *American* movement.[2]

When Thurlow Weed joined the Republicans in midsummer of 1855, he believed there was a chance for victory. "It is possible that the state may be carried this fall. There are elements enough, if combined, to effect it," he wrote to Seward. To achieve success, the new party had to build political machinery fast. It would be a mistake to assume that the Republican organization was easily established or that it was merely a slightly revamped version of the old Whig party. The Seward-Weed organization had been thrown into chaos by the events of the past two years. In some localities, enough of it survived to serve as a nucleus for the Republicans, but in other areas, the fusionists had to begin from scratch. Henry B. Stanton, formerly a prominent abolitionist and Free Democrat and now a Republican, worried about the lack of order. He informed Weed that

> Everything in the shape of *organization* is in utter chaos—I mean the kind of minute and detailed organization having for its chief object the bringing of votes to the polls. All old *Whig* committees are of course disabled and their substitutes are to a large extent yet to be appointed.

George E. Baker perceived a similar situation. He wrote to Seward: "I now see, what you saw long ago, how hard it is to break up an old party and organize a new one." Two weeks before election day, the New York *Tribune* expressed dismay at the absence of county committees and ward clubs in many crucial districts and appealed for swift action to remedy this defect.[3]

The Republicans urgently needed campaigners to canvass the state. Requests for speakers dominated Weed's correspondence. "Many Democrats are halting and a few words from [James W.] Nye or some other former Democrat would determine them," wrote one worker.[4] A special effort was needed to bring in conservative Whigs, many of whom withheld their aid from the new party. Stanton advised Weed that it was "important to have speakers who have been known throughout the state as *prominent Whigs.*" DeWitt C. Littlejohn, the speaker of the assembly, appealed for aid in Oswego. He reported that Whigs who were once in the habit of contributing freely were now in opposition and called a meeting to resuscitate the old party. The fusionists made great exertions in Lockport, the home of Washington Hunt, to offset his influence. Numerous writers begged Seward to take the stump, and the Senator responded. Together with Nye, he spoke in several cities along the Erie Canal.[5]

Republican leaders looked upon the campaign as an enterprise in mass education. They deemed it necessary to convince a confused electorate, dizzy with the proliferation of parties and crusades, that the prevention of slavery extension was the most pressing issue. Praising one of Seward's speeches for its instructional value, Baker observed that "if we fail this fall it will be because the people have read more about the Pope and Bishop [John] Hughes than about Slavery and Equal Rights." Seward, expressing his attitude toward the canvass, rejoiced that the revolution had commenced and was certain that it would ultimately prevail. He nevertheless, realized that there would be setbacks and temporary defeats. Republicans must remember that "they who work out political reformation through the action of popular suffrage under constitutional government must allow the people time, and calculate on many disturbances and caprices."[6]

The strategy of the Soft Shells was to take no definite stand on the slavery issue. Maintaining an equivocal position seemed the only way to ease the strain on the party. Did the Softs stand on John Van Buren's platform, which declared "fixed hostility to the extension of slavery into free territory," or was Tammany Hall correct when it declared this statement only an "abstract opinion" without practical application? The Softs deliberately left this question unanswered. By this plan, they hoped to attract the votes of antislavery Barnburners without alienating conservative Whigs and Democrats and their colleagues below the Mason-Dixon line.

John Van Buren stumped the state, attempting to revive his old standing with Radical Democrats. His speeches, re-affirming his Wilmot Proviso position of 1848, came under attack from the Washington *Union,* which called for his banishment from the party. If the Softs stood behind these heresies, warned the *Union,* they could not belong to the national Democratic party. "Prince John" welcomed this criticism. As he explained to Marcy, the attacks of the President's paper would be translated into thousands of votes for the Softs.[7]

At the same time that Van Buren toured the countryside, Horatio Seymour made a bid for conservative votes at home and Southern support at Cincinnati. He delivered a carefully prepared speech at Tammany Hall in which he lauded the principle of popular sovereignty and the Nebraska Act. Gently chiding the "border irregularities" committed by proslavery Missourians, he found ample provocation in the activities of Kansas emigrant societies. The Albany *Atlas* observed that Seymour's address "pitched the true keynote of the Democracy," and the Washington *Union* called it "thoroughly national," presenting "a platform on which northern and southern men can meet and join hands and heart for the perpetual preservation of the Union."[8]

At their state convention, the straight or Old Line Whigs refrained from naming a state-wide ticket. How then was an Old Liner to cast his vote? Both the Know-Nothings and the Softs had their own self-serving answers. Each party claimed that it had the only chance to defeat the Republicans; therefore, Whigs should do their patriotic duty. The New York *Commercial Advertiser,* the chief spokesman for the Whigs, urged its readers to vote so as to promote the welfare of the Union. Coming down to specifics, it acknowledged its uncertainty about the relative strengths of the Softs and the Know-Nothings, although it tended to favor the latter because of their superior organization and better candidates.[9]

The election result revealed a narrow Know-Nothing victory of nearly 12,000 votes over the Republicans. The state-wide returns for the head of the ticket (secretary of state) were: Joel T. Headley (Know-Nothing), 148,557; Preston King (Republican), 136,698; Israel T. Hatch (Soft), 91,336; Aaron Ward (Hard), 59,353.[10]

The Know-Nothings were delighted with their victory. In an off year election, they had increased their state-wide total by more than 25,000 votes. They made considerable gains in the eastern portion of the state. In 1854, the party had carried only five of the twenty-six counties comprising this region; in 1855, its total increased to fifteen.[11] They also registered gains in the heavily populated cities of Brooklyn and New York. As one nativist expressed it, "New York is covered with honor. Fusion—Seward, Weed, Greeley, Raymond are prostrate. The fusionists are not only astonished, but bitterly malignant; they fought with the desperation of pirates."[12]

New York Republicans shared in the reverses which the party suffered in most of the North. Besides New York, the Know-Nothings carried New Hampshire, Connecticut, Massachusetts, and Rhode Island. Only in Iowa, Michigan, and especially Ohio—where Salmon P. Chase was elected governor—did the fusionists triumph. New York City and other urban areas in the state delivered a sharp setback to the new party. In Brooklyn and New York, it received only 15.13 percent and 11.90 percent of the vote.[13] The combination of the Irish laborers' vote for the Softs and the merchants' support of the Hards and Know-Nothings swamped the fusionists. The anti-Republican vote, though overwhelming, was divided.

Conservative newspapers in New York City, regardless of party, were jubilant. The New York *Express*—whose editor, Erastus Brooks, had made a career out of baiting Archbishop John Hughes—concluded that efforts to create a sectional party were doomed. The paper hoped that the Know-Nothing party would gain new recruits as a result of its victory. Although disappointed that the Soft Shells were beaten, the New York *Journal of Commerce* was satisfied that the Republicans were "signally defeated." It remarked that "such a rebuke to that dangerous faction . . . is glory enough for one day." The voice of the straight Whigs, the New York *Commercial Advertiser,* rejoiced that "disunion and abolitionism" had been checked.[14]

The Republicans disputed the claims of newspapers which hastened to write their obituary. They had come close to victory in spite of their weak organization. The New York *Evening Post* offered this rejoinder:

> Considering that the Republican party was a sort of improvisation, an extempore affair, a spontaneous association of men not accustomed to act together, who came together reluctantly, and had no proper organization, it has done wonders.

Seward believed that Republican "wonders" would increase. "We have rather a tough beginning with our new organization, but it will work effectually in the end," he wrote to a friend. Greeley credited the Republicans with 20,000 more votes than the Know-Nothings at election time and attributed the fusionists' defeat to an inadequate organization—which allowed nativists, posing as Republicans, to destroy the latter's ballots. One prominent Whig, now a Republican, celebrated what he called "a sort of half victory this fall—a presage I trust of a whole one the next time—a republican triumph—and a hindoo and pro-slavery defeat."[15]

The primary reason for the Republicans' optimism was their success in central and western New York, the mainstay of the old Whig party. Many counties in the "infected district" had gone heavily Know-Nothing in 1854. This trend seemed to have been reversed, with the Republican party as the chief beneficiary. In 1854, the secret Order had carried eleven of the twenty-nine counties in the Burned-over-region; the following year the nativists carried only seven of these.[16] Fusionists were jubilant to find their predictions fulfilled. They noted that the Know-Nothing fever only appeared to last for one year in any locality before it died out. Of all the counties west of Cayuga Lake, only Wayne, Monroe, Niagara, and Wyoming had given pluralities against Daniel Ullman in 1854. In 1855, these four counties were still anti-Know-Nothing, and neighboring ones had been largely reclaimed.[17] Thurlow Weed was delighted:

> The REPUBLICAN PARTY needs no stronger or surer guarantees for the future, than the glorious WEST has furnished in its recent emphatic vote for FREEDOM. In Counties obscured for a brief season by the dark-lantern delusion, there is now light and liberty. With the WEST now, as formerly strong and firm in their devotion to FREEDOM, all is safe.[18]

The Soft Shells lost ground in the election, although they, too, were able to discover reasons for optimism. Collector Redfield admitted that he had hoped for a small plurality, but he was not disappointed with the result. He found comfort in the fact that the combined Hard and Soft Shell vote was still a majority. Redfield predicted that the total vote for 1855 would be 200,000 less than in 1856 and that those who abstained from balloting—in his judgment, mostly conservative Democrats who were disgusted by the divisions in the party brought about by profligate leaders—would support the Softs in the presidential campaign. The Collector assumed that in 1856 the leading Adamantines would join the Know-Nothings but that the rank and file would return to the Democracy.[19]

The election of 1855, like its predecessor, was inconclusive; the revolution in the New York party system had not yet been completed. As we have seen, all three major participants—the Know-Nothings, the Republicans, and the Softs—believed they had a good chance for success in the coming presidential campaign.

One highly significant result, however, did occur—the slavery extension issue emerged as the paramount subject before the electorate. Temperance, the most potent question of 1854, was reduced in importance. This fact had become apparent when the state temperance convention agreed to endorse the Republican ticket instead of nominating its own. The narrow victory of Know-Nothingism reflected the power of anti-foreign and anti-Catholic prejudice. Yet, Silver Gray managers were forced to renounce Article XII to hold antislavery nativists in the Burned-over-region, and they were hard pressed in emphasizing "Popery" rather than Kansas. The success of the American party was due to its excellent organization and not to the primacy of nativist objectives. The Softs also had to deal with the slavery issue, whereas in 1854, they had given exclusive attention to liquor. Because they refused to take an unequivocal stand against slavery in Kansas, they experienced great difficulty in keeping ex-Barnburners loyal.

If antislavery sentiments had come to dominate the people's response to the political upheaval, why, then, did New York Republicans fail to receive a preponderant endorsement at the polls? The inadequate organization of the new party was partly responsible for its defeat. Seward and Weed had hesitated to abandon the Whig party, because they anticipated the difficulty of establishing another one. Their apprehensions proved correct; much work remained before the Republican machine operated with the same effectiveness as the Know-Nothing's. However, even more important than the lack of an efficient party apparatus was the fact that no clear distinction on the slavery extension issue emerged between the Republicans and their principal opponents; during the canvass, the Soft Shells and the Know-Nothings also opposed the expansion of the South's "peculiar institution." Both of these parties found themselves facing the dilemma of having to satisfy both the antislavery attitudes of constituents and the demands of Southern colleagues. Confronted by the immediate problem of the 1855 election, these two parties felt compelled to adopt positions acceptable to local opinions. Many nativists who voted Know-Nothing believed that they were also voicing opposition to the spread of slavery. The same was true of a large number of Barnburners who were deceived by the statements of John Van Buren. In this way, thousands of ballots were lost to the Republicans.

The Republicans lost their first battle in 1855, but they took a giant step toward a subsequent victory. The fusionists had forced their opponents to fight on their terrain, differences on slavery and

its extension having become the dividing line between parties. The turning point was the success of the Republican party in the "infected district." This region had postponed temperance crusading and was growing disillusioned with nativism. Efforts to save Kansas from slavery had taken precedence over all other goals. With the election completed, attention focused on the drama unfolding in Kansas, and on Washington, where an anti-Nebraska House of Representatives would soon meet.

12

The Cincinnati Convention

Sectional tension within the national party brought severe difficulties to New York Democrats. But the problems of the Democratic organization in the Empire State also threatened the national party. By 1856, the Hard Shell-Soft Shell feud had become a matter of great concern to the entire Democracy. In three successive elections from 1853-1855, factionalism had resulted in Democratic defeat in New York; in each case the combined Hard-Soft vote had been a majority. Democrats throughout the nation appreciated the crucial importance of New York's thirty-five electoral votes, which had often been the decisive margin in presidential elections, and they demanded an end to this disastrous rift.

The Hard-Soft split also created other dilemmas. The Adamantines had recklessly reopened the bitter controversies of 1848 by accusing the Softs of free soilism. Having carried on the struggle for so long, the Hards were determined to bring their case before the Cincinnati convention. Since efforts to obtain unity had failed, the Softs resumed the denunciation of their rivals. They again indicted the Hards for complicity with the Know-Nothings; the Albany *Argus* even suggested that Dickinson was anxious for a spot on the nativists' presidential ticket.[1] By undermining confidence in the loyalty of New York Democrats, these charges and countercharges weakened the ties of mutual trust which bound the national party together.

The Soft Shells had powerful arguments in favor of their claim to being the regular Democrats of the state. They pointed to their superior voting strength in the past two canvasses and to their many newspapers. Nevertheless, they felt vulnerable. They feared that popularity at the polls would count for little at Cincinnati if their orthodoxy on the slavery issue were doubted

The Softs had reason for concern. Custom house and postal appointees had secured a grudging endorsement of the Nebraska Act, but they had been compelled to make concessions to antislavery sentiment. The 1854 state convention declared the Act "inexpedient and unnecessary," and the 1855 conclave adopted John Van Buren's resolution pledging "fixed hostility to the extension of slavery." Besides soothing the anger of many delegates, these "sweeteners" helped to hold many antislavery Democrats in the party. Although this ambiguous policy had relieved some immediate strains on the Softs, it exposed them to Adamantine charges of free soilism. With the election of 1855 over, Soft Shell leaders realized that they had to place their faction on unassailable national grounds.[2]

Great care was taken to insure that the Soft Shell convention of January 10-11, 1856 avoided dissension. Horatio Seymour assured Marcy that unmanageable radicals would be strictly excluded. The meeting was composed almost entirely of federal officeholders, and the Administration's wishes regarding the platform were solicited well in advance.[3] Lorenzo Shepard of Tammany—whose efforts to secure a blanket endorsement of the President's actions had been thwarted for two years—reported the resolutions.[4] The first pronouncement attacked the Republicans for attempting "to impair the security of the domestic institutions of the South." The Kansas-Nebraska Act and the principle of popular sovereignty received an *unqualified* endorsement; John Van Buren's amendment, adopted only three months before, was omitted. The last statement eulogized the Pierce Administration. These resolves passed with only one negative vote. The final order of business, the selection of delegates to contest the Hard Shells at Cincinnati, also went smoothly.

Soft Shell leaders were relieved that they had adopted pro-Administration resolutions. Secretary of State Marcy announced his satisfaction and so did the President and the Cabinet. William Cassidy, an editor of the Albany *Atlas,* had once opposed the Nebraska bill but was unwilling to sever his ties with the national Democracy over the issue. He explained his reasoning to former President Martin Van Buren: "It would be a folly and a crime to destroy a party organization to which the people have owed so much, since the very foundation of the government, for the sake of a few temporary and adventitious errors." The Albany *Argus* defended the deletion of John Van Buren's amendment. No one, it maintained, had the right to usurp the prerogatives of territorial citizens; should a majority of settlers include slavery in their constitution and apply for entry into the Union, they must be admitted.[5]

The Hard Shells would not allow their rivals to escape so easily from the stigma of free soilism; the Adamantines' only chance for recognition at Cincinnati depended on the credibility of this charge. Dickinson's organ, the New York *Daily News,* accused its foes of "groveling in the dust . . . acknowledging themselves hypocrites and pretenders . . . and sickening all beholders with a newly-assumed cant of nationality and patriotism." The *News* maintained that three-fourths of the delegates to the convention had supported the Buffalo Platform in 1848 and had taken a consistent free soil position afterwards. It warned Democrats in other states not to be deceived by these new professions.[6]

The Hard-Soft feud made New York a center of political intrigue for presidential aspirants. Maneuvering began in earnest after the election of 1855. Four men appeared as the most likely candidates —Secretary of State Marcy, President Pierce, Senator Douglas, and Minister James Buchanan. Each of these men had his adherents in the Empire State.

Marcy was the weakest contender for several reasons: he shared the opprobrium attached to the Nebraska bill, even though he had had no part in its formulation and had disapproved of it; the President desired a second term; and the Secretary could not depend on New York as a political base. The Hard Shells hated him and the Soft Shells were suspect in many parts of the country. Nevertheless, some of Marcy's friends hoped that in a deadlocked convention the "lightening" might strike him.[7]

It is rare that an incumbent President's desire for renomination can be resisted. The exceptions occur during periods of political crisis. In 1856, many Democrats held President Pierce responsible for the defeats suffered by the party, and they were determined to see him retired. Pierce possessed strength in the South and in New England and expected aid from the Softs in return for his patronage. However, his New York beneficiaries had only contempt for him; the New York *Tribune* correctly observed that the Softs used the same foul language to describe Pierce in private which the Hards used in public.[8] Although nominally committed, the Softs' real attitudes were well-known. This left the door ajar for secret overtures from the adherents of other candidates.

Stephen A. Douglas also coveted the nomination. He possessed an energetic agent in the Empire State, David T. Disney, a Cincinnati lawyer and former Congressman. Seeking to unite New York's feuding politicians behind Douglas, Disney traveled about the state speaking with the leaders of each faction. He repeated the same argument to all his conferees: both the Hards and the Softs faced a barren future if they presented contesting delegations; however, if they seized the opportune moment and rallied around the Illinois Senator, they could place themselves in a commanding position at Cincinnati.[9] Although confident that his reasoning would have the desired effect, Disney urged the Little Giant to assist him by sending some Southerner to New York. The Ohioan surmised that this would be particularly useful for its effect on Daniel S. Dickinson: "I may go up and see Dickinson but at present I think that in going to him it would be well for me to have as coadjutor some Southern man of standing—such a man and myself *can control Dickinson* . . . I say Southern because that location would weigh with Dickinson."[10]

Although James Buchanan had been a perennial aspirant for the nomination, the prize had always eluded his grasp, and he had to be satisfied with prominent roles in other men's administrations. Secretary of State in the Polk Administration, he had coveted the same office under Pierce, and was piqued when the State Department went to Marcy. Nevertheless, the Pennsylvanian accepted the position of Minister to the Court of St. James, an appointment which proved to be a blessing in disguise. Safely installed in London, he had the ocean between himself and the Kansas-Nebraska controversy. Buchanan subsequently announced his approval of the Administration's Nebraska policy but only after it had been established as a new maxim of Democratic orthodoxy;[11] thus he avoided the resentment of thousands of Democrats—both from the North and the South— who despised Douglas' measure.

In New York, Buchanan had significant support in the metropolis, especially among the merchants, who, although somewhat uneasy about his record as an expansionist, viewed him as a sound conservative. One of the envoy's earliest and most ardent adherents was George W. Butler, an editor of the New York *Journal of Commerce*. The former Tammanyite Daniel W. Sickles, recently Buchanan's Secretary of Legation at London, applied his genius for rascality in behalf of his former superior. He pursued the same difficult objective as David Disney—to unite Hards and Softs behind his friend. Sickles arranged a regal welcome for the Pennsylvanian upon his arrival from England in April of 1856. Buchanan rode triumphantly down Fifth Avenue to the Everett House on Union Square, where he met a large crowd and several speakers eulogized him.[12]

All the schemers who tried to unite the Hards and Softs behind a favorite candidate failed. They underestimated the bitterness which separated the two antagonists. The Hards and the Softs could not resolve their differences, even though this might have placed them in a powerful position. When the Cincinnati convention assembled on June 2, 1856, the problem of New York's divided delegation was referred to the committee on credentials.

The Adamantines briefly investigated the possibility of supporting Douglas but finally decided to cast their lot with Buchanan. Several considerations played a part in this decision. First, they and the former envoy, shared a mutual hatred for both Pierce and Marcy. Second, rumors of an understanding between Douglas and Pierce alarmed Dickinson and his friends; the success of either would ruin them. Third, Beverly Tucker, a leading National Democrat—whose paper, the Washington *Sentinel,* attacked the Administration at every opportunity—warmly supported Buchanan.[13] When the Hard Shells arrived in Cincinnati, Buchanan's partisans pledged their assistance to them in the coming contest with the Softs; in return, Dickinson promised to stand behind the Pennsylvanian.[14]

The Softs had no real choice. Dependent on the President and his adherents for gaining admittance to the convention, they had to support him, whether they liked him or not. Many leading Softs favored Marcy, but they found upon arrival that the Secretary of State had little strength. For the very reasons that made him attractive to the Hards, Buchanan was an unthinkable alternative. Secret hopes settled on the Little Giant. Should the opportunity arise, the Softs were ready to desert Pierce.

While the main body of the Cincinnati convention passed its platform, including the doctrine of popular sovereignty, the credentials committee listened to arguments from New York's feuding delegations. Horatio Seymour advocated the case of the Softs; Samuel Beardsley spoke for the Hards. Regretting the inclusion of John Van Buren's resolution in 1855, Seymour pointed to the January, 1856 pronouncements as representing the true position of his faction. Beardsley disparaged his rivals' latest position on Nebraska. He charged that it had been adopted at the eleventh hour with one object in mind—to deceive the national convention. It hid the free soil inclinations of the Softs, which, according to Beardsley, had been so apparent in their last campaign.[15]

The great importance accorded to these charges and counter charges revealed the sectional strains tearing the national party apart. The slavery question had thrust all traditional Democratic issues aside. An acceptable stand on slavery had become the *sine qua non* of party regularity. Deviation from the official party platform could deny a state organization its representation at the national convention. Democrats throughout the North resented the inquisitorial atmosphere at Cincinnati. Knowing the attitudes of New York's Radical Democrats, Secretary of State Marcy had sought to prevent a party test on Nebraska, but he had failed. Former Barnburners had previously denounced proceedings in which Southern Democrats and Northern doughfaces assumed the roles of prosecutor, judge, and jury. Many now resolved never to again go through this ordeal. After the Cincinnati convention, large numbers of Barnburners joined the Republican party.

Unable to agree, the credentials committee presented a majority and a minority report. The former recognized the Softs as the regular party and granted them 20 of New York's 35 votes, a distribution justified by the Softs' superior voting strength. The minority report —presented by Senator James Bayard of Delaware, a secret Buchanan supporter—favored a more equal distribution, 18 votes for the Softs, and 17 for the Hards. Bayard adopted Beardsley's argument that the Soft Shells' success had been achieved with a platform tinged with free soilism. Since this error had been corrected, Bayard would neither debar the Softs from the convention nor reward them by according them status as the regular party and a greater portion of New York's vote.[16]

The vote on the two reports represented a test of strength between the partisans of the major contestants. Douglas' and Pierce's followers supported the Softs, and Buchanan's delegates backed the Hards. The result was a narrow victory for the latter; the balloting stood 137 to 123.[17] Anson Herrick, the editor of the New York *Atlas,* wrote Buchanan that "the disposition of the 'New York difficulty' was a master stroke in political strategy and an achievement that entitles somebody to an exalted diplomatic position."[18]

With the New York question settled, the convention could proceed with the selection of its standard-bearer. The Hards fulfilled their bargain to vote for Buchanan, and the Softs reluctantly went for Pierce. When the first voting session ended, Buchanan was the front runner but still lacked the two-thirds majority necessary to nominate. That evening candles burned late in smoke filled rooms, and an agreement emerged to stop Buchanan. Pierce's adherents promised to support Douglas until either the Senator or a dark horse received the nomination.[19]

When the convention reassembled for the fifteenth ballot, everything went according to plan. New Hampshire withdrew Pierce's name and all who had supported him went for Douglas, New York Soft Shells among them. The decisive moment had now arrived. Douglas' floor manager abruptly withdrew the Senator's name. He read a letter from Douglas declaring his unwillingness to create bitterness among Democrats; the triumph of his principles meant much more to him than personal elevation. Although this announcement surprised everyone, its significance was clear: it assured Buchanan's nomination. When order was restored and the seventeenth ballot called, New York Softs, who, in common with many other delegates felt betrayed by the swift capitulation of Douglas, had no other choice than to join the stampede toward the Pennsylvanian. Before adjourning, the convention enjoined the Hards and the Softs to settle their differences and establish one organization. This they promised to do.[20]

The Hard Shells were jubilant over the result. Having long been denied all federal patronage and snubbed by Southern Democrats, they had suddenly found a powerful champion.[21] Samuel Beardsley wrote to Buchanan that he was "exceedingly gratified." Dickinson expressed his appreciation to "the Pennsylvania delegation and the 'Buchanan men' generally in taking our New York friends by the hand & carrying them through against the packed instruments of a most perfidious administration."[22]

Soft Shell leaders were humiliated and envious. Yet, most of them managed to control their anger. John Pruyn of Albany—a prominent lawyer and railroad promoter, who had been a delegate to the convention—felt that his faction had been treated with gross injustice. Noting that the Softs' position on the slavery issue had been acceptable to the delegations of North and South Carolina, Georgia, Alabama, and Mississippi, who had supported the majority report of the credentials committee, Pruyn believed that penalizing the Softs for alleged free soilism was both insulting and absurd. Nevertheless, he decided to swallow his pride and support Buchanan rather than cut his ties with the Democratic party. Horatio Seymour, although "intensely mortified with the position of New York," promised to go into the contest with vigor. The rancor of the editors of the Albany *Argus* briefly gained control over their discretion, and they printed a bitter article against partisans of Buchanan, singling out James W. Bayard of Delaware for special abuse. The next day party discipline prevailed; the *Argus* eulogized the Buchanan-Breckinridge ticket.[23]

The road toward reunion proved to be a difficult one; mutual suspicion impeded progress at every step. Only the twofold fear of Buchanan's anger, and of losing the state beyond redemption forced an alliance. An agreement was reached to hold a joint convention on July 30, 1856 for the purpose of selecting presidential electors and a state ticket. Several representatives of each faction coveted the gubernatorial nomination. Amasa J. Parker, a judge on the Court of Appeals, received the honor, mainly because he had stood aloof from the Hard-Soft feud and neither faction could take umbrage at his selection. A new Democratic State Committee emerged with equal representation accorded to the former opponents.[24]

Thus, an uneasy truce was established. Heretofore, New York Democrats had never been particularly alarmed when internal feuds enabled their political opponents to carry the state. Fairly certain of patching up differences when participating in a united campaign, they had always been confident of easily regaining control. In 1856, however, they embarked upon the campaign without the former optimism. Now that their fratricidal struggle had ended, they were appalled to discover the growing strength of the Republican party.

13

The Decline of Know-Nothingism

In 1856, the Know-Nothings had plans to capture the Presidency.
nd, for a period, this ambition did not seem unrealistic. An im-
ressive list of electoral triumphs, including one in the Empire State,
ncouraged the nativists. Yet, the events of previous years had re-
ealed that they were not immune from the forces breaking up the
ther national parties. In 1854, the New York Order had failed to
ppreciate the strength of temperance sentiment and suffered the
onsequences. In 1855, the re-election of Seward in New York, the
iumph of Governor Wise in Virginia, and the split in the Grand
ouncil at Philadelphia had demonstrated the difficulty of subordin-
ing sectional differences over slavery. Divisions in the party would
ave to be overcome if the party were to succeed further.

The opening session of the Thirty-fourth Congress in December,
855 presented nativists with an opportunity to reconcile their differ-
nces. Many unknown Congressmen from two new parties—the
epublican and the American—arrived in Washington during the
arly winter. They had been elected as a result of the revolution in
he nation's party politics. A formidable number of Representatives
rom both the North and the South had been elected with the Order's
upport. Although not a majority, the Know-Nothings held the
alance of power between the Democrats and the Republicans. If
ney could cooperate, they had an excellent chance of electing a
peaker favorable to their interests.[1]

Problems appeared even before the Congress convened. Southern
now-Nothings circulated a letter announcing an intention to not
ote for a candidate for Speaker unless he declared the finality of
xisting laws on slavery. Vespasian Ellis, the editor of the American
rgan, feared that this attempt to dictate the terms of cooperation

would destroy the party; it would drive off conservatives and others of the North. He urged Daniel Ullman to use his influence and to enlist Erastus Brooks, the co-owner of the New York *Express,* against the plan.[2]

When the House convened, a deadlock developed over the Speakership. The Democratic minority, refusing to yield to the anti-Nebraska majority, selected William A. Richardson of Illinois, the floor manager of the Nebraska bill, as its candidate. The Republicans concentrated their strength on Nathaniel P. Banks, a former Know-Nothing from Massachusetts. The Americans fell victim to the worst apprehensions of nationalists within the party. Unable to support a single candidate, they divided along sectional lines. Northern nativists split their votes between Henry M. Fuller of Pennsylvania, and Lewis D. Campbell of Ohio, and Southerners supported Humphrey Marshall of Kentucky. For two months the impasse continued.[3]

The letters of Solomon G. Haven—the law partner and political confidant of Millard Fillmore, who represented the city of Buffalo in Congress—illustrated the plight of nationalists in the Know-Nothing party. Haven tried "to stand upon purely conservative middle ground making the American question subordinate to no other and fighting extreme men north and south." However, he found that sectional feeling controlled even Know-Nothings. The Buffalo Congressman admitted that in his role as a would-be arbiter, he was "very nearly crushed out." New York's House contingent proved especially vulnerable to the polarizing process. Haven complained that Benjamin Pringle, Thomas T. Flagler, Russell Sage, Guy Pelton, Abram Wakeman, and James Stranahan—all of whom had been elected with Know-Nothing aid—had sunk "every other consideration in the Nebraska issue or folly and thereby became as essentially allied to Republicanism as if they were its born heirs and sole representatives."[4]

After months of fruitless balloting, the House agreed to change its rules and permit the Speaker to be elected by a plurality. All minor contenders were eliminated so that only two sectional candidates remained. Southern Know-Nothings generally voted for the Democratic choice—William Aiken, a wealthy South Carolinian slaveholder; most Northern members of the Order supported Banks. The final vote stood: Banks, 103; Aiken, 100.[5]

The Know-Nothings had another opportunity to resolve their differences when the National Grand Council, composed of delegates from the state councils, met at Philadelphia on February 18, 1856, only four days before the scheduled assembly of the presidential nominating convention. The problem was to seek a substitute for Article XII.

The sessions of the National Council were acrimonious; Northern representatives insisted that Article XII be omitted, and Southerners demanded its retention. After extremists had made their views known, the Council debated some of the complicated resolutions which had been drawn up as compromises. A series of pronouncements written by Vespasian Ellis, a platform previously adopted in the District of Columbia, was approved. However, several delegates remarked that the language was so unclear that the people would be unable to decipher it.[6]

The main feature of the platform adopted by the Grand Council resorted to an expedient adopted by the Soft Shells in 1854: It denounced the repeal of the Missouri Compromise but approved the principle of popular sovereignty. Interference with the "domestic and social affairs" of the territories was declared outside the power of Congress. One plank called for the perpetuation of the Union and another for the "non-interference by Congress with questions appertaining solely to the individual states. . . ." The word slavery did not appear in the platform.[7]

This "compromise" satisfied no one, but Northern delegates were particularly distressed. Many critics pointed out that the new creed did not make any substantive departure from Article XII. A few days later at the presidential nominating convention, a group of free state delegates gave vent to their discontent. They introduced a motion requiring that the standard-bearer of the party be "in favor of interdicting the introduction of slavery north of 36° 30'." When this move was defeated by the vote of 141 to 60, 42 representatives from Connecticut, Massachusetts, Rhode Island, Ohio, Indiana, New Hampshire, Iowa, and Pennsylvania bolted; 185 delegates, including the entire New York contingent, stayed in their seats. Following this disruption, the remaining delegates passed the platform agreed upon by the National Grand Council.[8]

Before proceeding with the outcome of the Philadelphia nominating convention, it is necessary to consider the struggle waged in New York for control of that state's delegation. The feud between the Daniel Ullman and the James Barker factions grew more embittered with the prospect of a national campaign and the likelihood that a New Yorker would be the presidential nominee. The Ullman clique backed ex-President Millard Fillmore for a second term. Barker and his allies supported George Law, a wealthy owner of a steamship company based in New York City. Formerly a Democrat, Law had joined the Know-Nothings because the new organization appeared to offer a more fertile field for his ambition.

Since each congressional district would send a representative to the Philadelphia nominating convention, the crucial struggle went on within the local lodges. Stephen Sammons, a rising politician who sided with Fillmore, warned "that unless steps are immediately taken and men selected who are unpurchasable everywhere a majority of the delegates will be lost. The Law men are constantly maturing their plans and will have (now have) men all over the State." Although confident of his law partner's nomination, Haven worried about the large amounts of money spent by Law's adherents and their reputed success in corrupting delegates.[9]

Despite Law's efforts, when the national convention assembled at Philadelphia, a majority of the delegates favored Fillmore. The ex-President received strong support from Southern Unionists, who remembered his services during the Compromise of 1850 and his signing of the Fugitive Slave Act. Although the first ballot revealed that the former President would become the standard-bearer, the vote from New York was disappointing: twenty of the state's thirty-five delegates went for Law. On the second roll call, which decided the nomination, the victor picked up only four more votes from the Empire State. The Know-Nothings, having selected a man with Northern Whig antecedents, sought to balance the ticket by choosing a Southerner with a Democratic past. The vice-presidential position went to Andrew Jackson Donelson of Tennessee.[10]

Failing to capture the nomination for their favorite, the partisans of George Law walked out of the meeting hall and joined the North American delegates who had departed during the platform fight. Law had previously endorsed Article XII, but now he condemned the Fillmore convention for its proslavery bias. The bolters issued an address calling for restoration of the Missouri Compromise, and some professed their intention to enter Republican ranks without delay. However, the majority, desiring to exert as much political leverage as possible, agreed to meet again in early June, just prior to the Republican national convention.[11]

Although slavery was the chief source of dissension, the Know-Nothings were confronted with another severe problem. They were under considerable pressure to dilute the professed objective of the party—the establishment of restraints upon the Catholic and foreign-born population. These efforts threatened to turn the American organization into a party without a program.

Northern Know-Nothings clamored for the admission into the party of Protestant citizens from Europe, who they argued were necessary for success at the polls; Southern Americans, especially in Louisiana, importuned for the entry of Catholics born in the United States. In New York, the Order had widened its appeal to include Protestants born abroad. It also tried to make a distinction between religious and political Catholicism; it professed to oppose only the latter.[12] Agitation for change reached its climax during the National Grand Council of 1856, and despite strong resistance, both foreign-born Protestants and native-born Catholics were accorded the privilege of membership. Henceforth, only the Catholic immigrant remained a suitable target for the Know-Nothings. Ironically, Silver Grays, who had seized upon "Americanism" to divert attention from the slavery controversy, found themselves in opposition to the Irish, the one ethnic group in agreement with their desire to quiet sectionalist discord.

After his retirement from the Presidency, Millard Fillmore went into retirement, but his ambition to return to the White House remained strong. He toured the country in 1854, ostensibly on a pleasure trip, but really to assess his strength. Throughout his travels, he maintained an unbroken silence on the Nebraska question. Although fully aware of the activities of his fellow Silver Grays, who were seeking to control the Know-Nothing organization, he made no public statement either praising or condemning the nativist fever sweeping the country. Even many of his old friends were uncertain of his views. James R. Thompson, whom Fillmore had appointed as Collector of the Port of Rochester, regretted that the former President had not destroyed Seward's power when he had had the opportunity. Since he had failed to seize his chance, Thompson continued, "it was a 'god send' for *us* that this new movement [Know-Nothingism] came up and he cannot blame his friends if they make the most of it."[13]

Fillmore waited to see if the new nativist party could mobilize sufficient strength before disclosing his hand. The election of 1854, with its important Know-Nothing victories, settled the question. He was now ready to place himself into a position of availability. In a letter intended for publication, the former President announced his nativist sympathies.[14] Having indicated his willingness to be a candidate, Fillmore did not wait at home for expected overtures. Heeding the bitter experience of others—the memory of Henry Clay's disastrous letter on the annexation of Texas in 1844 had not been forgotten—Fillmore set sail for Europe in March of 1855 to place the ocean between himself and letters on the slavery issue. He turned over the management of his interests to his friend Solomon G. Haven.

Contending against the forces disrupting the American party was not an easy task. Persistent rumors that Fillmore was not a member of the Order and that he would decline the nomination handicapped the Know-Nothing campaign. Haven believed that a formal letter of acceptance would restore confidence in the candidate and stimulate greater efforts for his election. Urging that this letter be carefully composed, he outlined those points which he wanted Fillmore to emphasize. First, the former President "must come out square American & a little smack protestant." Turning to the slavery dilemma, Haven revealed that he still adhered to the Silver Gray strategy of playing down this issue. He urged Fillmore to make the "Slavery question altogether subordinate. . . ." but treat all parties to that problem fairly. He must "acknowledge no extreme men" and promise to "stand in the center" and serve "as an absolute check & control upon all extremes."[15]

With the campaign still going badly, Fillmore's partisans asked him to leave Europe and return home so that he could infuse life into the faltering Know-Nothings. Haven believed that his friend's arrival would set things in motion and unlock the pockets of the tightfisted. Already by May of 1856, the coffers of the party were empty and efforts to raise funds met with little success.[16]

Fillmore arrived in New York City on June 22, 1856. Elaborate arrangements for a "spontaneous" show of enthusiasm insured a warm welcome.[17] Proceeding at a leisurely pace from city to city along the Erie Canal, enroute to his Buffalo home, he allowed himself to be "lured" into making brief speeches to the local citizenry. In these addresses he set forth his political creed.

Fillmore's oration at Albany on June 26, 1856, may serve as a model of the type of speech he repeated on other occasions. Here, as elsewhere, one theme prevailed: the Union was in danger from unbridled sectional agitation over slavery and only he could save it. He began by alluding to the troubled times surrounding the Compromise of 1850, when after the death of Zachary Taylor, he had assumed the Presidency. He then felt it his duty "to rise above sectional prejudice, and look to the welfare of the whole nation . . .

to overcome long cherished prejudices, and disregard party claims."
Thanks to the efforts of patriotic, unselfish men from the Democratic
and the Whig parties, who rallied around his Administration in the
crisis, peace and harmony were restored to a distracted country. But
"Where are we now?," asked the former President, rhetorically.
"Threatened at home with civil war. . . . ," he answered. He laid
the blame for this ruinous deterioration upon Pierce and the Democrats, who had "recklessly and wantonly" reopened the slavery issue.
Turning to the Republicans, he denounced them as a purely Northern party. Should they succeed in November, the South would withdraw from the Union, and Fillmore intimated his belief that secession
would almost be justified.[18]

It should be observed that neither the word "Americanism" nor
the word "Protestanism" appeared in Fillmore's address at Albany.
When he did mention "Americanism," it was in the diluted form
recently approved at the National Grand Council. He censured only
religious groups organized for political purposes. He would not
restrict immigration; on the contrary, he would "open wide the gates
and invite the oppressed of every land to our happy country. . . ."
The former President permitted himself only one concession to
nativist feeling: he stated his belief that as a general rule, "Americans should govern America."[19]

These speeches indicated that Fillmore realized that the strategy
of Haven and other Silver Grays needed modification. The candidate
downgraded the appeal to prejudice because events had shown that
this emotion could not hold Northern and Southern conservatives
together. The former President did retain one feature of the Silver
Gray plan: He tried to subordinate differences over slavery—but
this time to the overriding goal of maintaining the Union. He would
admit that grave problems existed, yet he would call upon the
patriotism of the people, both North and South, to overcome them.
Under Fillmore's aegis, the Know-Nothings' use of the term "Americanism" acquired a new emphasis—it came to mean "Unionism"
rather than anti-foreignism and anti-Catholicism.

The de-emphasis on nativism in Fillmore's speeches was also
apparent during the canvass in New York. This new course elicited
complaints from bigots. One Know-Nothing acknowledged his dissatisfaction with the campaigners sent to his area: "I hope you will
pardon me for saying that our speakers have said too little about the
great American principles." Opponents of the Order also recognized
the change. "Do you notice that Know-Nothingism has utterly sunk

all discussion of its leading principle," asked Erasmus Pershine Smith, formerly a Seward Whig and now a Republican. "It has nothing to say against foreigners, and its only allusion to Catholicism is in connection with the charge against Frémont."[20]

It would be an error to assume that *all* appeals to intolerance were abandoned. A powerful undercurrent of bias, especially against Catholics, still remained. This manifested itself, as Erasmus Smith observed, in the charge that John C. Frémont, the Republican presidential candidate, was a Catholic. Although false, this rumor did considerable damage to the Republican cause. If they did not actually manufacture this allegation, the Know-Nothings certainly exploited it. Stephen Sammons—who supervised the nativists' campaign in New York—wanted a pamphlet containing the "proofs" of Frémont's Catholicism printed and distributed in mass quantities. He directed that letters be written to Methodist, Baptist, and other religious organs "and gotten into these papers by hook or by crook, for love or for money—this would drive the last nail in his [Frémont's] political coffin."[21]

Another overture to religious prejudice was the nomination of Erastus Brooks—"that Prince of newspaper liars," according to one Republican—for governor. Brooks shared the editorship of the New York *Express* with his older brother, James. Both men had a long history of Silver Grayism. Grasping the potential of the Know-Nothing movement as a powerful weapon against Seward and Weed, they had given it their entire support. The younger Brooks had provoked a bitter controversy with Archbishop John Hughes. His triumphant re-election to the state senate from New York City in 1855 testified to his success at baiting the clergyman. His nomination for governor was a patent attempt to exploit anti-Catholic feeling. One Know-Nothing candidly admitted this fact. He wrote that Brooks' candidacy "will bring up the Hughes controversy involving the Catholic interference with our state politics, and that will bring us in tens of thousands to our whole ticket regardless of every other consideration."[22]

Fillmore and his advisers had conceived his remarks in New York to be his final statements during the campaign. They wished to emphasize sectional reconciliation without supplying the details. Printed in pamphlet form, the speeches were distributed throughout the nation. After congratulating his law partner on his oratory, Haven cautioned him against answering the inevitable flood of requests for opinions on "immaterial matters." "The true way I think now," advised Haven, "is to all such to point them to your past administration, to your messages & public papers & to your late speeches and tell them all you can promise will be to do as your judgement may dictate when the occasion arises, unpledged & uncommitted in any way."[23]

As Haven predicted, requests for further details and clarifications piled up on Fillmore's desk. Several correspondents informed the nominee that Democrats in the South construed his remarks at Rochester—in which he condemned the repeal of the Missouri Compromise (but was careful not to place the blame on Southern politicians)—to mean that he favored restoration of the Missouri line; another writer enclosed an article which maintained that Fillmore favored the ending of the slave trade and abolition of slavery in the District of Columbia. Allegedly the candidate's friends, they urged him to refute these charges.[24] Northerners demanded reassurance from Fillmore that he would oppose the extension of slavery. Know-Nothing campaigners in New York reported that Weed's lieutenants accused him of proslavery leanings and used his approval of the Fugitive Slave Act to substantiate the charge. Stephen Sammons searched for some way to blunt this Republican attack. Realizing that Fillmore could not personally address himself to the question, he proposed that a letter be prepared by some prominent person, preferably a judge, who should argue that signing the Act was a constitutional necessity. Sammons believed that such a letter was urgently needed in the rural areas of the state.[25]

Fillmore did clarify his position in some *private* letters. He assured one correspondent of his opposition to the extension of slavery. "All my education, all my sympathies, all my instincts are against it," he exclaimed. To Anna Ella Carroll, the author of several nativist tracts, he admitted that he favored restoration of the Missouri Compromise. "Were it possible, it would annihilate black Republicanism at a blow, and the Hydra-headed monster of disunion would be crushed. . . ." Yet, he recognized the futility of agitating the question, for the Senate would never give its consent to repeal. Confessing that he saw "no light leading from this dark and bewildering cave, but that which points to Kansas as a state," he promised, if elected, to repeal its obnoxious laws and make sure that only residents participated in framing its constitution; he did not care whether it became a slave or a free state, so long as the will of the people prevailed. Fillmore yielded to self pity and lamented the uselessness of proclaiming his position: "I am attacked at the South as an *abolitionist,* as you will see by a pamphlet recently issued from the *Union* press at Washington, and at the North as a *pro-slavery* man, as you see by the whole black Republican press." Discouragement strengthened Fillmore's resolve to resist the pressure exerted upon him and he refused to issue any further amplification of his views.[26]

Events in Kansas caused a further decline in the prospects of the American party. By the end of March, Seward's and Douglas' rival bills, which proposed antithetical plans for the admission of Kansas as a state, were helping to crystallize two hostile camps in the Congress. At this time hostilities had not yet broken out in the territory; nevertheless, the situation there had become critical. Subjected to the pressures of this sectional division over Kansas, many Know-Nothings abandoned commitments to the nativist party; Northern members of the Order joined the Republicans and Southerners, the Democrats. Haven deplored the fact that Congressmen elected from New York had revealed themselves to be turncoats of the same breed that returned Seward to the Senate. He wanted the press to "pitch into them." By early May, the Know-Nothings had been reduced to a small and ineffectual group. "Everybody who could be coaxed, frightened or driven has been operated against us," lamented Haven. "Our men in Congress have been demoralized & broken up holding no associations whatever."[27]

At the end of May, news from Kansas caused another blow to Know-Nothing unity. A sheriff's posse of proslavery men entered Lawrence, the stronghold of the free staters, and burned and looted several buildings. Shortly thereafter, in retaliation for the attack on Lawrence, John Brown and his sons brutally murdered five Southern sympathizers. This deed unleashed a full scale guerrilla war in the territory with much loss of life on both sides. These happenings, which excited the entire nation, accelerated the process of sectional polarization destroying the nativist party.

Nationalists within Know-Nothing ranks tried to restore calm in Kansas. George G. Dunn, an Indiana nativist Congressman, submitted a bill for the restoration of the Missouri Compromise line and the reaffirmation of the Fugitive Slave Law. Dunn sought to forge an alliance between Northern and Southern nativists behind his measure, but he found that he had only underlined irreconcilable differences.[28] Haven also discovered this fact to his dismay. He had supported the bill for several reasons. He knew that a negative vote would be difficult to explain to his constituents. Most important, he hoped his stand would aid the Know-Nothing cause throughout the North. The

Buffalo Congressman feared, however, that his vote would have bad consequences in the South. This proved to be the case. A week later, Fillmore learned that Southern Democrats had unleashed a bitter attack against him. "They [the Southern Democrats] are now in a terrible fever about my vote on Dunn's bill. . . . ," wrote Haven. "According to men from every where I defeat you effectually every vote I give." Southern harassment of Haven increased as the session came to a close. He confessed that he never felt his hands so tied: "I could blow those Republicans into a cocked hat in a week if I had no South to deal with, but as it is I am compelled to sit here and hold my peace."[29]

Haven's humiliation in the House reflected Fillmore's dismal prospects in the South. The second split of the party at Philadelphia had deepened the pessimism of Southern nativists to the point of despair. Their greatest concern centered about rumors of an imminent amalgamation of the North American bolters with the Republicans. This apprehension increased the suspicion that Fillmore could never carry the North and caused him severe damage. The former President became the victim of a crisis of confidence, which continued to grow. Haven described its operation in both sections:

> The democracy and republicans . . . join hands and efforts. The former in making the public believe you can carry nothing at the north so as to get everybody to vote with them south rather than throw their votes away. The latter in making the public believe you can carry nothing south so that no body need throw their votes upon you north.[30]

Many conservatives in the South announced a preference for Fillmore but regretfully admitted they would vote for Buchanan. "In this part of the Country, both in Georgia—and Alabama—strong—influential members of the American party—are leaving it in bodies," wrote a politician from Montgomery. "Men also would rejoice to see you elected, but they say that in the coming struggle the strength of the opposition to Free-Soilism must not be divided." Another Southerner reported that he had "frequently heard the wish expressed by your most devoted friends that your name had never been put in nomination *because* of the impossibility of success—Those who every way prefer you, will feel compelled to vote for Mr. Buchanan."[31]

New York Know-Nothings attempted to shore up the confidence of the South. The hard pressed Southern nativists were anxious for good news from the Empire State; this was the most effective argument against allegations that Fillmore's chances were hopeless in the North. The former Whig Governor of Kentucky, Robert P. Letcher, entreated

Fillmore to have his New York friends write daily to Southerners to assure them of their undoubted ability to carry the state. "If the public should be convinced of that fact," Letcher continued, "you may rely upon it, that your success is *almost, if not perfectly sure.*"[32] Fillmore's campaign managers met with little success when they tried to beat the Democrats at their own game and sought to persuade the South that the contest at the North would be narrowed down to Fillmore and Frémont.[33]

The resort area of Saratoga Springs, New York became a prominent electioneering post. Visitors from all over the country, but especially from below the Mason-Dixon line, came to bathe in the mineral waters. According to Stephen Sammons, Southerners vacationing at the spa sent hundreds of letters to friends back home, urging them to stand by the Know-Nothing ticket.[34]

All efforts failed to arrest the loss of Southern Know-Nothings to the Democratic party. The August elections in North Carolina, Kentucky, and Missouri went badly for the nativists.[35] Good news became increasingly rare at Fillmore headquarters.

The experience of the American party in 1856 vividly illustrated the overwhelming strains on the party system. Caught between irreconcilable extremes, the Know-Nothings were indeed being crushed out. The nativists' efforts to surmount differences generated by the slavery issue miscarried again and again. Sectional bitterness had triumphed over solemn oaths; Southern members of the Order joined the Democrats and Northerners, the Republicans. Fillmore's strategy of emphasizing Unionism and patriotism also failed to heal the division. The inability of the American organization to act together seemed to confirm the worst fear of nationalists—the forces dividing North and South were too powerful for any political party to overcome.

14

The Republican Triumph

The New York Republican party became the ultimate beneficiary of the revolution in the state's politics. The disruption of the party system had continued for three years; during this period, thousands had abandoned old partisan loyalties. The fusionists absorbed most of these. In 1855, the Republican party represented an alliance of Free Democrats, Seward Whigs, and temperance men. Barnburners and Soft Democrats, antislavery Know-Nothings, and conservative Whigs had participated in relatively small numbers. By 1856, the last three groups also contributed to the new grouping. The formation of a winning coalition was partly due to organizational improvements, but the outbreak of civil war in Kansas and the attack on Senator Charles Sumner of Massachusetts dramatized the Republican cause and gave it a tremendous boost. Also, after the presidential nominating conventions, neither the Know-Nothings nor the Softs could effectively combat the charge of Southern domination. Republican success rested upon the growing consensus that slavery extension was the foremost threat to the nation, and that all other issues must be postponed until this one had been solved.

Republican leaders ascribed defeat in their initial campaign to an inadequate organization, and immediately after the canvass, they attempted to remedy this defect. Primary responsibility for this task fell upon the Chairman of the Republican State Committee, Edwin D. Morgan. A wealthy merchant from New York City and a rising politician, Morgan brought to his job a businesslike efficiency, a capacity for hard work, and a zealot's enthusiasm. Through the exertions of Morgan and his aides, Republicans in New York acquired an organizational framework which permitted them to absorb thousands of new adherents. Republicans throughout the country subsequently recognized Morgan's abilities and appointed him the first Chairman of the National Republican Committee.

Although the diligence of local Republicans was an important factor in the growth of the party in the state, events outside of New York were of much greater importance. The full effects of the Kansas-Nebraska Act became evident when in the spring of 1856 civil war broke out in Kansas. Then, more dramatic news filled the newspapers. While writing letters at his desk on the Senate floor, Charles Sumner was assaulted and severely injured by the South Carolinian Congressman Preston Brooks.

These events had the same profound effect on politics in the Empire State that they had throughout the North. They impaired the efforts of straight Whigs, Democrats, and Know-Nothings to hold onto their constituencies. A significant number who had voted for these parties in the past now came over to the Republicans. The rival issues of prohibition, anti-Catholicism, and anti-foreignism fell into the background when compared with the emergency in Kansas and the outrage on the Senate floor. Many New Yorkers had wanted to believe the best about the situation in Kansas. Editorials in conservative papers had aided complacency by dismissing the possibility of armed conflict and accusing the New York *Tribune* of alarmism.[1] All at once, the warnings in the *Tribune* and other Republican journals seemed to have been borne out by facts.

Shocked by the bloodshed in Kansas and the attack on Sumner, some of the staunchest opponents of Republicanism—straight or Old-Line Whigs—found themselves wavering. These conservatives joined in the general expressions of indignation. A Sumner protest meeting at the Tabernacle, one of the largest churches in New York City, attracted many well-known straight Whigs. This gathering revived the hopes of Edwin D. Morgan—who, once confessing that the city was *"bad soil* for *free soil,"* had frequently been discouraged by the failure of his efforts in the metropolis. Believing that the Old Liners were gradually coming around to the Republican point of view, he noted that "the doubtful hesitating men are more excited now—than those who took the right ground early." The Tabernacle event also encouraged Thurlow Weed. "New York [City] is at last avowed," he declared. "There was a tremendous meeting last night. Light is breaking very rapidly upon our state."[2]

Many Old Line Whigs still felt themselves politically homeless. In 1855, such prominent conservatives as Hamilton Fish, Robert A. West, and Washington Hunt decided to remain with their dissolving party rather than join the Republicans, Know-Nothings, or Democrats. By 1856, this alternative was no longer practical, for it became increasingly apparent that the Whig party was moribund.

James A. Hamilton, a son of the former Secretary of the Treasury, tried to resuscitate the Whig organization. He invited famous Whigs from all over the nation to his home at Dobbs Ferry to discuss what should be done. The response was disheartening. When the date for the proposed conference arrived, only two others besides Hamilton were present. Letters from absentees brought little cheer. Most respondents agreed that Whigs should not hold a national convention to nominate their own candidates for President and Vice-President. Such an assembly would be impractical and dangerous; it would demonstrate the weakness and divisions of the party. Moreover, even if a measure of success could be attained in the North, the chaotic condition of Whiggery in the South would make it impossible to mount an effective campaign.[3]

Once it was established that the Whig party could not be resuscitated, the problem still remained—what were Old Liners to do in the forthcoming campaign? Daniel Dewey Barnard, an aged Silver Gray and bitter opponent of Seward and Weed, offered a solution. He urged Whigs to vote for Fillmore and maintained that it was their patriotic duty to do so. After writing a lengthy exposition of his views, which was subsequently printed in the Albany *Statesman,* Barnard informed Fillmore that he had tried to demonstrate the truth of the ex-President's remarks at Albany—"that nothing is wanting to a party of sectionalism like the Republican party but success, to make it necessarily a party of Disunion. Success is *ipso facto* Dissolution."[4]

Many straight Whigs, although considerably less enthusiastic about Fillmore than Barnard, considered voting for him. Disturbed by the intolerance of the Know-Nothings, they nevertheless looked upon Fillmore as the least objectionable candidate. Washington Hunt acknowledged his poor opinion of Fillmore and his distaste for Know-Nothingism, but he admitted that he might support the nativist nominee on "high considerations of patriotism."[5] James A. Hamilton was also half persuaded; he urged Hamilton Fish to abandon his objections to Fillmore, arguing that it was "the duty of conservative men of all parties to throw off all party obligations and interests; and if you please to choose the *least of evils.*"[6]

Robert A. West also considered Fillmore to be the only feasible alternative. His New York *Commercial Advertiser* announced that it would "support him [Fillmore] *in spite* of his being a member of the Know-Nothing or American order." The editor frankly admitted to the ex-President the reasons for his paper's endorsement: "As a Whig I am quite willing to acknowledge that the American party is the *chief* agency now existing. It is *chief* because of its greater numerical strength and *because* it is an *organization,* which the Whigs are not." The *Commercial Advertiser* considered backing Buchanan and even commended the Democratic convention for making such a good choice. However, the aggressive tone of the Democratic platform with regard to foreign policy posed an insuperable obstacle to further co-operation.[7]

A group of Old Liners claiming to speak for the New York Whig party met in Albany on August 14, for the purpose of selecting delegates to a national Whig convention in Baltimore on September 17, 1856. Both of these meetings adopted the Know-Nothing candidates of Fillmore and Donelson. These endorsements carried little weight, however; they were clearly the action of only a rump of the Whig party. Although Francis Granger traveled to Baltimore to represent New York, Washington Hunt, pleading poor health, stayed at home.[8]

Other straight Whigs proved more receptive to the Democratic nominee. A letter written by Rufus Choate, a prominent Massachusetts conservative, argued the case for Buchanan with important effect. Choate called upon all Whigs to stop the drift of the nation toward disunion by voting for the only candidate capable of winning. In New York, the *Journal of Commerce* reiterated the same idea. Lamenting the defection of so many Whigs to Buchanan, Daniel Barnard wrote that it was a "singular feature of this contest, that Fillmore, if defeated, will lose by the failure of those who believe that he is the best and safest man for the country."[9]

Other straight Whigs continued to enlist in the Republican party. Hamilton Fish was the most influential New Yorker to undergo conversion. The Senator had done everything in his power to foil the Republican party. His stand had alienated him from his close friend Thurlow Weed and in 1857 led to his replacement in the Senate by Preston King. As the hopelessness of reanimating the Whig party became apparent, however, Fish moved closer to the Republican point of view. Finally, in a carefully reasoned letter to James A. Hamilton, he declared his intention to vote for Frémont.[10] Jonathan Nathan, a former Columbia College classmate and close friend of Fish, perceived the fundamental reason for his own and the Senator's shift to the Republicans, and he stated it clearly:

The great difficulty in our position arises from the fact that the only issue between parties is *slavery.* There is no other dividing line, no other practical question . . . I contend that we must be either Democrat or Republican. Now if Republicanism means abolition I ain't there—but if the choice be presented to me of Abolitionism or slavery extension and Southern principles and predominance I ask you which must I take.[11]

Republicans never abandoned hope of winning over additional straight Whigs and made great efforts to secure their support. In New York City, the Frémont press denied charges of "radicalism" and sought to portray its candidate and party as truly conservative. These journals emphasized the point that the goal of Republicanism was only to prevent the extension of slavery and not its abolition. James Watson Webb judged this distinction to be vital. He warned Edwin D. Morgan that a man "who is not satisfied with opposition to *Slavery Extension* is too unreasonable to be entitled to further concessions." The party chairman agreed with Webb. He reassured one correspondent that "it is against the *aggressions* only that we wage war. I am in no sense an abolitionist, and will protect the South in all their *just rights,* as readily as I will do the same thing in the North."[12]

Republican newspapers also tried to allay the conservatives' fear of disunion. They scoffed at the pronouncements of prominent Southerners that Frémont's election would be the signal for the breakup of the nation. However, Republicans did not always believe their own assurances. John Bigelow anxiously queried Francis P. Blair concerning rumors about an alleged agreement between President Pierce and Jefferson Davis to permit secession.[13]

Thus, many Old Line Whigs who had first resisted the formation of a sectional party found themselves drawn to it. The reason was simple; they felt they had no other place to go. Three years of political upheaval had hurt conservatives. Their principal aim—harmony between North and South—seemed more and more elusive. They would have preferred to remain in the national Whig party, but they were forced to accept the fact of its destruction. Although the Know-Nothings made a vigorous attempt to enlist their support, many moderates could not overcome their revulsion for nativist intolerance. They deemed the name "American" party a disgraceful sham—for them, true "Americanism" meant equal opportunity for all regardless of religion or place of birth. Having discarded this possibility, they found themselves confronting the dilemma which Jonathan Nathan had described—either they must ally themselves with proslavery Democrats or with antislavery Republicans. Once the choice narrowed to these two alternatives, an increasing number of conservatives discovered the Republican party to be their only recourse.

New York's Republican leadership knew that success depended upon attracting antislavery Democrats. Since the 1830's, the Democracy had enjoyed a predominant position in the Empire State, a role which Whig leaders had deeply envied. Even during the period of factional strife from 1853-1855, the combined Hard and Soft Shell vote still constituted a majority of the ballots cast; hence, it was reasonable to believe that a united party would carry the state for Buchanan. By 1856, only a small vanguard of Democrats, led by Preston King, had joined the Seward Whigs. During the presidential election campaign, however, a large number of Democrats defected from their party and supported the Republican coalition.

Many Barnburners had hoped that their party would resist the pressure of Southern politicians. Soft Shell federal officeholders had tried to keep this faith alive. The resolutions, however, adopted by the Soft convention of January 10, 1856, which gave an unqualified endorsement of the Administration and made a transparent bid for Southern support at Cincinnati, alienated many Democrats. Republicans now saw a chance to gain the recruits they required. After reading an account of the latest Soft Shell convention, Seward observed to Weed: "I think you are through with the Softs in New York —what a pitiful conclusion!"[14]

Weed saw an immediate opportunity for a gesture to dissatisfied Democrats, and he took advantage of it. Concurrent with the Speakership battle in Washington, a similar struggle was taking place in Albany. Interminable balloting failed to elect a speaker of the assembly. The Know-Nothings cast approximately 45 votes, the Republicans 35, and the combined Hard and Soft Shell strength was estimated at about 40. Realizing that the Republicans could not win and wishing to prevent a nativist victory, Weed brought his followers to the aid of the Softs' nominee—Orville Robinson of Oswego, a former Barnburner—who was elected. Supporting a Democratic candidate was deemed the lesser evil by Republicans, who considered the nativists their most dangerous opponents.[15] But Weed's action was also a calculated overture to Radical Democrats outraged by the last Soft Shell convention. If they could overcome suspicions of "Whig tricks" and obtain assurance of fair treatment, they would constitute a valuable source of strength.

An important newcomer to Republican ranks was Henry H. Van Dyck—the co-editor of the Soft Shell organ, the Albany *Atlas*. He had grown increasingly dissatisfied with acquiescence to Southern demands and had alarmed party leaders when he voiced his misgivings in his paper. Undoubtedly, the expectation of a warm welcome from the opposition encouraged his boldness. Determined upon a break after the convention of January 10, the editor wrote Martin Van Buren this letter:

> You will undoubtedly have seen the doings of the state convention. It was wholly controlled by the officeholders. . . . If the 'Hards' should reconvene their convention and go *for Cuba and the opening of the African slave trade,* I am afraid they would be ahead of us. Without this I have no fear, as I am quite sure in no other way can they get South of our platform.

After selling his share in the *Atlas,* Van Dyck accepted Weed's invitation to run for Albany's congressional seat.[16]

Thousands of Democrats soon followed Van Dyck's example. Several well-known Softs—including past state officers and legislators, former Congressmen, and presidential electors—signed a pamphlet entitled the "Voice of the Radical Democracy of New York."[17] This manifesto began by attacking the Kansas-Nebraska Act and President Pierce for unnecessarily stirring up slavery agitation; Democrats throughout the free states had suffered defeat as a consequence of this policy. It then denounced the Soft Shell convention of January 10 for changing the position of the party from "ardent opponents of slavery extension into quiescent abettors of its diffusion." By submitting to Southern demands, which insist that Northern politicians worship at the "Moloch of slavery," the delegates had betrayed the views of most New York Democrats. Lest it be thought that Radical Democrats were actuated by "a morbid philanthropy toward the African race," they hastened to explain that their primary concern was the degrading effect of a slave system on free white labor. This document was a clear call to attract Barnburners.

Buchanan's partisans in New York could do little to halt the exodus. They pleaded with Democrats to beware of "Whig tricks," but these warnings had lost their former power. The Albany *Atlas and Argus,* the new party organ formed from a merger of the two papers, tried to expose the activities of bolters working in close conjunction with Weed; however, the editors could not deny that these plotters had once occupied honored places within the Democracy.[18]

Democratic prospects looked bleakest in the central and western portions of the state, the Burned-over-region, and in the northern counties, the former center of Barnburner strength. Ex-Lieutenant Governor Henry S. Randall concluded that "the Democratic party is annihilated, for the time being, in the centre." He feared that Frémont's majorities in the middle counties would overwhelm Buchanan's strong areas in Erie county, the Hudson Valley, and New York City. Another Soft Shell made a similar appraisal: "I consider success as very doubtful—with the precedent of 1840 before me I fear the effect of the excitement and popular cry that has been raised of 'freedom.'" Secretary of State Marcy was also pessimistic. He told George W. Newell that he was asked forty times a day how New York would go. "I do not reply positively that it will go against us," Marcy confided, "yet my apprehensions are so strong that they amount to a conviction that such will be the result."[19]

Several lifelong Democrats resisted the temptation to become Republicans. For these, loyalty to their party prevailed over dissatisfaction with its actions. Martin Van Buren, the former President and the presidential candidate of the Free Soilers in 1848, was one of these. Edwin D. Morgan invited him to preside over the Republican national convention, but the aged statesman had no intention of embarking on another free soil crusade. Although he deplored the repeal of the Missouri Compromise and disliked Buchanan, he believed that the Democratic party provided the only hope for keeping the Union intact.[20]

Republicans made every effort to allay Democratic fears. The prominence of men like Seward and Weed in the new party—for whom most Democrats had an abiding suspicion—made this necessary. Gathered in convention for the purpose of choosing candidates for the state offices, New York fusionists adhered to the policy of the previous year and distributed nominations equally among former Whigs and former Democrats. In 1855, Preston King, a Democrat, had headed the slate. In 1856, John A. King, the son of Rufus King and a Whig, secured the nomination for governor. Morgan explained the reason why Henry R. Selden, a well-known Soft and a signer of the "Voice of the Radical Democracy," received the lieutenant governor's slot: "The nomination of Mr. King for Gov. made it advisable to put on a Democrat in antecedents for Lt. Gov. Consequently Mr. Selden was taken—none better from that branch of our party could have been selected."[21]

Democrats such as Preston King, John Bigelow, William Cullen Bryant, and Abijah Mann, Jr., played an important role in the new party, but former Whigs predominated. Morgan attested to this fact when he assured the arch-Whig James Watson Webb that only friends of Seward would be placed on the ticket. Erasmus P. Smith also knew where real power rested: "Put our party in power & we will lead them [the Democrats] twelve years more—We are the Whig party after all and they but an appendix." The ambition which Seward and Weed had harbored for a generation—to make significant gains at the expense of their powerful rival—appeared to have been achieved. The Republican party chairman, a former Whig himself, expressed his own satisfaction at the course of events: "The changes from the Soft division of the late Democratic Party in this State in favor of Frémont, and of prominent men are very numerous making our position eminently safe here."[22]

The defection of so many Democrats would never have been possible without the intervening three years of political crisis. The events of this period had placed an unbearable strain on the New York Democracy. Soft Shell leaders had managed to keep losses to a minimum in 1854 and 1855, but they could not avoid indefinitely Southern pressure for an unqualified acceptance of the Nebraska Act and all its bitter consequences. Many Barnburners resented what they regarded as the unreasonable proslavery demands of Southern Democrats. They had rebelled against tests of Democratic orthodoxy in the past, and when the Nebraska policy was rigidly imposed at Cincinnati, they bolted again. The powerful bonds of loyalty holding the Democratic party together had finally broken.

New York Republican leaders recognized that nativist sentiment remained a potent political force within the state. No one appreciated this fact better than Thurlow Weed. The boss did not share the attitude of one optimist who considered Fillmore's nomination to be "a joke." Weed saw no humor in the situation; he judged the candidacy of his old Buffalo adversary as a formidable threat.[23]

Weed looked for some way to neutralize Know-Nothing strength. He had always been attracted to the possibility of embracing the antislavery and nativist issues within a single party. He realized that such an amalgam would have irresistible strength among Protestant and native-born voters who wanted to express their hostility to the expansion of slavery, but who also desired to strike a blow at immigrants and Catholics. Loose coalitions of anti-Nebraskaites and Know-Nothings had worked together in most Northern states, but the dominance of Silver Grays within the Order in New York had prevented similar cooperation. Nevertheless, the potentialities in mingling the two causes had encouraged Weed to secretly foster the Know-Something movement, which combined a strong anti-Nebraska sentiment with a mild nativism. His support revealed that the powerful editor was prepared to make concessions to "Americanism." He insisted, however, that the antislavery crusade be paramount and that anti-Catholicism and anti-foreignism be kept in the background.

During the winter and spring of 1856, Weed negotiated with the leaders of the North Americans who had bolted the Philadelphia convention which had nominated Fillmore. They were ideal instruments for his purpose; as moderate nativists, they could widen the appeal of Republicanism. Weed made important progress when he enlisted George Law, who was bitter over his defeat for the Know-Nothing nomination.[24]

Seward deplored Weed's willingness to cooperate with the North Americans. The target of bigots ever since his proposal for state supported Catholic schools, the Senator feared that any coalition with nativists would close the door on his ambition for the Presidency. He had persistently discouraged attempts to bring about a union of anti-Nebraska Know-Nothings and Republicans. Invited by Francis P. Blair, Sr. to discuss such a coalition, he declined to do so.[25] Seward wrote to Weed that he "must distinctly protest against any combination with 'Know-Nothings.' "[26]

Weed was sorry that his friend had refused Blair's invitation. He could see no reason for not cooperating in preliminary plans of organization. Seward acceded to the views of his adviser and participated in subsequent efforts to bring all antislavery forces together. Nevertheless, he continued to argue that by courting the Know-Nothings, the Republicans were losing their grip on the party and sacrificing their principles.[27]

Despite Seward's misgivings, Weed continued to pursue an understanding with antislavery North Americans. He also sought to discourage the rising demand among New York Republicans for an aggressive campaign to obtain the presidential nomination for Seward. Weed frustrated the desire of Seward and his boosters, because he believed that the time was not ripe for the Senator's nomination. He preferred to wait until 1860, when the Republicans would be stronger and could assure victory. Also, he reasoned that in four years the nativist fever would subside and objections to Seward would diminish.[28]

Other prominent Republicans agreed with Weed's analysis. Erasmus P. Smith observed that Seward should not run "till we feel *sure*." The best candidate, according to Smith, would be one who could draw enough votes to make the Republican party a powerful organization. Then we can "sweep the field with Seward" in 1860. Samuel Wilkeson, an editor of the Albany *Evening Journal* and the Senator's close friend, tried to soothe Seward's disappointment. He praised him as the "completest exponent of Republicanism" and for being at the "head of American political civilization." Unfortunately, the delegates to the Republican convention would clamor for a lesser man, but Wilkeson was confident that in 1860 they would be ready for their true leader.[29]

Having made his decision to woo nativist votes and to delay Seward's bid for the Presidency, Weed had to find another candidate. Widely mentioned as a possibility was John McLean of Ohio, an Associate Justice of the Supreme Court. McLean's advanced age and lackluster personality appealed to conservatives but failed to generate any enthusiasm among the more radical elements of the party. Weed distrusted him; he feared that the Ohioan would betray his party, much as Tyler and Fillmore had done in the past. Jonathan Nathan reported the boss' unflattering appraisal of McLean: "He [Weed] would go for a democrat in preference to that 'white liver'd hollow-hearted-Janus faced rascal' Judge ML—I think he prefixed 'd—d.' " The state nominating convention revealed that New York Republicans shared this distaste for the Justice. His name failed to inspire any support.[30]

As the Republican national convention drew near, the prospects of John C. Frémont of California rose rapidly. The famous pathfinder benefited from the advocacy of such influential men as Francis P. Blair, Sr., John Bigelow, William Cullen Bryant, and Nathaniel Banks. Seward reported that Republicans in Congress were overwhelmingly in favor of the Californian. Weed, along with other leading politicians, sensed the strong appeal of Frémont and decided to join his supporters. As might be expected, the state nominating convention was most enthusiastic for Seward; its favorable attitude toward Frémont, however, revealed that the explorer was the second choice of most delegates.[31]

The close cooperation which Weed had established with North American leaders proved of great importance in unifying antislavery forces behind Frémont. The Pathfinder's supporters were worried about the forthcoming North American convention, scheduled to assemble in Philadelphia on June 12, 1856, only five days before the Republican meeting. This date had obviously been chosen to afford the maximum leverage over Republican nominations. The problem confronting Frémont's backers was a difficult one. If the first convention refused to nominate the explorer and the Republicans did select him, this would divide antislavery strength into two tickets. If, however, the Know-Somethings supported Frémont, foreign-born voters, who had the balance of power in several key states, would turn against him, and the Republicans might be forced to find another candidate.[32]

Republican leaders devised a plan to solve this dilemma. The North Americans must be persuaded to nominate Banks for President and Governor William F. Johnston of Pennsylvania for Vice-President with the understanding that Banks would resign in favor of Frémont and the Republican's vice-presidential candidate would yield in favor of Johnston. By such a bold stroke, antislavery nativists and Republicans could be united behind one ticket and sweep the North. This scheme appealed to Weed, and he and his lieutenants—Morgan, King, and Spaulding—came to Philadelphia to use their influence with Know-Something delegates. It was rumored that when ordinary methods of persuasion failed, bribery succeeded. Weed's alliance with George Law was also an important factor in achieving the desired result. The North American convention nominated Banks and Johnston and chose Law as the chairman of a committee to confer with the Republicans. It then adjourned, to convene again two days after the Republicans had nominated their slate.[33]

Fulfilling the bargain made with the North Americans was a more difficult matter. When the Republican national convention assembled at Philadelphia on June 17, George Law and his committee asked for permission to confer upon candidates for President and Vice-President. Empire State delegates took the lead in advocating their participation. DeWitt C. Littlejohn of Oswego, the former speaker of the New York assembly who had once been the special target of Know-Nothing enmity, urged all friends of freedom to unite; consequently, he advocated that the North Americans should have one candidate on the ticket. Joshua R. Giddings of Ohio, for more than a generation the opponent of slavery in the House of Representatives, opposed any deal with the Know-Somethings. If the Republicans parleyed with a committee of native-born Americans, he argued, they should also treat with a committee of foreign-born citizens. He, for one, was there to speak for all the people of the United States, regardless of birth.[34]

Giddings' speech had the desired effect; George Law and the Know-Somethings did not play the role which they and Thurlow Weed had intended. The Republicans nominated Frémont for President but refused to acknowledge the agreement made with the North Americans concerning the Vice-Presidency. Governor Johnston failed to receive second place on the ticket, but William Dayton of New Jersey was chosen instead.

Reconciling the North Americans to the Frémont-Dayton ticket proved to be difficult. When they reconvened their convention, several delegates angrily attacked the Republicans, a few even threatening to support the Fillmore-Donelson ticket. Cooler heads prevailed, however, and the majority agreed to withdraw Banks and substitute Frémont, but it refused to drop Johnston for Dayton.[35]

Confusion now existed throughout the North; some ratification meetings endorsed the Frémont-Dayton ticket and others the Frémont-Johnston slate. Primary responsibility for resolving this dilemma fell into Morgan's hands. At various times, he attempted to persuade both Johnston and Dayton to resign, but both refused. A solution was finally found when Johnston met with Frémont and received assurances of "fair treatment" in the event of Republican victory. He then withdrew from the campaign.[36]

All of these intrigues were designed to achieve one purpose—to unite those voters with both nativist and antislavery inclinations behind the Republican candidates. The bargaining power of the North Americans derived from their claim to represent this constituency. Of course, deals between political chieftains are not always ratified at the grass roots level, and the crucial question still remained unanswered: Would antislavery Know-Nothings abandon Fillmore and support Frémont? The answer appeared to be in the affirmative. Republican leaders were gratified by evidence of mass defections. Erasmus P. Smith observed that "it looks as if there was to be an explosion of those who have never believed, what we have always told them, that they were sold to the Silver Grays."[37] By the summer of 1856, Republicans in New York breathed easier. The great nativist excitement appeared to be waning and giving way to antislavery enthusiasm.

While recruiting new adherents from the ranks of conservative Whigs, Democrats, and Know-Nothings, Republicans sought to maintain the allegiance of temperance men. Although the fusionist platform of 1855 remained silent on the question of enforcing New York's Maine Law, prohibitionists had still supported the new party, thus revealing a willingness to subordinate the anti-liquor to the antislavery cause. A new problem arose when in March of 1856 the state's Court of Appeals declared the prohibition act unconstitutional. Would this be the signal for a new crusade to restore the law? Would it force the Republicans to take a more definitive stand against alcoholic beverages? These questions perplexed Republican leaders.

Thurlow Weed again preferred to remain silent, thereby alienating neither temperance advocates nor their opponents. Greeley agreed; he repeated his 1855 appeal which entreated prohibitionists to suspend agitation and concentrate on "the sole object of freedom in Kansas and non-extension of slave territory." Governor Myron H. Clark, once the leader of anti-liquor forces in the legislature, assured Weed that the issue could be avoided, because temperance leaders had agreed not to press their cause. Once again, they refused to divert both energies and votes needed for the struggle against slavery. The liquor issue, which had dominated the election of 1854 and was subordinated in 1855, was almost totally ignored in 1856. The distribution of political rewards aided this outcome. Wesley Bailey, editor of the Utica *Teetotaler,* received the Republican nomination for state prison inspector. By election time, New York's temperance organizations and newspapers were solidly behind Frémont and King.[38]

Defections from the straight Whigs, the Democrats, and the Know-Nothings had swelled the New York Republican organization and the confidence of its leadership. A powerful coalition opposed to the extension of slavery and resolved to subordinate all other issues had formed. Reports from campaign workers were especially encouraging from the Burned-over-region. "In the western counties, where I spent the last fifteen days, our prospects are good and you will be astonished at the majorities which some of them will give for the Republican ticket," wrote one of Morgan's correspondents. Haven, running for re-election from Buffalo, and Washington Hunt, seeking the Orleans-Niagara congressional seat as the American candidate, were special targets for Republican efforts, and it appeared that these influential politicians would be defeated. After a speaking tour in Oneida and Herkimer, Greeley predicted that these counties would "give Frémont some 15,000 votes to 7,000 for Buchanan, and 4,000 for Fillmore. Jefferson, Lewis, Onondaga, Madison, Otsego —all formerly against us, are as good." The editor believed that Frémont's state-wide plurality would be closer to 100,000 than the 50,000 he had originally estimated.[39]

So promising did the canvass appear that one politician advised the party chairman that the forensic abilities of Joshua Giddings were wasted in the "infected district" of the state. He suggested that speakers of Giddings' calibre be sent to the Hudson River counties, where a contest still existed, or better yet, to Pennsylvania, which seemed to be the real battlefield.[40]

Although the Republicans failed to carry the presidential election, the New York branch of the party fulfilled the expectations of its chieftains. (See Table I)

TABLE I

Presidential Votes in 1856 [41]

	National Total	New York
Buchanan	1,838,169	198,878
Frémont	1,347,264	276,007
Fillmore	874,534	124,604

Frémont carried the state by a substantial plurality; the state ticket also won handily, carrying with it a large majority in the assembly.[42] For the first time in three years, the combined Democratic vote failed to constitute a majority, an important indication that the Democracy had sustained heavy losses. Fillmore ran third in New York as he did in the nation. Within a year, the Know-Nothings had suffered a fatal decline, falling from first to last place at the polls.

The heavy pluralities and majorities which the Republicans piled up in the western, central, and northern portions of the state overwhelmed the pockets of Know-Nothing and Democratic strength in eastern and southern New York. The Fillmoreites' hope of building a powerful base in the "infected district" had been crushed. Failing to carry a single county in this region, they lost their former strongholds to the Republicans;[43] in most cases, the decline in their vote was precipitous. Neither Haven nor Hunt escaped the rout: the former ran third in a bitter three cornered race, in which the popular Democrat, Israel T. Hatch, narrowly beat Elbridge G. Spaulding, the Republican candidate; the latter lost by a large margin to his Republican opponent, Silas Burroughs. The nativists also sustained losses in the Hudson River counties and New York City, but these were not as significant. Astounded by the result, Stephen Sammons exclaimed that "people acted as if they were bereft of their senses."[44]

The Democrats were most successful in the downstate area, especially in New York and Kings counties, where they garnered 52.65 percent and 46.21 percent of the vote, respectively. As usual, they obtained overwhelming majorities in the Irish wards. They also received a significant number of votes from wealthier sections of the city, thus revealing that many conservative merchants, who had formerly voted Whig and then Know-Nothing, had turned full circle and supported their old enemies. Their reasons were clear and openly professed: Buchanan appeared stronger than Fillmore and therefore better able to defeat Frémont. Democrats also showed vitality in the Hudson River counties, an area where the economy was closely tied to New York City. Henry H. Van Dyck—the former editor of the Albany *Atlas,* who defected to the Republicans—was beaten by the influential and wealthy Erastus Corning in a hotly contested canvass for Albany's congressional seat. Democrats won other victories in congressional races and gained a total of eleven seats.[45]

These successes could not hide the fact that the Democrats had suffered a serious setback. Like the Know-Nothings, the Democracy had been routed in the "infected district." A review of the election returns prompted one Buchanan supporter to complain that the party was "hopelessly prostrate and except in N.Y.C. & Bklyn can hardly be said to exist in the state." Horatio Seymour agreed with this assessment:

> We are badly beaten in this state notwithstanding our best efforts to uphold the democratic party. I am mortified at the result. In central and western New York we were swept away by the popular feeling. In Oneida county we put our best speakers and most active men into the field, but the majority against us is nearly five thousand.

David A. Ogden admitted that he had never engaged in a campaign like the last and hoped never to do so again. According to Odgen, the people of the North went berserk: "They would not reason or hardly think, but the Republican party moved forward in solo column like the crusaders of old—excited, fanatical, abusive, & irresistible."[46]

New York Republicans had expended great efforts to attain a national victory, and they were naturally disappointed over Frémont's defeat. Nevertheless, they were elated over their victory at home. Especially gratifying were the large majorities from upstate. "It is with pride that I look upon the rural districts of our state and with a very different feeling—at the *cotton* portion of it," wrote Edwin Barber Morgan. "That the interior should wipe out the 30,000 majority of N. York City and its twin sister Brooklyn & pole [*sic*] up 30 or 40,000 more is consoling." While watching the election returns come in on the telegraph, Erasmus P. Smith wrote a letter which articulated the Republicans' pleasure:

> The more the figures come in, the larger is the victory in this state . . . We have now a party which contains the elite of the Whigs & the Democrats—all that gave either of them strength is with us—all that weakened either is left with the Hindoos & Democrats. It has ceased to be a coalition & has become a chemical union . . . We have the strongest party that ever took the field & four years hence, it will sweep the country.[47]

The victory of the New York Republican party climaxed three years of political upheaval. The chaotic canvass of 1854 had broken down old party loyalties, but it failed to reveal a pattern for the future. In 1855, though the antislavery issue had clearly become paramount and nativism subordinate, the Know-Nothings, having reached the peak of their power, won by a small plurality. In 1856, however, the revolution in the party system attained a definitive stage; the Republicans' decisive triumph and growing strength revealed that a dominant party had emerged in the Empire State.

The Republicans had put together a winning coalition. Seward Whigs, who comprised the largest and controlling contingent; Free Democrats, who had striven to mold an antislavery fusion for years; Barnburners, who had rebelled against the Nebraska test of Democratic loyalty; conservative Whigs, who were convinced that Southern demands were insatiable; temperance reformers, who decided to fight against slavery now and against alcohol later; and Know-Somethings, who were disgusted with Southern domination of the Know-Nothings, all joined the new party. Why did this amalgam take shape and succeed in 1856?

The clarification of doctrine with regard to the slavery extension issue contributed greatly to the Republican victory. Uncertainty had prevailed concerning the precise position of the Know-Nothings and the Democrats on this vital question. Both of these parties, realizing the strong feeling against the Nebraska Act, had adopted state platforms which could be and were interpreted as hostile to Douglas' measure. In 1855, the nativists' Binghamton resolves, omitting Article XII of the national platform, and the Softs' declaration against further encroachment of free territory, had lessened the distinction between them and the Republicans. However, one year later, no such confusion was possible. New York's Know-Nothing and Soft Shell leadership submitted to the discipline of their national organizations, both of which were dominated by the Southern point of view. Only the Republicans stood firmly for the admission of Kansas as a free state. The election revealed that the people of the Empire State had had enough acquiescence; what they wanted now was resistance.

The outbreak of guerrilla war in Kansas and the assault on Charles Sumner persuaded many that prohibition and legislative discrimination against foreigners and Catholics would have to wait until slavery's expansion had been checked. Although fearful of secession, a growing number of Old Line Whigs had also come to the conclusion that appeasement of the South should be ended.

The political skill of Thurlow Weed played an important part in bringing temperance advocates and nativists into the Republican coalition; he adroitly hinted at the possibility of his aid to these other crusades, although secretly he had only contempt for them. Nowhere did Weed's strategy have greater impact than in the Burned-over-region. During the period 1854-1855, the "infected district" had been attracted to both Know-Nothingism and temperance reform. However, in 1856, this region gave its overwhelming support to the antislavery movement.

Another factor in Republican success was the wide appeal of the "non-extension" principle. Even many abolitionists, who were dedicated to the total eradication of slavery, convinced themselves that the Republicans would eventually support this position. Straight Whigs, on the other hand, were reassured by the limited objectives of Republicanism and the repeated professions of conservatism by its leaders. Republicans deliberately cast a wide net and succeeded in unifying individuals who had formerly been at opposite ends of the political spectrum.

The election of 1856 brought the revolution in New York politics to an end. The great confusion caused by the existence of numerous parties and crusades had been largely resolved: A new two party system was emerging, and the Empire State had joined other Northern states in support of the growing demand that slavery be confined and placed upon the road to ultimate extinction. The pattern of party alignments and power which emerged during the Frémont campaign persisted for many years to come. The American party, having sustained a crippling blow, never regained its former promise and finally merged with the Republicans in 1860. The Democrats lost control of the Empire State, in both national and local contests, until 1862. Never again would they occupy the preponderant position which they had enjoyed in the past. The Republicans prevailed in all the crucial contests before secession. Although failing to place Seward in the Presidency, they carried their state for Abraham Lincoln in 1860.

ABBREVIATIONS USED IN NOTES AND BIBLIOGRAPHY

AHR	*American Historical Review*
AmQ	*American Quarterly*
CUL	Columbia University Library
HSP	Historical Society of Pennsylvania
JAH	*Journal of American History*
JNH	*Journal of Negro History*
JSH	*Journal of Southern History*
LC	Library of Congress
MVHR	*Mississippi Valley Historical Review*
NEQ	*New England Quarterly*
NYH	*New York History*
NYHS	New-York Historical Society
NYHSQ	*New York Historical Society Quarterly*
NYPL	New York Public Library
NYSL	New York State Library
PUL	Princeton University Library
SAQ	*South Atlantic Quarterly*
SUNY	State University of New York at Oswego
UCL	University of Chicago Library
URL	University of Rochester Library
YUL	Yale University Library

Notes & References

INTRODUCTION

1. The name "Barnburners" arose from the charge of an opponent who claimed that they were similar to the Dutch farmer who burned his barn to eliminate the rats. The term "Hunkers" emerged from the accusation that this group always "hankered" after office.

2. The most detailed account of the schism and reunion of the Democratic party is Ferree, "The New York Democracy."

3. The most detailed account of the Whig party during the years 1848-1852 is Donald, "Prelude to Civil War."

4. One recent statement of this view has been made by McCormick, *The Second American Party System*, p. 353.

CHAPTER 1

1. R. Russel, "The Issues in the Congressional Struggle," *JSH*, XXIX (May, 1963), 197; New York *Evening Post*, Jan. 5, 1854.

2. R. Nichols, "The Kansas-Nebraska Act" *MVHR*, XLIII (Sept. 1956), 187-212.

3. New York *Evening Post*, Feb. 17, Mar. 8, 25, May 31, 1854; New York *Tribune*, Feb. 23, 28, Mar. 17, 1854.

4. New York *Evening Post*, Jan. 31, 1854; P. Foner, *Business & Slavery*, pp. 91-99.

5. New York *Evening Post*, Feb. 18, 20, 1854.

6. John Mitchell, the editor of the Irish paper, the *Citizen*, professed his desire for a rich plantation in Alabama, well-stocked with Negro slaves. Horace Greeley feared that this avowal would only increase the popularity of Mitchell's journal. See the New York *Tribune*, Jan. 14, 1854 and Greeley to Alvan E. Bovay, Mar. 7, 1854, quoted in F. Curtis, *The Republican Party*, Vol. I, pp. 174-77.

7. The New York *Tribune* enjoyed an extensive circulation in central and western New York and throughout the Northwest. See Isely, *Horace Greeley*, p. 53.

8. New York *Times*, Jan. 24, 1854; New York *Courier and Enquirer*, Jan. 25, 1854; New York *Commercial Advertiser*, Jan. 24, 1854; New York *Evening Post*, Jan. 24, Feb. 14, 1854; New York *Journal of Commerce*, Jan. 7, 21, 1854; Erastus Brooks to Beekman, Feb. 12, 1854, Beekman Papers, NYHS.

9. See text, pp. 27-28, for a discussion of Pierce's motivation.

10. New York *Evening Post*, Jan. 6, Feb. 7, 8, 13, 1854.

11. See text, pp. 18-19.
12. Van Dyck to Marcy, Feb. 10, 1854, Redfield to Marcy, Feb. 27, 1954, Marcy Papers, LC.
13. See Ch. 3.
14. New York *Journal of Commerce,* Jan. 7, 21, Feb. 3, 18, 1854.
15. New York *Evening Post,* Feb. 20, Mar. 17, 1854.
16. Ellis, "The Yankee Invasion of New York," *NYH,* XXXII (Jan. 1951), 3-17; G. Barnes, *The Anti-Slavery Impulse,* pp. 3-16, 79-87; Tyler, *Freedom's Ferment,* pp. 489-99; Cross, *The Burned-over District,* pp. 217-25. In this study, I have followed Professor Cross' boundary for the Burned-over-region as that portion of New York State lying west of the Catskill and Adirondack mountains. *Ibid.,* p. 4.
17. *Cong. Globe,* 33 Cong., 1 Sess., 520, 521, 550, 1321, 1324; App. 338-42, 550, 788. For a breakdown of the vote in the Senate, see Russel, "Issues in the Congressional Struggle," 208-9.
18. New York *Evening Post,* May 9, 11, 1854; W. H. Seward to Weed, Jan. 8, 1854, Weed Papers, URL.
19. Weed to Fish, March 21, 1854, Fish Papers, LC; Weed to Patterson, Mar. 31, 1854, Weed Papers, URL; New York *Tribune,* Mar. 17, Apr. 7, 1854.
20. New York *Tribune,* May 8, 13, 1854; New York *Evening Post,* May 9, 23, 25, 1854; Nichols, *Franklin Pierce,* pp. 337-38.
21. *Cong. Globe,* 1 Sess., 1254-55; New York *Evening Post,* May 23, 25, 1854; Russel, "Issues in the Congressional Struggle," 209.
22. King to Flagg, May 20, 1854, Flagg Papers, CUL.
23. Cross, *Burned-over District,* pp. 211-16; Tyler, *Freedom's Ferment,* pp. 318-19.
24. Dow, *The Reminiscences of Neal Dow,* pp. 306-7.
25. Krout, *The Origins of Prohibition,* pp. 283-96, 303-4.
26. This account of the origins of prohibition legislation in New York is derived from Krout, "The Maine-Law," *Proceedings of the New York State Historical Association,* XVII (Jul. 1936), 262-65.
27. Ellis, "Yankee Invasion of New York," 3-17.
28. *United States Census,* 1860, p. XIX; *New York State Census,* 1865, p. LXXXIX.
29. A. Tyler makes the point that Democratic idealism spilled over into nativism in New York. Tyler, *Freedom's Ferment,* p. 351.
30. This account of the American-Republican movement is derived from I. Leonard, "The Rise and Fall of the American-Republican Party in New York City, 1843-1845," *NYHSQ,* L (Apr. 1966), 166-68, 182-91.
31. This account of the origins of the Know-Nothing movement is derived from Curran, "The Know-Nothings" (1963), pp. 65-109.
32. L. D. Scisco placed great weight on the attractive novelty of a secret political organization in his explanation of nativist appeal in the rural counties of the state. Scisco, *Political Nativism,* p. 12. It is interesting that only a generation before, central and western New York had been aroused to a high pitch of fury *against* another secret organization, the Free Masons. See Tyler, *Freedom's Ferment,* pp. 351-58.
33. W. Bean stresses the importance of antislavery sentiment in promoting political nativism. In Massachusetts, this was more important than the religious motive. Bean, "Puritan and Celt, 1850-1860," *NEQ, VII* (Mar. 1934), 70-89.

CHAPTER 2

1. Shepard to Marcy, Jan. 18, 1854, Newell to Marcy, Jan. 25, 1854, Marcy Papers, LC.
2. Theodore Sedgwick to Marcy, Feb. 4, 1854, George R. Davis to Marcy, Feb. 21, 1854, *Ibid.*
3. Butts to Abel French [Marcy's secretary], Feb. 8, 1854, *Ibid.*

4. Albany *Atlas,* Jan. 9, 16, 1854; Albany *Argus,* Jan. 18, 1854.

5. Albany *Atlas,* Jan. 26, 1854.

6. Newell to Marcy, Jan. 27, 1854, Marcy Papers, LC. Pierce's Attorney General, Caleb Cushing, considered by many contemporaries the most influential man in the Cabinet, gained notoriety for his phrase "crushing out," by which he meant purging free soilers from the Democratic party. See Fuess, *Cushing,* Vol. II, pp. 136, 139ff.

7. Washington *Union,* Jan. 22-31, Feb. 17, 24, 1854; Newell to Marcy, Feb. 15, 1854, Marcy Papers, LC.

8. Washington *Union,* Mar. 1, 2, 1854; Albany *Atlas,* May 23, 27, 1854.

9. Nichols, "Kansas-Nebraska Act," 201-4; Foner, "The Wilmot Proviso Revisited," 269-71; Foner, *Free Soil,* pp. 155-59.

10. Nathaniel P. Banks of Massachusetts gave this account of how Pierce consented to Repeal: "Douglas called upon the President to talk about Nebraska and by arrangement [Senator David R.] Atchison [of Missouri] dropped in soon after and they lead Pierce along step by step until they got him to suggest their Amendment which was finally adopted and called the principle of the bill, himself. When he did so Douglas proposed to him to put the Amendment or proposition in writing. He did so at once. And that they hold as evidence against him and hence his inability to back out of his position. This was done without consulting with any member of his Cabinet who were quite taken by surprise when they learned what their Chief had done but none of them had courage enough to break their connexion [*sic*] with him!!" Bigelow to Francis P. Blair, Sr., undated, Blair-Lee Papers, PUL. Pierce had asked Douglas to consult Marcy before he went ahead with his plans. The Senator went to Marcy's home but did not find him in, and he made no further effort to see him. See Nichols, *Pierce,* p. 323.

11. Marcy's biographer, Spencer, considered Marcy's decision "the most important of his life and certainly the most unfortunate. Against his better judgment, he had stayed in the Pierce administration and had even used his influence, half-heartedly, in favor of the unwise policy." Spencer, *The Victor and the Spoils,* p. 282.

12. Marcy to Seymour, Feb. 11, 15, 1854, typescripts, Seymour Papers, NYHS; Seymour to Marcy, Feb. 21, 1854, Marcy Papers, LC.

13. Newell to Marcy, Jan. 25, 1854, Marcy Papers, LC; New York *Tribune,* Feb. 11, 1854; Dix to Benton, Apr. 15, 1854, Dix Papers, CUL.

14. Cochrane to Marcy, Jan. 23, 1854, Shepard to Marcy, Jan. 28, 1854, Marcy Papers, LC.

15. New York *Evening Post,* Feb. 4, 1854; Shepard to Marcy, Feb. 7, 1854, Marcy Papers, LC.

16. J. Van Buren to Marcy, Feb. 12, 1854, Marcy Papers, LC.

17. Shepard to Marcy, Jun. 28, Jul. 7, 1854, Levi S. Chatfield to Marcy, Jul. 10, 1854, Fernando Wood to Marcy, Jul. 12, 1854, *Ibid.*

18. Marcy to Seymour, Jul. 2, 1854, typescript, Seymour Papers, NYHS; Marcy to Seymour, Jul. 12, 1854, Seymour to Marcy, Jul. 6, 1854, Marcy Papers, LC.

19. New York *Evening Post,* July 12, Aug. 4, 5, 1854.

CHAPTER 3

1. Albany *Argus,* Jan. 9, 1854.

2. Marcy to Seymour, May 27, Jun. 18, 1853, typescripts, Seymour Papers, NYHS.

3. Marcy to Seymour, Dec. 4, 1853, typescript, *Ibid.*

4. New York *Evening Post,* Jan. 4, 5, 1854.

5. *Cong. Globe,* 33 Cong., 1 Sess., 190-94.

6. *Ibid.,* App., 117-20.

7. *Cong. Globe,* 33 Cong., 1 Sess., 191-92.

8. Dickinson to Theo N. Corn, Oct. 21, 1860, Dickinson Misc. MSS, NYHS.

9. Hammond to Seward, Feb. 28, 1854, Seward Papers, URL.
10. Seward to Weed, Jan. 7, 1854, Weed Papers, URL; Nichols, *Pierce,* p. 318.
11. Albany *Argus,* Jan. 10, Feb. 4, 14, Mar. 15, 16, 1854.
12. J. J. Jones to Marcy, Feb. 7, 1854. Jones added, however, that the Hard Shell rank and file shared the opposition of the people. See also S. M. Shaw to Marcy, Feb. 14, 1854, Marcy Papers, LC.
13. Albany *Argus,* Jan. 10, 12, 14, 18, 1854.
14. *Ibid.,* Jan. 14, Feb. 8, 1854.
15. Burke's editorial was copied in the New York *Evening Post,* May 2, 1854.
16. *Ibid.,* Mar. 22, 1854; *Cong. Globe,* 33 Cong., 1 Sess., 701-2.
17. New York *Evening Post,* Mar. 28, 29, 30, 1854; *Cong. Globe,* 33 Cong., 1 Sess., 759-64.
18. Baker to Seward, May 14, 1854, Seward Papers, URL; Albany *Argus,* Apr. 4, 13, 25, May 23, 1854.
19. These dissidents included James Maurice, John Wheeler, Jared V. Peck, Rufus W. Peckham, Andrew Oliver. Albany *Argus,* Jun. 1, 3, 1854.
20. Newell to Marcy, Mar. 3, 1854, Marcy Papers, LC; James T. Brady to Rufus Peckham, undated, letter appearing in the New York *Tribune,* Jul. 8, 1854.
21. Albany *Argus,* Jul. 13, 14, 1854.
22. *Ibid.*

CHAPTER 4

1. Patterson to Weed, Mar. 16, 1854, N. Darling to Weed, Feb. 12, 1854, Weed Papers, URL; Greeley to Schuyler Colfax, Jul. 7, 1854, Greeley-Colfax Papers, NYPL.
2. Seward to Weed, Jan. 8, 1854, Weed Papers, URL; Nichols, "Kansas-Nebraska Act," 205. Seward's latest and most thorough biographer, Glyndon Van Deusen, thinks it "altogether likely that Seward made some such suggestion to Dixon and Jones." But he believes it also probable "that the idea of outright repeal was already in the air when Seward talked with the two men. The Senator from New York was not at all averse to magnifying the importance of his acts." Van Deusen, *William Henry Seward,* pp. 150-51. See also the note, pp. 586-87. The Washington correspondent of the New York *Evening Post* may have made a shrewd guess when he noted that while Seward spoke effectively in opposition, it is "universally conceded that its [Nebraska's] passage would be of more service to the political prospects of Mr. Seward than the combined efforts of ten thousand friends; *this is so generally conceded, that most of the knowing politicians here impute to his management the present agitation of the problem.*" (my italics) New York *Evening Post,* Feb. 24, 1854.
3. More than two years after the introduction of the Nebraska bill, Erasmus Pershine Smith, a trusted political ally of Seward and Weed, observed that "the South will come to know after a while that Seward is the only man who can stand between them and the retribution they are provoking. The hatred they have felt for him is being very rapidly diluted for it now has to be divided among Sumner, Wade, Fessenden & c . . . There will be little left soon but *respect* for his boldness will remain." Smith to Henry C. Carey, Apr. 11, 1856, E. Gardiner Collection, HSP.
4. Hunt to Fish, Feb. 7, 1854, Henry H. Elliot to Fish, Feb. 7, 1854, Fish Papers, LC; Fish to Weed, Jan. 25, 1854, Weed Papers, URL.
5. Weed to Fish, Feb. 19, 1854, Fish Papers, LC; Albany *Evening Journal,* Mar. 13, May 15, 19, 1854; Van Deusen, *Thurlow Weed,* p. 196.
6. Call for the "New York State Convention to be Held at Saratoga Springs, Aug. 16, 1854," Webb Papers, YUL.
7. Blue, "A History of the Free Soil Party," pp. 235-40.

8. *National Era,* May 22, 1854.

9. Minutes of the Free Democratic League for 1853-1854, NYHS; *Whig Almanac,* 1854.

10. New York *Tribune,* Aug. 11, 15, 16, 1854; Raymond to Weed, Aug. 8, 1854, Weed Papers, URL. Joseph Blunt and John Jay were prominent Free Democrats. Jay, the son of the first Chief Justice of the United States, was president of the New York Free Democratic League.

11. Greeley to Alvan E. Bovay, Mar. 7, 1854, quoted in Curtis, *Republican Party,* Vol. I, pp. 174-77; New York *Tribune,* Jul. 10, 11, 1854.

12. Greeley to Colfax, Jun. 20, 1854, Greeley-Colfax Papers, NYPL.

13. Hunt to Fish, Aug. 2, 1854, Fish Papers, LC; Isely, *Horace Greeley,* p. 87.

14. Seward to Weed, May 29, Jun. 24, 1854, Weed Papers, URL.

15. Seward to Weed, Jun. 24, 1854, *Ibid.* Henry Wilson—formerly a Whig, but soon to be elected to the United States Senate as an anti-Nebraska Know-Nothing— was upset by what he believed was Seward's desire "to keep up the union of the Northern and Southern Whigs." Wilson admitted that he would like to see Seward as President; however, he would rather vote for Douglas should the New Yorker run as the candidate of the united Whig party. Wilson to Seward, May 28, 1854, Seward Papers, URL.

16. Albany *Evening Journal,* Jul. 8, 31, 1854; Van Deusen, *Thurlow Weed,* pp. 197-99.

17. Hunt to Fish, Aug. 2, 1854, Fish Papers, LC.

18. Morgan to Weed, Aug. 11, 1854, Weed to Patterson, Jul. 11, 1854, Orson Nichoson to Weed, Aug. 11, 1854, Elbridge G. Spaulding to Weed, Aug. 8, 1854, Weed Papers, URL.

19. Hunt to Fish, Aug. 2, 1854, Fish Papers, LC; Greeley to Weed, Aug. 10, 13, 1854, Weed Papers, URL; Greeley to Colfax, Jul. 26, 1854, Greeley-Colfax Papers, NYPL; Isely, *Horace Greeley,* pp. 92-100.

20. This account of the Saratoga convention is derived from the New York *Evening Post,* Aug. 17, 1854; New York *Tribune,* Aug. 17, 1854; Albany *Argus,* Aug. 18, 19, 1854; New York *Times,* Aug. 17, 1854.

21. King to F. P. Blair, Sr., Jul. 16, 1854, Blair-Lee Papers, PUL; King to Tilden, Jul. 10, 1854, Tilden Papers, NYPL; Muller, "Preston King," pp. 535-40.

CHAPTER 5

1. Marcy to Seymour, Feb. 11, 15, 1854, typescripts, Seymour Papers, NYHS; Cochrane to Marcy, Jan. 23, Feb. 9, 1854, Marcy Papers, LC.

2. New York *Evening Post,* Jun. 26, 1854.

3. Redfield to Marcy, Jul. 15, 1854. See also D. A. Ogden to Marcy, Jul. 23, 1854, Marcy Papers, LC; New York *Tribune,* Aug. 8, 1854.

4. Newspapers recorded that the Barnburners controlled the delegations from districts in Utica, Orange, Livingston, Albany, Ontario, Delaware, Queens, Schenectady, Buffalo. New York *Evening Post,* Aug. 29, Sept. 5, 1854; New York *Tribune,* Aug. 30, 1854; Albany *Argus,* Sept. 4, 5, 1854.

5. Albany *Argus,* Sept. 4, 5, 1854.

6. *Ibid.,* Aug. 22, Sept. 5, 1854; James G. Dickie to Marcy, Sept. 3, 1854, Marcy Papers, LC.

7. Bigelow to F. P. Blair, Sr., Aug. 30, 1854, Blair-Lee Papers, PUL; New York *Evening Post,* Sept. 7, 8, 9, 1854.

8. This account of the Soft Shell convention is derived from the New York *Evening Post,* Sept. 7, 8, 9, 1854.

9. King to F. P. Blair, Sr., Aug. 29, 1854, Blair-Lee Papers, PUL; King to Hamlin, Aug. 29, 1854, Hamlin Papers, CUL (microfilm).

10. Mann subsequently charged Ludlow with packing the resolutions committee and cutting off debate in return for the lieutenant governor's nomination. Ludlow denied these charges. See the New York *Evening Post*, Sept. 11, 16, 1854.

11. Albany *Atlas*, Sept. 9, 1854.

12. New York *Evening Post*, Sept. 15, 1854 (semi-weekly edition).

13. For quotations from these papers, see the Albany *Argus*, Sept. 18, 21 25, 1854 and the New York *Tribune*, Sept. 18, 26, 1854.

14. *National Era*, Sept. 21, 1854.

15. New York *Tribune*, Sept. 4, 8, 1854.

16. Redfield to Marcy, Jul. 15, 1854, Marcy Papers, LC.

17. New York *Evening Post*, Jun. 22, July 19, Sept. 7, 1854.

18. John A. Dix was a good example of a prominent Barnburner who reluctantly went along with the bolt of 1847-1848. He considered the Nebraska bill a disaster and opposed it, but he had no intentions of participating in a new rebellion. Dix to F. P. Blair, Sr., Feb. 25, 1854, Dix to Benton, Apr. 15, 1854, Dix Papers, CUL.

19. The Albany *Atlas*, Sept. 7, 1854, encouraged this line of thought. Nothing in the Nebraska Act, the editors averred, required drastic action; before any new organization could take the field, Nebraska and Kansas would find their way into the Union as free states.

20. Tilden to (?), Aug. 26, 1854, Tilden Papers, NYPL.

21. Albany *Atlas*, Aug. 17, 1854.

CHAPTER 6

1. Weed to Patterson, Mar. 31, 1854, Patterson to Weed, Apr. 3, 1854, Weed Papers, URL; E. D. Morgan to Fish, May 2, 1854, Fish Papers, LC.

2. Seymour's veto is printed in Charles Z. Lincoln, ed., *Messages from the Governors of New York State*, Vol. 4, p. 687.

3. New York *Tribune*, Mar. 31, 1854; Weed to Patterson, Mar. 31, 1854, Weed Papers, URL. It should be noted that the New York *Evening Post*, Mar. 31, 1854, which was not friendly to Seymour, could not see any advantage in antagonizing the temperance forces in the state, armed as they were with powerful resources, zealous advocates, and in alliance with pulpit and press. The editors admitted their surprise at the veto and considered it one of the Governor's rare acts of selflessness.

4. Hunt to Fish, Apr. 8, 1854, Fish Papers, LC.

5. New York *Tribune*, Jun. 9, Aug. 9, 1954.

6. *Ibid.*, Apr. 1, Jun. 8, 13, 1854.

7. See text. pp. 13-14.

8. Vivus W. Smith to Seward, Sept. 4, 1854, Seward Papers, URL; Nichoson to Weed, Sept. 16, 1854, Weed to Patterson, May 10, 29, Sept. 17, 1854. Weed Papers, URL.

9. See Curran, "Know-Nothings of New York," p. 104.

10. The contents of this letter were communicated to Weed by Thomas R. Horton, Aug. 5, 1854, Weed Papers, URL.

11. J. Oshander to Robert Wetmore, Aug. 2, 1854, E. F. Hovey to Ullman, Aug. 7, 1854, L. S. Parsons to Ullman, Sept. 14, 16, 1854, George R. Babcock to Ullman, Sept. 16, 1854, Ullman Papers, NYHS.

12. Weed to Patterson, Sept. 17, 23, 1854, Lyman A. Spaulding to Weed, Aug. 3, 1854, Weed Papers, URL; D. L. Pettee to Ullman, Sept. 18, 1854, Ullman Papers, NYHS.

13. R. B. Warren to Marcellus Ells, Aug. 7, 1854, Socrates Smith to Ells, Aug. 11. 1854, Ullman to D. Andrews, Sept. 16, 1854, copy, N. G. King to Ullman, Sept. 16, 1854, Ullman Papers, NYHS.

14. Hunt to Fish, Apr. 8, 1854, Fish Papers, LC; Patterson to Weed, May 8, 1854, Weed to Patterson, May 10, 29, 1854, Weed Papers, URL.

15. Weed to Patterson, Sept. 23, 1854, Weed Papers, URL.

16. John M. Bradford to Weed, Jun. 24, 1854, Myron H. Clark to Weed, Sept. 19, 1854, Weed Papers, URL; L. S. Parsons to Ullman, Sept. 16, 1854, N. G. King to Ullman, Sept. 8, 14, 1854, Ullman Papers, NYHS.

17. New York *Tribune*, Sept. 21, 1854.

18. Greeley to Seward, Oct. 5, Nov. 17, 1854, Seward Papers, URL; Isely, *Horace Greeley*, p. 80.

19. New York *Tribune*, Sept. 21, 1854.

20. Weed to Patterson, Sept. 17, 1854, Weed Papers, URL.

21. The following account of the various Auburn conventions is derived from the New York *Evening Post,* Sept. 29, Oct. 3, 1854 and the New York *Times,* Sept. 26, 27, 1854.

22. For charges of Whig sharp dealing, see the letter of a Free Democrat, "How the Auburn Convention was BeWhigged," in the New York *Evening Post,* Oct. 3, 1854.

23. Snodgrass subsequently took part in several abolitionist meetings. At a meeting of the American Anti-Slavery Society in May of 1855, he debated William Lloyd Garrison, criticizing him for his aloofness from the electoral process. Snodgrass said that he had lived most of his life in the South. He was vice-president of the American Settlement Company of New York, an organization dedicated to sending immigrants to Kansas. See the New York *Tribune,* May 11, 1855.

CHAPTER 7

1. New York *Herald,* Oct. 7, 1854; New York *Tribune,* Oct. 6, 9, Nov. 3, 1854.

2. J. P. Faurot to Ullman, Sept. 27, 1854, Ullman Papers, NYHS.

3. The New York *Tribune* ran a continual discussion of these charges. See the *Tribune* for Oct. 13, 26, 28, 30, 31, Nov. 2, 6, 7, 1854. Ullman claimed to have been born in Wilmington, Delaware.

4. J. P. Faurot to Ullman, Oct. 20, 1854, L. L. Pratt to Ullman, Oct. 19, 1854, Darius Perrin, S. W. D. Moore, and James R. Thompson to Ullman, Nov. 13, 1854, Ullman Papers, NYHS.

5. New York *Tribune,* Oct. 24, 1854; Albany *Argus,* Sept. 30, 1854. Among Ullman's correspondents there were several editors of Silver Gray papers who were Know-Nothings. All ostensibly supported the Whig ticket. See L. L. Pratt to Ullman, Oct. 17, 1854, J. T. Henry to Ullman, Oct. 10, 1854, Alexander Mann to Ullman, Oct. 9, 1854, Ullman Papers, NYHS. Pratt was editor of the Fredonia *Advertiser,* Henry of the Cattaraugus *Union,* and Mann of the Rochester *Union.*

6. Henry Sherman to Ullman, Oct. 9, 1854, Ullman to D. Andrews, Sept. 16, 1854, copy, Ullman Papers, NYHS.

7. One supporter informed Ullman that in Buffalo both the temperance folks and the rum sellers favored him. Charles G. Irish, Jr., to Ullman, Oct. 16, 1854, *Ibid.* Greeley feared that many anti-Nebraska and anti-rum men would be swindled into voting for Ullman: "The wire workers whisper to them that Ullman is as much of their way of thinking as Clark, and thus dupe them into aiding the triumph of Seymour, Slavery, and Liquor!" New York *Tribune,* Nov. 4, 1854.

8. John J. Bowen to Ullman, Oct. 30, 1854, George O. Jones to S. Sammons, Oct. 28, 1854, L. L. Pratt to Ullman, Oct. 17, 1854. Ullman also learned that great enthusiasm prevailed in the lake counties—Orleans, Niagara, and Monroe. N. G. King to Ullman, Nov. 2, 1854, Ullman Papers, NYHS.

9. For the McKeon incident, see text, pp. 22-23.

10. Seymour to Marcy, Sept. 9, 1854, Marcy Papers, LC; Seymour to Douglas, Apr. 14, 1854, Douglas Papers, UCL.

11. Henry S. Randall to Marcy, Jun. 24, 1854, Marcy Papers, LC; S. B. Garvin, Dean Richmond, and William Cassidy to Seymour, Sept. 7, 1854, Marcy to Seymour, May 28, 1854, typescripts, NYHS.

12. Seymour to Marcy, Sept. 9, 18, 29, 1854, Jonathan B. Skinner to Marcy, Sept. 28, 1854, Marcy Papers, LC (Skinner was the postal official from Washington); Nichols, *Pierce*, pp. 363-64.

13. Redfield to Marcy, Jul. 15, 1854, Marcy Papers, LC; Albany *Atlas,* Sept. 25, 1854; New York *Tribune,* Oct. 10, 1854.

14. John E. McMahon to Seymour, Oct. 29, 1854, Seymour Papers, NYHS; Robert Kelly to Seymour, Oct. 7, 1854, Seymour Papers, NYSL.

15. Bronson's letters were printed in the New York *Weekly Mirror,* Oct. 14, 1854.

16. Albany *Atlas,* Sept. 22, 1854; William A. Searer to Seymour, Nov. 6, 1854, Seymour Papers, NYSL; Journal of Van Schaik Lansing Pruyn, Oct. 23 to Nov. 1, 1854, Journal No. 1, NYSL.

17. See Sammons to Ullman, Oct. 18, 1854, Ullman Papers, NYHS.

18. New York *Courier and Enquirer,* Sept. 30, 1854; New York *Commercial Advertiser,* Sept. 30, 1854; New York *Evening Post,* Oct. 30, 1854.

19. Hunt to Weed, Oct. 21, 1854, Raymond to Weed, Oct. 28, 1854, Weed Papers, URL; Buffalo *Telegraph,* quoted in the Albany *Argus,* Sept. 30, 1854.

20. Hunt to Weed, Oct. 21, 1854, Hanson A. Risley to Weed, Nov. 2, 1854, A. J. Upham to Weed, Nov. 1, 1854, Weed Papers, URL; Greeley to Colfax, Nov. 6, 1854, Greeley-Colfax Papers, NYPL.

21. A correspondent of Seward suggested the idea of a "backfire" against the Know-Nothings. V. W. Smith to Seward, Sept. 4, 1854, Seward Papers, URL.

22. New York *Tribune,* Oct. 30, 1854; Syracuse *Chronicle,* quoted in the *Tribune,* Nov. 3, 1854; G. O. Jones to Sammons, Oct. 28, 1854. J. W. Coley warned Ullman against a number of Choctaws who were "doing their best to divide and go for Clark." Coley promised "to meet them and confront them at every point possible." Coley to Ullman, Oct. 17, 1854, Ullman Papers, NYHS.

23. *Whig Almanac,* 1853, 1855.

24. *Ibid.,* 1855.

25. Baker to Seward, Nov. 10, 1854, Seward Papers, URL.

26. Examples of normally Whig counties which went heavily for the Know-Nothings include: Ontario, Livingston, Orleans, Cattaraugus, Chautauqua. See the New York *Tribune,* Nov. 17, 1854 and the New York *Times,* Nov. 8, 1854; *Whig Almanac,* 1855.

27. Curran, "Know-Nothings of New York," p. 308; Patterson to Seward, Nov. 8, 1854, Seward Papers, URL; L. L. Pratt to Ullman, Nov. 9, 1854, Ullman Papers, NYHS.

28. New York *Tribune,* Oct. 16, Nov. 2, 9, 11, 14, 1854; Greeley to Colfax, Nov. 6, 1854, Greeley-Colfax Papers, NYPL; Greeley to Seward, Nov. 17, 1854, Seward Papers, URL.

29. L. S. Parsons to Ullman, Nov. 11, 1854, Granger to Ullman, Nov. 14, 1854, A. Mann to Ullman, Nov. 16, 1854, Ullman Papers, NYHS; Jacob G. Sanders to Beekman, Nov. 19, 1854, Beekman Papers, NYHS.

30. H. Seymour to J. Seymour, Nov. 22, 1854, Seymour Papers, NYHS; Henry S. Randall to Seymour, Dec. 26, 1854, Robert Kellog to Seymour, Nov. 15, 1854, Seymour Papers, NYSL.

31. Quoted in Crandall, *The Early History of the Republican Party,* p. 25.

32. The vote in Binghamton, the home of Dickinson and an area where he was reputed to have power, looked especially suspect: Ullman, 479; Clark, 76; Bronson, 41; Seymour, 14. See the New York *Times,* Nov. 11, 1854. The Albany *Atlas,* Nov. 11, 1854, accused the Hards of complicity with the nativists: "Thus professing rigid principles, they have gone for a party professing no principles except proscription."

CHAPTER 8

1. *Whig Almanac,* 1855, p. 54.

2. New York *Tribune,* Nov. 22, 1854, Jan. 29, 1855; Albany *State Register,* quoted in *Ibid.,* Dec. 29, 1854; Roswell Hart to Ullman, Jan. 25, 1855, L. L. Pratt to Ullman, Jan. 27, 1855, Ullman Papers, NYHS.

3. John Sanders to Beekman, Feb. 17, 1855, Beekman Papers, NYHS; Albany *Argus,* Mar. 22, 23, 1855; Curran, "Seward and the Know-Nothings," *NYHSQ,* LI (Apr., 1967), 156-58.

4. New York *Tribune,* Feb. 2, 6, 1855; Albany *Argus,* Feb. 6, 1855; *Journal of the New York Assembly,* 78th Sess., p. 264.

5. Seward to Weed, Feb. 7, 1855, Weed Papers, URL.

6. See, for example, Jacob G. Sanders to Beekman, Feb. 6, 1855, John Sanders to Beekman, Aug. 10, 1855, Beekman Papers, NYHS; James R. Thompson to Ullman, Mar. 15, 1855, Ullman Papers, NYHS.

7. Hammond to Seward, Apr. 2, 1855, George Geddes to Seward, Feb. 7, 1855, Seward Papers, URL; Henry Morgan to Weed, Feb. 8, 1855, Weed Papers, URL.

8. Rayner to Ullman, January 22, 1855, Ullman Papers, NYHS.

9. William E. Cunningham (Norfolk, Va.) to Ullman Apr. 10, 1855, George M. Wise (Charlottesville, Va.) to Ullman, Apr. 14, 1855, Joseph Segar (Roseland, Va.) to Ullman, Jan. 5, 1855, *Ibid.*

10. Rayner to Ullman, May 8, 1855, Samuel H. Hammond to Ullman, Apr. 20, 1855, J. Timberlake (Charlottesville, Va.) to Ullman, May 30, 1855, *Ibid.*

11. Rayner, for example, wrote that the Know-Nothings must leave the question of slavery exactly where the institutions of the country had left it, and not "to hazard the integrity of the Union by discussing or agitating the question, either at the North or the South. On this subject we have fanatics, agitators, and disunionists at both ends of the Union. Our order shall lend no encouragement to either." Rayner to Ullman, Jan. 22, 1855. See also Vespasian Ellis to Ullman, Nov. 17, 1855, *Ibid.*

12. New York *Tribune,* Jun. 14, 23, 1855.

13. Rayner voted for Barker's re-election as president of the National Grand Council. He wrote Ullman that he hoped this action would not stand in the way of their friendship. Rayner to Ullman, Aug. 21, 1855, Ullman Papers, NYHS.

14. Sammons to Ullman, Jun. 15, 1855, *Ibid.*

15. Killian Miller to Ullman, Jun. 24, 1855, J. D. Colver to Ullman, Jun. 24, 1855, H. F. Pultz to Ullman, Jun. 22, 1855, James R. Thompson to Ullman, Jun. 28, 1855, *Ibid.*

16. Edwards to Ullman, Jun. 15, 19, 23, 1855, Thompson to Ullman, Jun. 26, July 10, 1855, J. P. Faurot to Ullman, Jul. 10, 1855, *Ibid.*

17. New York *Tribune,* Aug. 29, 30, 1855; Thompson to Ullman, Aug. 14, September 8, 1855, Ullman Papers, NYHS.

18. New York *Weekly Mirror,* Sept. 8, 1855; New York *Journal of Commerce,* Sept. 4, 1855.

CHAPTER 9

1. King to Flagg, Mar. 5, 1855, Flagg Papers, CUL; Hammond to Seward, Apr. 2, 1855, Seward Papers, URL.

2. John M. Bradford to Fish, Dec. 12, 1854, Fish Papers, LC; Weed to Seward, July 23, 1855, Seward Papers, URL.

3. This address—dated Aug. 6, 1855 and signed by John Jay, president, and William R. King, secretary—was printed in the New York *Tribune,* Aug. 7, 1855.

4. King to Seward, Sept. 19, 1854, Seward Papers, URL; King to F. P. Blair, Sr., Jul. 16, Oct. 14, 1854, Blair-Lee Papers, PUL: King to Flagg, Mar. 5, 1855, Flagg Papers, CUL. Erasmus Smith subsequently revealed his high esteem for King: "His

[King's] great quality is *backbone*. We ran him for Secty of State last fall, having the winter before put him on the N.Y. Harbor commission, without asking, as an overture to the Demo Free soilers. There is nothing Soft about him & he is as [illegible] honest as a Loco Foco can be." Smith to Henry C. Carey, Oct. 17, 1856, Gardiner Collection, HSP.

5. New York *Tribune,* Aug. 24, 1855.
6. *Ibid.,* Sept. 28, 1855; Stanton, *Random Recollections,* p. 91.
7. Alonzo Johnson to Weed, Aug. 17, 1855, Weed Papers, URL; New York *Tribune,* Sept. 28, 1855.
8. Abijah Mann, Jr., to Weed, Sept. 29, 1855, Weed Papers, URL.
9. Albany *Argus,* Apr. 17, 1855; New York *Tribune,* Sept. 29, 1855; N. Darling to Weed, Sept. 20, 1855, Weed Papers, URL.
10. New York *Tribune,* Jul. 25, Aug. 1, 1855.
11. *Ibid.,* Sept. 24, 26, 28, 1855.
12. *Ibid.,* Sept. 29, Oct. 3, 1855.
13. Hunt to Weed, Aug. 10, 1855, Weed Papers, URL; Fish to Hunt, Oct. 5, 1855, Letter Copy Book, Vol. 196, Fish Papers, LC; New York *Commercial Advertiser,* Jul. 19, 1855.
14. Fish to Hunt, Oct. 5, 1855, Letter Copy Book, Vol. 196, Hunt to Fish, Oct. 7, 1855, Fish Papers, LC. Several Silver Grays met in New York City to denounce the abandonment of the Whig party. The New York *Tribune,* Oct. 5, 1855, and the New York *Courier and Enquirer,* Oct. 6, 1855, accused them of shedding crocodile tears; for years they had done their best to destroy the Whig organization and were presently enrolled as Know-Nothings.
15. New York *Tribune,* Aug. 22, 1855. See also the New York *Courier and Enquirer,* Oct. 6, 1855.
16. Hunt to Fish, Oct. 7, 1855, Fish Papers, LC; Albany *State Register,* quoted in the New York *Tribune,* Oct. 25, 1855; Baker to Seward, Oct. 5, 8, 1855, Seward Papers, URL; New York *Commercial Advertiser,* Oct. 24, 1855.
17. Crouthamel, "Webb and the New York *Courier and Enquirer,* 1827-1861," p. 727.
18. New York *Courier and Enquirer,* Jul. 11, 12, 21, Sept. 29, Oct. 2, 6, 18, 1855; Webb to Seward, Oct. 2, 1855, Seward Papers, URL; Edward Harte to Webb, Nov. 25, 1855, Webb Papers, YUL.

CHAPTER 10

1. Albany *Argus,* January 29, Feb. 1, 19, Mar. 9, 18, Apr. 2, Jun. 8, 12, 16, 1855. Formerly the Hard Shell organ, the *Argus* had changed ownership in Jan. of 1855 and was now a Soft paper.
2. This account of the proceedings of the Hard Shell convention is derived from *Ibid.,* Aug. 24, 25, 1855.
3. New York *Evening Post,* Aug. 24, 1855; Seymour to Marcy, August 27, 1855, Marcy Papers, LC.
4. F. S. Edwards to Ullman, Dec. 10, 1854, Sammons to Ullman, Nov. 27, Dec. 15, 1854, Tucker to Ullman, Dec. 15, 1854, Ullman Papers, NYHS; Albany *Argus,* Jan. 16, 27, 1855.
5. Seymour to Douglas, Feb. 7, 1855, Douglas Papers, UCL; Marcy to Seymour, Feb. 25, 1855, copy, Seymour to Marcy, Feb. 8, 28, Jul. 31, 1855, Marcy to J. Van Buren, Apr. 8, 1855, copy, Marcy Papers, LC.
6. This account of the proceedings of the Soft Shell convention is derived from the Albany *Argus,* Aug. 30, 31, Sept. 1, 1855.
7. Shepard wrote to Marcy that he had never felt more indignant at Van Buren's "natural proclivity to mischief," and he believed that "the Prince's" action was

meant to damage the Secretary. Van Buren gave his own explanation for his behavior. He had no wish to hurt Marcy or to sabotage the Soft campaign. Quite the contrary. He hoped that his action would be condemned by the Washington *Union,* the Administration paper, and the Southern press. Such denunciations, Van Buren observed, would enhance his own influence with anti-Nebraska Democrats and would greatly aid the Softs in the coming canvass. Shepard to Marcy, Sept. 8, 1855, J. Van Buren to Marcy, Sept. 20, 1855, Marcy Papers, LC.

8. Seymour to Marcy, Aug. 27, 1855, *Ibid.;* Newell to Tilden, Sept. 18, 1855, Tilden Papers, NYPL.

9. New York *Journal of Commerce,* Sept. 8, 1855; Shepard to Marcy, Sept. 8, 1855, Marcy Papers, LC.

10. New York *Journal of Commerce,* Sept. 29, 1854, June 12, Sept. 8, Nov. 3, 1855.

11. New York *Evening Post,* Aug. 31, Sept. 1, 8, 1855; Abijah Mann, Jr., to Weed, Sept. 29, 1855, Weed Papers, URL; Clapp, *Forgotten First Citizen,* p. 96; Bigelow and Bryant to Tilden, Sept. 3, 1855, Tilden Papers, NYPL.

CHAPTER 11

1. F. S. Edwards to Ullman, Feb. 21, 1855, Thompson to Ullman, Mar. 8, 1855, Ullman Papers, NYHS; Patterson to Weed, Feb. 17, 1855, Weed Papers, URL.

2. Thompson to Ullman, Sept. 1, 1855, Ullman Papers, NYHS.

3. Weed to Seward, Jul. 23, 1855, Baker to Seward, Oct. 19, 1855, Seward Papers, URL; Stanton to Weed, Oct. 15, 1855, Thurlow Weed Misc. MSS, NYHS; New York *Tribune,* Oct. 20, 31, 1855.

4. George Barker to Weed, Oct. 20, 1855, Weed Papers, URL. Nye, a former Soft who had joined the Republicans, was a highly esteemed political orator.

5. Stanton to Weed, Oct. 15, 1855, Weed Misc. MSS, NYHS; Littlejohn to Weed, Oct. 15, 1855, L. A. Spaulding to Weed, Oct. 5, 1855, Weed Papers, URL.

6. Baker to Seward, Oct. 13, 1855, Seward to E. A. Stansbury, Sept. 14, 1855, Seward Papers, URL.

7. Washington *Union,* quoted in the Albany *Evening Journal,* Oct. 29, 1855; J. Van Buren to Marcy, Sept. 20, Nov. 13, 1855, Marcy Papers, LC; Henry D. Rich to J. Van Buren, Nov. 21, 1855, included in the Tilden Papers, NYPL. See notes for Ch. 10, note 7.

8. The Albany *Atlas* and the Washington *Union,* quoted in the New York *Evening Post,* Oct. 4, 1855. Marcy approved of the speech. See Seymour to Marcy, Sept. 9, Oct. 5, 1855, Marcy Papers, LC, and Marcy to Seymour, Sept. 12, 1855, typescript, Seymour Papers, NYHS.

9. Albany *Argus,* Oct. 29, 1855; Albany *State Register,* quoted in the New York *Tribune,* Oct. 25, 1855; New York *Commercial Advertiser,* Nov. 5, 6, 1855.

10. *True American's Almanac and Political Manual,* 1857.

11. Curran, "Know-Nothings of New York," p. 311. Curran attributes the nativists' poor showing in eastern New York in 1854 to the fact that pro-Renter Daniel Ullman headed the ticket. Although most powerful in the 1840's, anti-Rentism remained an important factor in the politics of the Hudson Valley a decade later. See *Ibid.,* p. 198.

12. John Sanders to Beekman, Nov. 19, 1855, Beekman Papers, NYHS.

13. Curran, "Know-Nothings of New York," p. 312. The Albany *Evening Journal,* Nov. 8, 1855, attributed the Republicans' defeat to the solid vote of New York City and Brooklyn, "those huge ulcers upon the body politic."

14. New York *Express,* Nov. 13, 1855; New York *Journal of Commerce,* Nov. 8, 1855; New York *Commercial Advertiser,* Nov. 7, 1855.

15. New York *Evening Post,* Nov. 9, 1855; Seward to Willard McKinstry, Nov. 8, 1855, Bradford to Seward, Nov. 27, 1855, Seward Papers, URL; Greeley to Colfax, Nov. 13, 1855, Greeley-Colfax Papers, NYPL.

16. In twenty-three of the twenty-nine counties in the Burned-over-region, the Republicans made gains as compared with the percentage of the vote received by the Whigs in 1854. See Curran, "Know-Nothings," pp. 308-9.

17. Bradford to Fish, Nov. 8, 1855, Fish Papers, LC; New York *Tribune,* Nov. 12, 1855.

18. Albany *Evening Journal,* Nov. 8, 1855. The dark lantern was a symbol used by the Know-Nothings. Seward wrote that "all the west has partially or fully redeemed itself. . . ." Seward to (?), Nov. 10, 1855, quoted in F. W. Seward, *William Henry Seward at Washington,* p. 258.

19. Redfield to Marcy, Nov. 27, 1855, Marcy Papers, LC.

CHAPTER 12

1. Albany *Argus,* Dec. 20, 1855, Apr. 30, May 1, 2, 15, 1856.

2. The Marcy Papers include an article clipped from the Maysville [Kentucky] *Weekly Express,* Sept. 11, 1855, which praises the Hard Shells for the nationality of their platform and condemns the Softs' position as thoroughly antislavery. Presumably, this type of commentary alarmed the Secretary of State and other Softs.

3. Seymour to Marcy, Sept. 9, 1855, James G. Dickie to Marcy, Dec. 24, 1855, Marcy Papers, LC.

4. This account of the Soft Shell convention is derived from the Albany *Argus,* Jan. 12, 1856.

5. Marcy to Seymour, Jan. 18, 1856, typescript, Seymour Papers, NYHS; Cassidy to M. Van Buren, Jan. 13, 1856, Van Buren Papers, LC; Albany *Argus,* Jan. 7, 11, 1856.

6. New York *Daily News,* quoted in the New York *Tribune,* Jan. 16, 1856.

7. John Stryker to Marcy, May 7, 27, 1856, S. M. Shaw to Marcy, May 3, 1856, Marcy Papers, LC.

8. New York *Tribune,* Oct. 3, 1854.

9. Disney to Douglas, Feb. 28, 29, 1856, Douglas Papers, UCL.

10. Disney to Douglas, Feb. 29, 1856. Douglas could not comply with this request. He did not know of any suitable Southerner that he could send. See Douglas to James W. Singleton, Mar. 16, 1856. Disney made some vague promises where he thought they would do the most good: "I have *hinted* that *Dickinson* may be assured that he will be cared for in case of your success—I however phrased it in general terms and spoke of it as a natural matter of course thing." Disney to Douglas, undated, *Ibid.*

11. Buchanan to John Slidell, Dec. 28, 1855, Buchanan Papares, HSP.

12. Sickles to Buchanan, Nov. 25, 1855, Feb. 3, 19, May 24, 1856, *Ibid.*

13. Sickles had to restrain Tucker from coming out prematurely for Buchanan. Sickles to Buchanan, Feb. 19, 1856, *Ibid.*

14. Disney's belief that this last minute deal converted the Hard Shells from an original preference for Douglas is doubtful. Disney to Douglas, Jun. 7, 1856. Douglas Papers, UCL.

15. New York *Tribune,* Jun. 5, 1856.

16. *Official Proceedings of the National Democratic Convention, June 2-6, 1856,* pp. 34-37. The Albany *Atlas and Argus,* Jun. 12, 13, 1856, printed the minority and majority reports of the credentials committee. These do not appear in the official proceedings. Nichols, *The Disruption of American Democracy,* pp. 18-32.

17. *Official Proceedings,* p. 36. The New York *Tribune's* correspondent, Jun. 10, 1856, observed that the rejection of the majority report was the first important demonstration of Buchanan's power in the convention. By neutralizing the vote of New York and alarming the officeholders who supported Pierce, it paved the way for the Pennsylvanian's nomination on the next day.

18. Herrick to Buchanan, Jun. 8, 1856. Herrick was an early supporter of Buchanan. See Herrick to Buchanan, Feb. 13, 1856, Buchanan Papers, HSP.

19. *Official Proceedings,* pp. 39-42; Nichols, *Disruption,* p. 31.

20. *Official Proceedings,* pp. 45-49, 60-61.

21. Many politicians concurred in the belief that if the Hard Shells were excluded from Cincinnati, they would then have gone over completely to the Know-Nothings. James R. Thompson worried about a large influx of Adamantines. He felt that they would endanger Silver Gray control of the party. Thompson to Ullman, Apr. 23, 1856, Ullman Papers, NYHS. Another nativist, however, looked forward to a large Hard Shell contingent. N. K. Hall to Millard Fillmore, Mar. 23, 1856, Fillmore Papers, SUNY. Republicans feared that an alliance between the Hards and the Know-Nothings would be too strong to overcome. E. Smith to Henry C. Carey, Feb. 9, 1856, Gardiner Collection, HSP. Daniel Sickles warned Buchanan that Dickinson sought a place on the American ticket, either for President or Vice-President, in case his faction was denied recognition by the national convention. Sickles to Buchanan, Dec. 25, 1855, Buchanan Papers, HSP.

22. Beardsley to Buchanan, Jun. 15, 1856, Dickinson to Buchanan, Jun. 10, 1856, Buchanan Papers, HSP.

23. Journal of John V. S. L. Pruyn, Jun. 6, 1856, Journal No. 1, NYSL; Pruyn to Buchanan, Jun. 12, 1856, Seymour to Buchanan, Jun. 6, 1856, Buchanan Papers, HSP; Albany *Argus,* Jun. 6, 7, 1856.

24. Albany *Atlas and Argus,* Jul. 31, Aug. 1, 2, 1856.

CHAPTER 13

1. The exact number of Know-Nothing Congressmen is difficult to determine Various estimates of the size of the contingent exist. Allan Nevins assesses the number to be as low as forty-three, Jeter Isely at about seventy-seven, and Thomas Curran at approximately ninety. Nevins, *Ordeal of the Union,* Vol. II, p. 414; Isely, *Horace Greeley,* p. 143; Curran, "Know-Nothings," p. 218. Part of the problem arises from the fact that several Representatives were elected as Whigs and Democrats but were secretly endorsed by the Order. The *Know-Nothing Almanac,* 1855, for example, claimed nineteen of New York's thirty-three Congressmen; however, all of these had run as Whigs. Confusion is compounded when it is remembered that many Northern Representatives were professed anti-Nebraskaites as well as recipients of nativist aid.

2. Ellis to Ullman, Nov. 11, 1855, Ullman Papers, NYHS.

3. *Cong. Globe,* 34 Cong., 1 Sess., pt. 1, 2-337; Nevins, *Ordeal,* Vol II, pp. 412-16; Isely, *Horace Greeley,* pp. 143-45.

4. Haven to Ullman, Dec. 13, 16, 1855, Ullman Papers, NYHS.

5. *Cong. Globe* 34, Cong., 1 Sess., pt. 1, 337; Nevins, *Ordeal,* p. 415; Isely, *Horace Greeley,* 143-45.

6. Ellis to Fillmore, Jul. 31, 1856, Fillmore Papers, SUNY; Ellis to Ullman, Mar. 2, 1856, Ullman Papers, NYHS.

7. New York *Times,* Feb. 20, 21, 1856.

8. *Ibid.,* Feb. 26, 1856; New York *Tribune,* Feb. 23, 1856.

9. Sammons to Ullman, Nov. 26, 1855, Ullman Papers, NYHS; Haven to Fillmore, Jan. 20, 1856, Fillmore Papers, SUNY.

10. New York *Times,* Feb. 26, 1856; Ellis to Ullman, Feb. 17, 1856, Ullman Papers, NYHS.

11. New York *Times,* Feb. 26, 1856.

12. New York *Express,* Nov. 13, 1855.

13. Rayback, *Millard Fillmore,* pp. 390-91; Thompson to Ullman, Mar. 15, 1855, Ullman Papers, NYHS.

14. Fillmore to Isaac Newton, Jan. 3, 1855, printed in Frank Severance, ed., *Fillmore Papers,* Vol. II, pp. 347-49.

15. Haven to Fillmore, Apr. 24, May 11, 25, 1856, Fillmore Papers, SUNY.

16. Haven to Fillmore, May 11, 25, 1856, *Ibid.*

17. Haven to Fillmore, May 11, 1856, *Ibid.*

18. Fillmore's speech at Albany and other orations at different cities along his route are conveniently printed in Severance, *Fillmore Papers,* Vol. II, pp. 18-33.

19. Fillmore's remarks concerning "Americanism" were contained in his speech at Newburgh, New York. See *Ibid.,* pp. 16-17.

20. D. C. Calvin to Ullman, Oct. 13, 1856, Ullman Papers, NYHS; Smith to Carey, Oct. 31, 1856, Gardiner Collection, HSP.

21. Sammons to Fillmore, July 24, 25, 1856, Fillmore Papers, SUNY. Several pamphlets were subsequently written. See, for example, "Frémont's Romanism Established: Acknowledged by Archbishop Hughes," NYSL.

22. A. B. Parmelee to John A. King, Oct. 6, 1856, King Papers, NYHS; A. H. Wells to Fillmore, Jul. 15, 1856, Fillmore Papers, SUNY.

23. Haven to Fillmore, Jul. 4, 1856, Fillmore Papers, SUNY.

24. John W. Syme (Petersburg, Va.) to Fillmore, Jul. 2, 1856, Leonard F. Doyal (Georgia) to Fillmore, Jul. 13, 1856, *Ibid.,* Fillmore's Rochester speech may be found in Severance, *Fillmore Papers,* Vol. II, pp. 23-26.

25. Blanchard Fosgate to Fillmore, Jul. 5, 1856, Ephraim Schutt to Fillmore, Oct. 21, 1856, Sammons to Fillmore, illegible date (probably Aug. 25, 1856), Fillmore Papers, SUNY.

26. Fillmore to Henry Dana Ward, Sept. 2, 1856, copy of letter in Ward's diary, NYPL; Fillmore to Carroll, Sept. 8, 1856, Carroll Papers, Baltimore Historical Society; D. O. Kellogg to Fillmore, Nov. 18, 1856, Isaac Hazlehurst to Fillmore, Oct. 18, 1856, Fillmore Papers, SUNY.

27. Haven to Ullman, Apr. 23, 1856, Ullman Papers, NYHS; Haven to Fillmore, May 11, 1856, Fillmore Papers, SUNY.

28. *Cong. Globe,* 34 Cong. 1 Sess., pt. 2, 1815-17. Haven informed Fillmore that Dunn was his ardent supporter. Haven to Fillmore, Jul. 29, 1856, Fillmore Papers, SUNY. The Republicans voted for Dunn's bill, but many secretly hoped it would fail. Greeley, for example, worried that it would provide a solution for Kansas and thus deprive the Republicans of their most effective campaign issue. Delighted that sectional lines had been established, he wanted Congress to adjourn and leave them that way. See Isely, *Horace Greeley,* p. 184.

29. Haven to Fillmore, Jul. 29, Aug. 5, 25, 1856. Vespasian Ellis was also afraid that the Northern Know-Nothings' support for Dunn's bill would ruin the nativists in the South. Ellis to Fillmore, Jul. 31, 1856, Fillmore Papers, SUNY.

30. Haven to Fillmore, Mar. 28, 1856, *Ibid.*

31. Henry W. Hilliard (Montgomery) to Fillmore, Jun. 26, 1856, E. Root (Stewart county, Georgia) to Fillmore, Jun. 26, 1856, *Ibid.*

32. Letcher to Fillmore, Jul. 12, 1856. Granger promised to assure Letcher that a vigorous effort would secure New York. Granger to Fillmore, Aug. 9, 1856, *Ibid.*

33. E. R. Jewett to Haven, Jul. 27, 1856, Sammons to Fillmore, Jul. 18, 1856, *Ibid.*

34. Sammons to Fillmore, Jul. 18, 1856, *Ibid.*

35. Haven to Fillmore, Aug. 15, 1856, Isaiah Fuller to Fillmore, Aug. 15, 1856, *Ibid.*

CHAPTER 14

1. New York *Tribune,* Dec. 7, 1855, Feb. 18, Apr. 29, 1856.

2. Morgan to John Niles, Mar. 18, 1856, Morgan to John Bigelow, Jun. 2, 1856, Morgan Papers, NYSL; Weed to Dear Governor (probably Seward), May (?) (probably May 31, 1856), Weed Misc. MSS, NYHS.

3. Robert A. West to Fish, Dec. 13, 15, 1855, James A. Hamilton to Fish, February 2, 1856, Fish Papers, LC; J. Prescott Hall to Hamilton, Jan. 5, 1856, Hunt to Hamilton, Jan. 5, 1856, James A. Hamilton Misc. MSS, NYHS; Edward Everett to Hamilton, Dec. 3, 17, 1855, Everett Misc. MSS, NYPL.

4. Barnard to Fillmore, Jul. 26, 1856, Fillmore Papers, SUNY.

5. Hunt to Fish, Jan. 16, 1856, Fish Papers, LC. Hunt eventually supported Fillmore and ran for Congress as a Know-Nothing.

6. Hamilton to Fish, Mar. 7, 1856, *Ibid.* Hamilton subsequently abandoned Fillmore and voted for Frémont.

7. New York *Commercial Advertiser,* Feb. 26, Jun. 6, Nov. 1, 3, 1856; West to Fillmore, Jun. 26, 1856, Fillmore Papers, SUNY; West to Fish, Mar. 22, 1856, Fish Papers, LC.

8. C. D. Brigham to Fillmore, Aug. 12, 1856, Granger to Fillmore, Aug. 9, 16, 1856, Edward Bates to Fillmore, Sept. 19, 24, 1856, Fillmore Papers, SUNY.

9. Barnard to Fish, Sept. 23, 1856, Fish Papers, LC.

10. Fish to Hamilton, Sept. 12, 1856, Fish Misc. MSS, NYPL. This letter was highly prized by Republican leaders and received wide publicity. Bigelow wrote F. P. Blair, Sr., that it would influence many of the wavering. Bigelow to Blair, Sept. 27, 1856, Blair-Lee Papers, PUL. Even Weed warmly thanked Fish for his valuable aid. Weed to Fish, Sept. 27, 1856, Fish Papers, LC.

11. Nathan to Fish, undated (received by Fish on Apr. 26, 1856), Nathan Papers, CUL.

12. Webb to Morgan, Mar. 31, 1856, Morgan to E. I. Woolsey, Sept. 19, 1856, Letter Copy Book Vol. V, Morgan Papers, NYSL. The abolitionists, of course, were not satisfied with opposition to slavery extension. To dramatize their discontent, the National Radical Abolitionists, composed of such men as Lewis Tappan and Frederick Douglass, assembled at the same time and in the same city (Syracuse) as a Republican state convention. They issued an address which condemned slavery wherever it existed and attacked the Republicans for failing to adopt a similar stand. New York *Tribune,* May 29, 1856. Gerrit Smith and the Liberty party also refused to endorse Republican candidates on the same grounds. Albany *Atlas and Argus,* Apr. 14, 1856.

13. Bigelow to F. P. Blair, Sr., Sept. 27, 1856, Blair-Lee Papers, PUL.

14. Seward to Weed, Jan. 15, 1856, Weed Papers, URL.

15. Weed to Fish, Jan. 17, 1856, Fish Papers, LC; Smith to Carey, Jan. 19, 1856, Gardiner Collection, HSP; Haven to Fillmore, Jan. 20, 1856, Fillmore Papers, SUNY.

16. William Cassidy to Seymour, Sept. 26, 1855, Seymour Papers, NYSL; Van Dyck to Van Buren, Jan. 14, 1856, Van Buren Papers, LC; Nicholas Hill, Jr., to Tilden, Jan. 14, 1856, Tilden Papers, NYPL.

17. This document may be found in the Martin Van Buren Papers, LC.

18. Albany *Atlas and Argus,* Feb. 25, Mar. 1, 4, Jul. 7, 1856.

19. Randall to M. Van Buren, Sept. 5, 1856, Van Buren Papers, LC; Chas. H. Haswell to Marcy, Sept. 10, 1856, Marcy Papers, LC; Marcy to Newell, Oct. 20, 1856, Marcy Misc. MSS, NYHS.

20. Morgan to F. P. Blair, Sr., May 14, 1856, Morgan Letter Copy Book, Vol. V, Morgan Papers, NYSL; F. P. Blair, Sr., to M. Van Buren, May 17, 1856, Van Buren Papers, LC; M. Van Buren to Tilden, Sept. 1, 1856, Tilden Papers, NYPL. Azariah Flagg, the highly respected comptroller of New York City, followed the lead of Van Buren. However, Benjamin F. Butler, Jackson's former Attorney General, was an early convert to Republicanism.

21. Morgan to Webb, Sept. 19, 1856, Webb Papers, YUL.

22. *Ibid.;* Smith to Carey, Nov. 21, 1856, Gardiner Collection, HSP; Morgan to James Nye & B. Marrierre, Jul. 7, 1856, Morgan Papers, NYSL.

23. Augustus Porter to Seward, Mar. 13, 1856, Weed to Seward, Feb. 27, 1856 (incorrectly catalogued as Feb. 27, 1855), Mar. 5, 1856, Seward Papers, URL.

24. Weed to Seward, March 5, 1856, *Ibid.*
25. Seward to F. P. Blair, Sr., Dec. 29, 1855, Blair-Lee Papers, PUL. This meeting was an important planning session. Senators Salmon P. Chase and Charles Sumner, Gamaliel Bailey, editor of the *National Era,* Nathaniel Banks, Speaker of the House, and Preston King attended.
26. Seward to Weed, Dec. 31, 1855, Weed Papers, URL.
27. Weed to Seward, Jan. 3, Mar. 5, 1856, Seward Papers, URL; Seward to Weed, Mar. 13, 1856, Weed Papers, URL.
28. Weed to Seward, Mar. 5, 1856, Seward Papers, URL.
29. Smith to Carey, Mar. 17, May 2, 16, 1856, Gardiner Collection, HSP; Samuel Wilkeson to Seward, Jun. 15, 1856, Seward Papers, URL.
30. Nathan to Fish, undated (received by Fish on Apr. 17, 1856), Nathan Papers, CUL; Morgan to Bigelow, Jun. 2, 1856, Morgan Papers, NYSL.
31. Seward to Weed, Apr. 4, 1856, Weed Papers, URL; Morgan to Bigelow, Jun. 2, 1856, Morgan Papers, NYSL.
32. Greeley to Colfax, May 6, Jun. 1, 1856, Greeley-Colfax Papers, NYPL; New York *Tribune,* Jun. 11, 1856; Harrington, "Frémont" *AHR* XLIV (Jul. 1939), 843; Nevins, *Frémont,* p. 430.
33. Weed to Seward, Mar. 5, 1856, Seward Papers, URL; New York *Herald,* Jun. 16, 1856; Harrington, "Frémont," 843-45; Nevins, *Frémont,* pp. 430-31.
34. *Proceedings of the Philadelphia Republican Convention of 1856,* pp. 57-58.
35. New York *Tribune,* Jun. 20, 21, 1856.
36. Weed to Morgan, Aug. 3, 1856, Morgan to William Dayton, Jul. 10, 1856, Letter Copy Book, Vol. V, Morgan Papers, NYSL; Harrington, "Frémont," 846-48; Nichols, "Some Problems of the First Republican Presidential Campaign" *AHR* XXVIII (Apr., 1923), 492-94.
37. Smith to Carey, Feb. 26, 1856, Gardiner Collection, HSP.
38. New York *Tribune,* Apr. 30, May 3, 1856; Clark to Weed, Sept. 26, 1856, Weed Papers, URL; Albany *Atlas and Argus,* Oct. 1, 20, 1856.
39. V. M. Rice to Morgan, Nov. 1, 1856, Morgan Papers, NYSL; Smith to Carey, Oct. 31, 1856, Gardiner Collection, HSP; Greeley to Colfax, Sept. 26, 1856, Greeley-Colfax Papers, NYPL.
40. Elias W. Leavenworth to Morgan, Oct. 24, 1856, Morgan Papers, NYSL.
41. *Tribune Almanac and Political Register,* 1857.
42. The state voting figures for the head of the ticket (governor) were: John A. King (Republican), 264,400; Amasa J. Parker (Democrat), 198,616; Erastus T. Brooks (American), 130,870. The assembly would consist of eighty-one Republicans, eight Americans, thirty-one Democrats, eight Americans and Democrats. *Ibid.*
43. The Know-Nothings lost control of Tompkins, Orleans, Seneca, Ontario, Chautauqua, Livingston, Steuben. *Ibid.*
44. E. G. Spaulding to Seward, Nov. 7, 1856, Seward Papers, URL; Smith to Carey, Nov. 6, 1856, Gardiner Collection, HSP; Sammons to Fillmore, Nov. 7, 1856, Fillmore Papers, SUNY.
45. P. Foner, *Business & Slavery,* Ch. 6; *Tribune Almanac and Political Register,* 1857; Albany *Atlas and Argus,* Nov. 7, 1856.
46. Seymour to Marcy, Nov. 12, 1856, D. A. Ogden to Marcy, Nov. 30, 1856, Marcy Papers, LC.
47. Edwin Barber Morgan to Seward, Nov. 6, 1856, Seward Papers, URL; Smith to Carey, Nov. 6, 1856, Gardiner Collection, HSP.

Bibliography

Manuscript Collections

Daniel D. Barnard Papers, New York State Library
James W. Beekman Papers, New-York Historical Society
John Bigelow Papers, New York Public Library
Blair Family Papers, Library of Congress
Blair-Lee Papers, Princeton University Library
Luther Bradish Papers, New-York Historical Society
James Buchanan Papers, Historical Society of Pennsylvania
Benjamin F. Butler Papers, Princeton University Library
Anna Ella Carroll Papers, Baltimore Historical Society
Salmon P. Chase Papers, Historical Society of Pennsylvania
Daniel S. Dickinson Miscellaneous Manuscripts, New-York Historical Society
John A. Dix Papers, Columbia University Library
Stephen A. Douglas Papers, University of Chicago Library
Millard Fillmore Papers, Buffalo Historical Society
Millard Fillmore Papers, State University of New York at Oswego
Millard Fillmore Miscellaneous Manuscripts, New York Public Library
Hamilton Fish Papers, Library of Congress
Hamilton Fish Miscellaneous Manuscripts, New York Public Library
Azariah C. Flagg Papers, Columbia University Library
Francis and Gideon Granger Papers, Library of Congress
Francis Granger Miscellaneous Manuscripts, New-York Historical Society
Horace Greeley Papers, Library of Congress
Horace Greeley Papers, New York Public Library
Greeley-Colfax Papers, New York Public Library
Horace Greeley Miscellaneous Manuscripts, New-York Historical Society
James A. Hamilton Miscellaneous Manuscripts, New-York Historical Society
Hannibal Hamlin Papers, Columbia University Library (microfilm)
Washington Hunt Miscellaneous Manuscripts, New-York Historical Society
Washington Hunt Miscellaneous Manuscripts, New York State Library
John A. King Papers, New-York Historical Society
Knollenberg Collection of Miscellaneous Manuscripts, Yale University Library
William L. Marcy Papers, Library of Congress

156

William L. Marcy Miscellaneous Manuscripts, New-York Historical Society
Edwin D. Morgan Papers, New York State Library
Jonathan Nathan Papers, Columbia University Library
George W. Newell Papers, New York State Library
George W. Patterson Papers, University of Rochester Library
John Van Schaick Lansing Pruyn Papers, New York State Library
Henry J. Raymond Papers, New York Public Library
Samuel B. Ruggles Miscellaneous Manuscripts, New-York Historical Society
Samuel B. Ruggles Miscellaneous Manuscripts, New York Public Library
William H. Seward Papers, University of Rochester Library
William H. Seward Miscellaneous Manuscripts, New-York Historical Society
Horatio Seymour Papers, New-York Historical Society
Horatio Seymour Papers, New York State Library
Erasmus Pershine Smith Papers, Edward Carey Gardiner Collection, Historical
    Society of Pennsylvania
Samuel J. Tilden Papers, New York Public Library
Daniel Ullman Papers, New-York Historical Society
Martin Van Buren Papers, Library of Congress
James Watson Webb Papers, Yale University Library
Thurlow Weed Papers, University of Rochester Library
Thurlow Weed Miscellaneous Manuscripts, New-York Historical Society

Newspapers

Albany *Argus*
Albany *Atlas*
Albany *Atlas and Argus*
Albany *Evening Journal*
Albany *State Register*
New York *Anti-Slavery Standard*
New York *Commercial Advertiser*
New York *Courier and Enquirer*
New York *Evening Post*
New York *Express*
New York *Herald*
New York *Journal of Commerce*
New York *Tribune*
New York *Weekly Mirror*
Washington *National Era*
Washington *Union*

Other Publications

Alexander, DeAlva S. *A Political History of the State of New York.* 4 vols.
    Henry Holt & Co., 1906-23. (Reprinted Kennikat Press, 1969).
Alexander, Thomas B. *Sectional Stress and Party Strength: A Study of Roll-Call
    Voting Patterns in the United States House of Representatives, 1836-1860.*
    Vanderbilt University Press, 1967.

Bancroft, Frederick. *The Life of William H. Seward.* 2 vols. Harper & Bros., 1900.

Barnes, Gilbert H. *The Anti-Slavery Impulse.* D. Appleton-Century Co., 1933.

Barnes, Thurlow Weed. *Memoir of Thurlow Weed.* Houghton, Mifflin & Co., 1884.

Bartlett, Ruhl J. *John C. Frémont and the Republican Party.* Ohio State University Press, 1930.

Beals, Carleton. *Brass-Knuckles Crusade: The Greatest Know-Nothing Conspiracy, 1820-1860.* Hastings House, 1960.

Bean, William   G. "An Aspect of Know-Nothingism—The Immigrant and Slavery." *SAQ,* XXIII (October, 1924), 319-34.

———. "Puritan and Celt." *NEQ,* VII (March, 1934), 70-89.

Benson, Lee. *The Concept of Jacksonian Democracy: New York as a Test Case.* Princeton University Press, 1961.

Benton, Thomas Hart. *Thirty Years' View.* 2 vols. F. Parker, 1856.

Berger, Max. "The Irish Emigrant and American Nativism." *The Pennsylvania Magazine of History and Biography,* LXX (April, 1946), 146-60.

Berwanger, Eugene H. *The Frontier Against Slavery.* University of Illinois Press, 1967.

Bigelow, John. *The Life of Samuel J. Tilden.* 2 vols. Harper & Bros., 1895.

———. *Retrospections of an Active Life.* 5 vols. Baker & Taylor Co., 1909.

Billington, Ray A. *The Protestant Crusade 1800-1860: A Study of the Origins of American Nativism.* Macmillan, 1938.

Blue, Frederick J. "A History of the Free Soil Party." Ph.D. dissertation, University of Wisconsin, 1966.

Buchanan, James. *The Works of James Buchanan.* Edited by John B. Moore. 12 vols. J. B. Lippincott Co., 1911.

Byrne, Frank. *Prophet of Prohibitionism: Neal Dow and His Crusade.* State Historical Society of Wisconsin, 1961.

Campbell, Stanley W. *The Slave Catchers: Enforcement of the Fugitive Slave Law, 1850-1860.* W. W. Norton & Co., 1972.

Carman, Harry J. and Luthin, Reinhard H. "The Seward-Fillmore Feud and the Disruption of the Whig Party." *NYH,* XXIV (July, 1943), 335-57.

———. "Some aspects of the Know-Nothing Movement Reconsidered." *SAQ,* XXXIX (April, 1940), 213-34.

Carroll, Anna Ella. *The Great American Battle; or, The Contest between Christianity and Political Romanism.* Miller, Orton & Mulligan, 1856.

Chalmers, Leonard. "Fernando Wood and Tammany Hall: The First Phase." *NYHSQ,* LII (October, 1968), 379-402.

Chambers, William N. and Burnham, Walter D., eds. *The American Party Systems: Stages of Political Development.* Oxford University Press, 1967.

Chase, Salmon P. *Diary and Correspondence of Salmon P. Chase. Annual Report* of the American Historical Association, 1902.

Clapp, Margaret. *Forgotten First Citizen: John Bigelow.* Little, Brown & Co., 1947.

Clephane, Lewis. *Birth of the Republican Party.* Gibson Bros., 1889.

Cole, Arthur C. *The Whig Party in the South.* American Historical Association, 1913.

Cole, Charles C. *The Social Ideas of the Northern Evangelists, 1826-1860.* Columbia University Press, 1954.

Crandall, Andrew W. *The Early History of the Republican Party 1854-1856.* Richard G. Badger, 1930.

Cross, Whitney R. *The Burned-Over District: The Social and Intellectual History of Enthusiastic Religion in Western New York, 1800-1850.* Cornell University Press, 1950.

Crouthamel, James L. *James Watson Webb: A Biography.* Wesleyan University Press, 1969.

Curran, Thomas J. "The Know-Nothings of New York State." Ph.D. dissertation, Columbia University, 1963.

————. "Seward and the Know-Nothings." *NYHSQ*, LI (April, 1967), 141-61.

Curtis, Francis. *The Republican Party: A History of Its Fifty Years' Existence and a Record of Its Measures and Leaders.* 2 vols. G. P. Putnam's Sons, 1904.

Dickinson, Daniel S. *Speeches, Correspondence, Etc., of the Late Daniel S. Dickinson of New York.* Edited by John R. Dickinson. 2 vols. G. P. Putnam & Sons, 1867.

Dix, John A. *Memoirs of John Adams Dix, Compiled by his Son.* 2 vols. Harper & Bros., 1883.

Donald, Aida DiPace. "The Decline of Whiggery and the Formation of the Republican Party in Rochester, 1848-1856." *Rochester History*, XX (July, 1958), 1-19.

————. "Prelude to Civil War: The Decline of the Whig Party in New York, 1848-1852." Ph.D. dissertation, University of Rochester, 1961.

Donovan, Herbert. *The Barnburners: A Study of the Internal Movements in the Political History of New York State and of the Resulting Changes in Political Affiliation, 1830-1852.* New York University Press, 1925.

Douglas, Stephen A. *The Letters of Stephen A. Douglas.* Edited by Robert W. Johannsen. University of Illinois Press, 1961.

Dow, Neal. *The Reminiscences of Neal Dow.* Evening Express Publishing Co., 1890.

Duberman, Martin B., ed. *The Antislavery Vanguard: New Essays on the Abolitionists.* Princeton University Press, 1965.

Dumond, Dwight L. *Antislavery, The Crusade for Freedom in America.* University of Michigan Press, 1961.

Durden, Robert F. *James Shepherd Pike.* Duke University Press, 1957.

Ellis, David M. "The Yankee Invasion of New York, 1783-1850." *NYH*, XXXII (January, 1951), 3-17.

Ernst, Robert. *Immigrant Life in New York City, 1825-1863.* King's Crown Press, 1949 (Reprinted Kennikat Press, 1965).

Ferree, Walter L. "The New York Democracy, Division and Reunion, 1847-1852." Ph.D. dissertation, University of Pennsylvania, 1953.

Field, Henry M. *The Life of David Dudley Field.* Charles Scribner's Sons, 1898.

Filler, Louis. *The Crusade Against Slavery 1830-1860.* Harper & Bros., 1960.

Fillmore, Millard. *Fillmore on the Great Questions of the Day. The Arrival, Reception, Progress and Speeches of Millard Fillmore.* R. M. DeWitt, 1856.

————. *Millard Fillmore Papers.* Edited by Frank Severance. 2 vols. Buffalo Historical Society, 1907.

Flick, Alexander C., ed. *History of the State of New York.* 10 vols. Columbia University Press, 1933-37. (Reprinted Kennikat Press, 1962)

————. *Samuel Jones Tilden: A Study in Political Sagacity.* Dodd, Mead & Co., 1939.

Flower, Frank A. *History of the Republican Party.* Union Publishing Co., 1884.

Foner, Eric. *Free Soil, Free Labor, Free Men: The Ideology of the Republican Party Before the Civil War.* Oxford University Press, 1970.

————. "Politics and Prejudice: The Free Soil Party and the Negro, 1849-1852." *JNH,* L (October, 1965), 232-56.

————. "Racial Attitudes of the New York Free-Soilers." *NYH,* XLVI (October, 1965), 311-29.

————. "The Wilmot Proviso Revisited." *JAH,* LVI (September, 1969), 262-79.

Foner, Philip S. *Business and Slavery: The New York Merchants and the Irrepressible Conflict.* University of North Carolina Press, 1941.

Fox, Dixon Ryan. *Yankees and Yorkers.* New York University Press, 1940.

Frémont, The Conservative Candidate. Correspondence between Hon. Hamilton Fish, U.S. Senator from New York, and Hon. James A. Hamilton, Son of Alexander Hamilton, n.p., 1856.

Frémont's Romanism Established: Acknowledged by Archbishop Hughes. n.p., 1856.

Fuess, Claude M. *The Life of Caleb Cushing.* 2 vols. Harcourt, Brace & Co., 1923.

Gibson, Florence E. *The Attitudes of the New York Irish Toward State and National Affairs, 1848-1892.* Columbia University Press, 1951.

Greeley, Horace. *Recollections of a Busy Life.* J. B. Ford & Co., 1869 (Reprinted Kennikat Press, 1971).

Gusfield, Joseph R. *Symbolic Crusade: Status Politics and the American Temperance Movement.* University of Illinois Press, 1963.

Hammond, Jabez D. *The History of Political Parties in the State of New York, from the Ratification of the Federal Constitution to December, 1840.* 2 vols. H. & E. Phinney, 1846.

————. *Life and Times of Silas Wright, Late Governor of the State of New York.* A. S. Barnes & Co., 1848.

————. *Political History of the State of New York from January 1, 1841 to January 1, 1847.* L. W. Hall, 1852.

Harlow, Ralph V. *Gerrit Smith, Philanthropist and Reformer.* Henry Holt & Co., 1939.

Harrington, Fred H. *Fighting Politician, Major General N. P. Banks.* University of Pennsylvania Press, 1948.

————. "Frémont and the North Americans." *AHR,* XLIV (July, 1939), 842-48.

Hartman, William J. "Politics and Patronage: The New York Custom House, 1852-1902." Ph.D. dissertation, Columbia University, 1952.

Holt, Michael F. *Forging a Majority: The Formation of the Republican Party in Pittsburgh, 1848-1860.* Yale University Press, 1969.

Horton, John T.; Williamson, Edward; and Douglas, Harry S. *A History of Northwestern New York; Erie, Niagara, Wyoming, Genesee and Orleans Counties.* Lewis Historical Publishing Co., 1943.

Hunt, H. Draper. *Hannibal Hamlin of Maine: Lincoln's First Vice-President.* Syracuse University Press, 1969.

Isely, Jeter A. *Horace Greeley and the Republican Party 1853-1861.* Princeton University Press, 1947.

Jay, John. *America Free—or America Slave, An Address on the State of the Country.* Office of the New York *Tribune*, 1856.

Jellison, Charles A. *Fessenden of Maine, Civil War Senator.* Syracuse University Press, 1962.

Johannsen, Robert W. "Stephen A. Douglas, Popular Sovereignty and the Territories." *Historian,* XXII (August, 1960), 378-95.

Julian, George W. "The First Republican National Convention." *AHR,* IV (January, 1899), 313-22.

———. *Political Recollections, 1840-1872.* Jansen, McClurg & Co., 1884.

Kelly, John. *The Union of the New York Democracy—The Kansas-Nebraska Act Vindicated. Speech of Hon. John Kelly of New York Delivered in the House of Representatives May 26, 1856.* n.p. 1856.

Know-Nothing Almanac and True Americans' Manual, 1855, 1856.

Kraditor, Aileen S. *Means and Ends in American Abolitionism: Garrison and His Critics on Strategy and Tactics, 1834-1850.* Pantheon Books, 1969.

Krout, John A. "The Maine-Law in New York Politics." *Proceedings of the New York State Historical Association,* XVII (July, 1936), 260-72.

———. *The Origins of Prohibition.* Alfred A. Knopf, 1925.

Leonard, Ira M. "The Rise and Fall of the American Republican Party in New York City, 1843-1845." *NYHSQ,* L (April, 1966), 151-93.

Lichterman, Martin. "John Adams Dix: 1798-1879." Ph.D. dissertation, Columbia University, 1952.

Litwack, Leon F. *North of Slavery: The Negro in the Free States, 1790-1860.* University of Chicago Press, 1961.

McClain, Richard H. "The New York Express: Voice of Opposition." Ph.D. dissertation, Columbia University, 1955.

McCormick Richard P. *The Second American Party System.* University of North Carolina Press, 1966.

McGuire, James K., ed. *The Democratic Party of the State of New York.* 3 vols. New York United States History Co., 1905.

McKay, Ernest. *Henry Wilson: Practical Radical, A Portrait of a Politician.* Kennikat Press, 1971.

Marsh, John. *Temperance Recollections. Labors, Defeats, Triumphs. An Autobiography.* Charles Scribner & Co., 1866.

Mathews, Lois K. *The Expansion of New England: The Spread of New England Settlement and Institutions to the Mississippi River, 1620-1865.* Houghton Mifflin Co., 1909.

Mayer, George H. *The Republican Party 1854-1966.* Oxford University Press, 1967.

Meyers, Marvin. *The Jacksonian Persuasion, Politics and Belief.* Vintage Books, 1960.

Miller, Douglas T. *Jacksonian Aristocracy: Class and Democracy in New York 1830-1860.* Oxford University Press, 1967.

Milton, George F. *The Eve of the Conflict: Stephen A. Douglas and the Needless War.* Houghton Mifflin Co., 1934.

162   THE REVOLUTION IN THE NEW YORK PARTY SYSTEMS

Mitchell, Robert S. *Horatio Seymour of New York.* Harvard University Press, 1938.
Morrison, Chaplain W. *Democratic Politics and Sectionalism: The Wilmot Proviso Controversy.* University of North Carolina Press, 1967.
Muller, Ernest P. "Preston King: A Political Biography." Ph.D. dissertation, Columbia University, 1957.
New York Hards and Softs: Which is the True Democracy? A Brief Statement of Facts for the Consideration of the Democracy of the Union, Showing the Origin and Cause of the Continued "Division of the Party." Daily News Job Office, 1856.
New York State Government Documents:
  Census of the State of New York, 1845, 1855.
  Civil List and Constitutional History of the Colony and State of New York. 7 vols. n.p. 1855-1889.
  Journal of the Assembly of the State of New York, 1853-56.
  Journal of the Senate of the State of New York, 1853-56.
  The Laws of New York State, 1840-60.
  Messages from the Governors. Edited by Charles Z. Lincoln. 11 vols. J. B. Lyons Co., 1909.
Nevins, Allan. *The Emergence of Lincoln.* 2 vols. Charles Scribner's Sons, 1950.
———. *The Evening Post: A Century of Journalism.* Boni & Liveright, 1922.
———. *Frémont, Pathfinder of the West.* Longmans, Green & Co., 1955.
———. *Hamilton Fish, The Inner History of the Grant Administration.* Dodd, Mead & Co., 1937.
———. *Ordeal of the Union.* 2 vols. Charles Scribner's Sons, 1947.
Nichols, Roy F. *The Democratic Machine 1850-1854.* Columbia University Press, 1923.
———. *The Disruption of American Democracy.* Macmillan, 1948.
———. *Franklin Pierce: Young Hickory of the Granite Hills.* University of Pennsylvania Press, 1931.
———. "The Kansas-Nebraska Act: A Century of Historiography." *MVHR,* XLIII (September, 1956), 187-212.
———. "Some Problems of the First Republican Presidential Campaign." *AHR,* XXVIII (April, 1923), 492-96.
———. *The Stakes of Power 1845-1877.* Hill & Wang, 1961.
O'Connor, Thomas H. *Lords of the Loom: The Cotton Whigs and the Coming of the Civil War.* Charles Scribner's Sons, 1968.
Official Proceedings of the National Democratic Convention, Held in Cincinnati, June 2-6, 1856. Enquirer Company Steam Printing Establishment, 1856.
Official Proceedings of the Republican Convention Convened in the City of Pittsburgh, Pennsylvania, on the 22nd of February, 1856. Republican Association of Washington, 1856.
Overdyke, William D. *The Know-Nothing Party in the South.* Louisiana State University Press, 1950.
Paul, James C. *Rift in the Democracy.* University of Pennsylvania Press, 1951.
Pessen, Edward. *Jacksonian America: Society, Personality, and Politics.* The Dorsey Press, 1969.
Pike, James S. *First Blows of the Civil War.* The American News Co., 1879.

Porter, Kirk H. and Johnson, Donald B., comps. *National Party Platforms 1840-1956.* University of Illinois Press, 1956.

Proceedings of the Democratic National Convention; Held at Baltimore, June 1-5, 1852, for the Nomination of Candidates for President and Vice-President of the United States. J. R. Armstrong, 1852.

Proceedings of the Philadelphia Republican Convention of 1856. n.p., n.d.

Ratner, Lorman. *Powder Keg: Northern Opposition to the Antislavery Movement, 1831-1840.* Basic Books, 1968.

Rawley, James A. *Edwin D. Morgan 1811-1883, Merchant in Politics.* Columbia University Press, 1955.

————. *Race and Politics: "Bleeding Kansas" and the Coming of the Civil War.* J. B. Lippincott Co., 1969.

Rayback, Joseph G. *Free Soil: The Election of 1848.* University Press of Kentucky, 1970.

Rayback, Robert J. *Millard Fillmore: Biography of a President.* Buffalo Historical Society, 1959.

Richards, Leonard L. *"Gentlemen of Property and Standing," Anti-Abolition Mobs in Jacksonian America.* Oxford University Press, 1970.

Russel, Robert R. "Constitutional Doctrines with Regard to Slavery in the Territories." *JSH,* XXXII (November, 1966), 466-86.

————. "The Issues in the Congressional Struggle Over the Kansas-Nebraska Bill, 1854." *JSH,* XXIX (May, 1963), 187-210.

Schlesinger, Arthur M., Jr. *The Age of Jackson.* Little, Brown & Co., 1945.

Scisco, Louis D. *Political Nativism in New York State.* Columbia University Press, 1901.

Seward, Frederick W., ed. *Seward at Washington As Senator and Secretary of State.* 3 vols. Derby & Miller, 1891.

Seward, William H. *The Works of William H. Seward.* Edited by George E. Baker. 5 vols. Houghton Mifflin & Co., 1889.

Sewell, Richard H. *John P. Hale and the Politics of Abolition.* Harvard University Press, 1965.

Sharrow, Walter G. "William Henry Seward: A Study in Nineteenth Century Politics and Nationalism, 1855-1861." Ph.D. dissertation, University of Rochester, 1965.

Silbey, Joel H. *The Shrine of Party, Congressional Voting Behavior 1841-1852.* University of Pittsburgh Press, 1967.

————, ed. *The Transformation of American Politics, 1840-1860.* Prentice-Hall, 1967.

Smith, George W. "Arphaxed Loomis—His Career and Public Services." *Papers Read Before the Herkimer County Historical Society,* II (1899-1902), 109-27.

Smith, William E. *The Francis Preston Blair Family in Politics.* 2 vols. Macmillan, 1933.

Smith, Theodore C. *The Liberty and Free Soil Parties in the Northwest.* Longman, Green & Co., 1897.

————. *Parties and Slavery.* Harper & Bros., 1906.

The Softs, The True Democracy of New York. n.p. 1856.

Sorin, Gerald. *The New York Abolitionists: A Case Study of Political Radicalism.* Greenwood, 1970.

Spencer, Ivor D. *The Victor and the Spoils: A Life of William L. Marcy.* Brown University Press, 1959.

————. "William L. Marcy Goes Conservative." *MVHR,* XXXI (September, 1944), 205-24.

Stanton, Henry B. *Random Recollections,* Harper & Bros., 1887.

Stewart, James B. *Joshua R. Giddings and the Tactics of Radical Politics.* Press of Case Western Reserve University, 1970.

Strong, George T. *Diary of George Templeton Strong.* Edited by Allan Nevins and Milton H. Thomas. 4 vols. Macmillan, 1952.

Swanberg, W. A. *Sickles the Incredible.* Charles Scribner's Sons, 1956.

Thomas, John L. "Romantic Reform in America, 1815-1865." *AmQ,* XVII (Winter, 1965), 656-81.

Tilden, Samuel J. *The Writings and Speeches of Samuel J. Tilden.* Edited by John Bigelow. 2 vols. Harper & Bros., 1885.

Trefousse, Hans L. *Ben Butler: The South Called Him Beast.* Twayne Publishers, 1957.

————. *Benjamin Franklin Wade: Radical Republican from Ohio.* Twayne Publishers, 1963.

————. *The Radical Republicans, Lincoln's Vanguard for Racial Justice.* Alfred A. Knopf, 1969.

Tribune Almanac and Political Register, 1857.

Tyler, Alice F. *Freedom's Ferment: Phases of American Social History to 1860.* University of Minnesota Press, 1944.

United States Government Documents:

    Biographical Directory of the American Congress, 1774-1927. Government Printing Office, 1928.

    A Compilation of the Messages and Papers of the Presidents, 1789-1897. Edited by James D. Richardson. Government Printing Office, 1896-99.

    Congressional Globe, Containing the Debates and Proceedings, 1833-1873. 109 vols. Blair and Reeves, et al., editors and publishers, 1834-73.

    7th Census, 1850. R. Armstrong, public printer, 1853.

Van Deusen, Glyndon. *Horace Greeley: Nineteenth Century Crusader.* University of Pennsylvania Press, 1953.

————. *The Jacksonian Era 1828-1848.* Harper, 1959.

————. *Thurlow Weed: Wizard of the Lobby.* Little, Brown & Co., 1947.

————. "Why the Republican Party Came to Power." *The Crisis of the Union 1860-1861.* Edited by George H. Knowles. Louisiana State University Press, 1965.

————. *William Henry Seward.* Oxford University Press, 1967.

Weed, Thurlow. *Autobiography of Thurlow Weed.* Edited by Harriet A. Weed. Houghton, Mifflin & Co., 1884.

Whig Almanac, 1853, 1854, 1855.

White, Philip L. *The Beekmans of New York in Politics and Commerce, 1647-1877.* The New York Historical Society, 1956.

Wilson, Henry. *History of the Rise and Fall of the Slave Power in America.* 3 vols. James R. Osgood & Co., 1876.

Wilson, Major L. "The Repressible Conflict: Seward's Concept of Progress and the Free-Soil Movement." *JSH,* XXXVII (November, 1971), 533-56.

Index

165